Zhao the Orphan

赵氏孤儿

Ji Junxiang
纪君祥（元）
Adapted by Wang Jianping and Ren Yutang
王建平　任玉堂　改编
Revised by Liu Yousheng
刘幼生　审订

New World Press
新世界出版社

First Edition 2001

Translated by Paul White
Edited by Zhang Minjie
Book Design by He Yuting

ISBN 7 – 80005 – 565 – 5

Published by
NEW WORLD PRESS
24 Baiwanzhuang Road, Beijing 100037, China

Distributed by
NEW WORLD PRESS
24 Baiwanzhuang Road, Beijing 100037, China
Tel: 0086 – 10 – 68994118
Fax: 0086 – 10 – 68326679
E-mail: nwpcn@public. bta. net. cn

Printed in the People's Republic of China

赵盾

赵氏孤儿

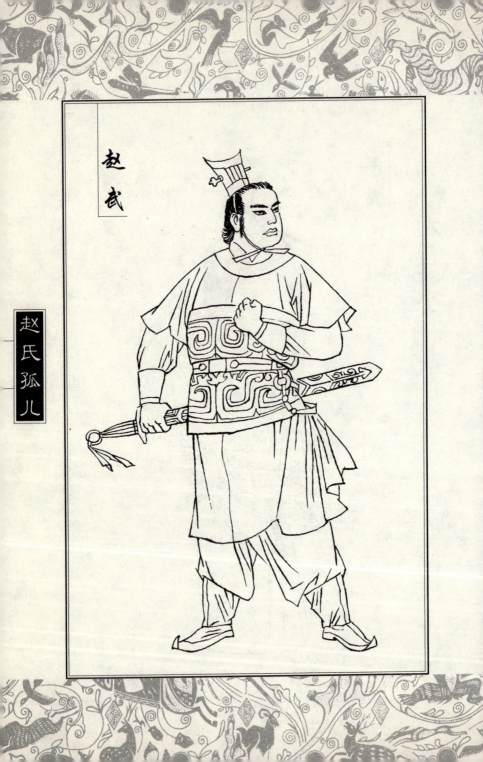

赵武

赵氏孤儿

程嬰

赵氏孤儿

屠岸贾

赵氏孤儿

Foreword

The drama *Zhao the Orphan* by Ji Junxiang (also known as Ji Tianxiang) is a tragedy steeped in Chinese folklore. The plot is a somewhat simplified version of a tale that dates as far back as in the *Zuo Zhuan*, and was written over 2, 000 years ago. Other classic works, such as Sima Qian's *Records of the Historian*, and the *New Annals* and *Garden of Tales* of Liu Xiang, also contain versions of the same story. The details contained in these works laid the foundation for the plot of the drama. The script of the drama has considerably altered the historical content of the story: for instance, the period has been shifted from the reign of Duke Jing of the State of Jin to that of Duke Ling; instead of Zhao the Orphan concealing himself in the palace, Cheng Ying smuggles him out in a medicine box; the boy does not grow up deep in the mountains, but in the home of his adoptive father Tu'an Gu; Han Jue does not ask for an estate for Zhao the Orphan, but dies a righteous death to get Cheng Ying expelled from the palace; and as for the retainers of the Zhao family, Cheng Ying and Gongsun Chujiu, the former is transformed into a humble physician who is an intimate of the Zhao family and the latter into a fellow court official of Zhao Dun who retires to live as a hermit. These changes serve to render the clashes and antagonisms of the play sharper and more vivid, and strengthen the dramatic impact.

The theme of *Zhao the Orphan* is the conflict between "loyalty" and "treachery" both inside and outside the court of the State of Jin during the Spring and Autumn Period. Throughout, the focus of the struggle against oppression thus engendered is Zhao the Orphan. Woven around this is the heart-stopping hunt for, and the rescue of the orphan boy; as the hunt gets closer, various measures are taken to save him. When the search reaches the palace, the princess sacrifices her life to save him; at the palace gate, Han Jue dies a chivalrous death to save him; and when the hunt becomes nationwide, Cheng Ying gives up his own son, and Gongsun Chujiu his own life, to save him. One after the other, these loyal ministers and heroes go nobly to their deaths, tragic sacrifices, for the sake of Zhao the Orphan. Because he has the muddle-headed ruler of Jin under his thumb, the dastardly Tu'an Gu's arrogance knows no bounds. As a result, the righteous people who oppose him are forced to undergo all kinds of dangers and oppression, a circumstance which permeates the whole dramatic structure with a tangible aura of tragedy. But at the same time, a thread of hope runs through the story, as in the end the orphan is saved, and extirpates evil and wreaks revenge. In the midst of all the lamentable martyrdom, there is a stirring sense of righteousness which inspires the protagonists with faith in the belief that good will triumph over evil in the end. At the same time, there is a sense of dramatic irony that the wicked minister is gradually weaving a snare in which he will eventually trap himself. There is a distinct folk flavor about this aspect of the plot.

The drama successfully portrays a range of high-minded tragic characters who are individually delineated, the most outstanding of whom are Cheng Ying and Gongsun Chujiu. Following the massacre of the Zhao clan, the former risks his life to save Zhao the Orphan. Not only that. He has to undergo the terrifying ordeal of an interrogation at the gate of the palace, the heartbreak of having to substitute his own son for the orphan, the heartrending anguish of witnessing the deaths both of his infant and his friend Gongsun Chujiu, and twenty years of humiliation and insults. These ordeals underline the sublime integrity of Cheng Ying. Gongsun Chujiu nurtured a passionate hatred for wickedness, which led him to refuse to participate in a government dominated by degenerate ministers. Unflinching, he goes to his death in an awe-inspiring display of rectitude. Besides these two, the descriptions of the selfless heroism of Han Jue, the way Ti Miming sacrifices himself for his master, Ling Zhe's bearing the carriage on his shoulder, etc., although they are little more than quick sketches, highlight distinct heroic personalities.

The tale of Zhao the Orphan has circulated both inside and outside of China for thousands of years. Within China, every form of dramatic tradition has adapted it for the stage. In the 18th century, it reached France and England, where it was translated and published in book form. It was also adapted for the stage in Germany and Austria.

This present version has preserved the unadorned style of language of the original text, and is basically faithful to the original plot. However, we have taken the liberty of adding some minor details and psychological descriptions —— firstly, as regards the licentious antics of Duke Ling and the brutalities of Tu'an Gu, and secondly, as regards the psychological tension between Cheng Ying and Gongsun Chujiu in the scene in Taiping Village in which the latter meets his end. In this new version of Zhao the Orphan we have striven to keep the plot tight and the pathos effective, revolving round the main theme of the search for and the rescue of the orphan. We have tried to make the psychological mechanism finely detailed, and the language flowing and elegant, so that it is more readable than the original poetic drama form.

Also, the original drama presents the clash between Zhao Dun and Tu'an Gu in terms of the incompatibility of civil and military court officials. This tends to obscure the antagonism between good and evil, and so we have made suitable adjustments.

It is our hope that we have made some contribution towards increasing the popularity of classical Chinese drama with this book. But as our abilities are limited, there are bound to be some shortcomings, and we sincerely welcome criticism and suggestions from the readers.

Contents
目　录

赵氏孤儿

Chapter One
Remonstration in the Peach Garden

It is said that Duke Ling of the State of Jin during the Warring States Period, who came to the throne as a child, was a petulant youngster of unstable temperament. But, fortunately for his realm, the influence of his benign forebears, dukes Wen and Xiang, still lingered, and the people were content and industrious. In addition, there were at court able and loyal ministers and generals, such as Zhao Dun and Han Jue, to ensure that Jin remained undefeated amid the incessant wars between the various states of China in those days.

As the years went by and Duke Ling attained manhood, his nature became even more depraved, his extravagance knew no bounds, and he plundered the people mercilessly to pay for an orgy of constructing palaces and pleasure domes. He held human life in complete disregard; if anything, no matter how slight, irritated him, he would unleash a whirlwind of executions of innocent people. The warnings and remonstrances from upright officials such as Zhao Dun fell on deaf ears, and provoked only resentment. Now Zhao Dun was the son of Zhao Shuai, who had accompanied Duke Wen, the previous ruler of Jin, on his 19-year exile, and who had done much work to restore the fortunes of the state. Zhao Dun had also served Duke Wen. In addition, he was a man of noble character and high prestige, so that Duke Ling treated him with a mixture of hatred, respect and fear.

As dynasties rose and dynasties fell, just as there appeared loyal and honest ministers, so also crafty and scheming courtiers mounted the political

第一章　桃园进谏

　　话说春秋时代晋国的国君晋灵公,幼年即位,骄纵成性,喜怒无常。幸而晋国承继文公、襄公的余泽,百姓也还能安居乐业;加上朝中又有赵盾、韩厥等忠臣良将鼎力辅佐,在列国争战之中,晋国依旧立于不败之地。

　　春去秋来,转眼就是十几年过去了,灵公已经长大成人。可惜他却越发荒淫暴虐,一味横征暴敛,搜括民财,大兴土木,挥霍无度。常常因为一些鸡毛蒜皮的小事,稍不如意,便滥杀无辜,视人命如同儿戏。赵盾等大臣多次犯颜直谏,灵公不但听不进去,反而对赵氏产生了猜忌怨恨。这是因为赵盾乃是当年跟随晋文公流亡在外十九年,曾为晋国立下汗马功劳的赵衰之子,本人又是两朝元老,托孤重臣,德高望重,威势赫赫,甚至执掌着废立大权。灵公对他也只得恨三分,敬三分,惧怕四分。

　　历朝历代,朝廷中多有忠直之臣,却也总免不了有些奸佞小人。当时晋国朝中有一位大夫,姓屠岸,名贾,出身将门之后。此人生得五大三粗,腰圆膀厚,鹰

stage from time to time. A prime example of the latter, Tu'an Gu, had the ear of Duke Ling at this time. Tu'an Gu came from a military family. He was a hefty individual, with a nose as hooked as a hawk's claw and narrow eyes. His very forehead exuded guile and wickedness. Having practiced martial arts from an early age, he was immensely strong, and so had come to the notice of Duke Ling, who appointed him head of the palace guard. Tu'an Gu was as cunning as a fox and an accomplished flatterer, as well as being adept at reading a person's thoughts. He soon had the ordinary court officials eating out of his hand, and as for Duke Ling, manipulating him was child's play for Tu'an Gu. The duke, in turn, doted on his chief bodyguard, who never left his side whenever he went out on jaunts. If perchance, Tu'an Gu happened to be absent on any occasion, Duke Ling was as distressed as if he had lost his right arm.

Early perceiving that Duke Ling cared for nothing but satisfying his appetites, Tu'an Gu used all his guile and flattery to wheedle out of the duke what he most desired. Then he had a park constructed in the eastern part of the royal palace in Jiangyi City, the capital of Jin. Crystal-clear streams and shady paths meandered around lofty halls, terraces and pavilions. Rare and exotic plants were brought from all over Jin and planted in the park, so that fine trees were in bloom all the year round, and lush lawns breathed their fragrance. Of all the flowers that bloomed in their turn, those of the peach trees were the most numerous. Everywhere the eye turned, it alighted on peach blossoms. In the season when the buds started to ripen, the air seemed to be filled with a rosy mist hovering over the rows of emerald-green buds, giving the park the aspect of an embroidered and perfumed picture. Shimmering in a warm breeze, the peach blossoms had a fairyland like quality about them and their scent wafted for miles around. For this reason, the park was given the name the Peach Garden.

With the opening of the Peach Garden, Duke Ling was overjoyed. He cast aside all thoughts of state affairs, and flung himself into an endless round

钩鼻,三角眼,眉宇之间蕴有几分凶狠狡诈之气。因为自幼练得一身好功夫,又力大无比,灵公便封他做了司寇,掌管宫中侍卫。这屠岸贾智计千条,诡诈百出,惯会察颜观色,阿谀奉承,玩些小忠小信的把戏来邀媚取宠,摆弄灵公如弄小儿。灵公因此对他宠幸无比,言听计从。凡是灵公游乐出猎,屠岸贾从来不离左右。偶然有一次不在场,灵公便如失膀臂,魂不守舍。

这屠岸贾看出灵公是个只知吃喝玩乐的国君,便用心奉承,揣摩着灵公的喜好,在绛邑城内的王宫东侧修筑了一座花园。园内殿阁轩峻,亭台参差,清流环绕,幽径纵横。又在国内广求奇花异卉,移植园中,一年四季佳木葱茏,芳草如茵;又有各类鲜花递相开放,其中尤以桃花为盛,目光所及,处处皆是。花发时节,葩吐丹霞,芽叠翠玉,满园内烂若锦绣,芳香馥郁。若有一阵暖风吹拂,那落红飘飘洒洒,真是仙境一般,就是几里地之外也能闻到香味,所以起名为"桃园"。

这晋灵公自从有了"桃园",恰似如鱼得水,越发将朝政置之脑后,日夜吃喝游乐,撒着欢儿地大玩儿特玩儿起来:有时在华亭上猜拳饮酒,有时在玉堂中掷骰赌博,有时在树丛内张弓射鸟,更不堪触目的是常与宫女在光天化日之下赤身取乐,无所不至。哪里还有个国君的样子? 难怪晋国朝野上下提起灵公来

of pleasure —— sometimes carousing in the Flowery Pavilion, sometimes dicing in the Jade Hall, sometimes shooting at birds in the trees, and sometimes romping naked with his harem. There was no excess he did not indulge in. Both in the palace and in the streets, whenever the duke's name was mentioned, heads would be shaken sorrowfully and groans would be heard: "He's not like a ruler at all!"

Tu'an Gu's scheming knew no bounds. Seeing his master abandoned to riotous dissipation, he not only did not censure him, but went so far as to devise a way to sink him further into the slough of debauchery. He secretly summoned master craftsmen from all corners of the land, and instructed them to build a terrace three stories high by the entrance to the Peach Garden. Atop the terrace was erected the Crimson Cloud Tower. This tower was most magnificently appointed, with soaring eaves and flying buttresses, carved beams and decorated rafters, bright red pillars and jade-green steps. On all four sides it was surrounded by intricate painted rails and balustrades. The tower commanded a panoramic view which reached to the horizon; the whole of the capital city and its inhabitants came under the gaze of the viewer from its height. Duke Ling was transported with joy to receive this unexpected present from Tu'an Gu, and straightaway concluded that his chief bodyguard was the most devoted, loyal and capable of all his subjects.

One fine spring day, Zhao Dun, as was his custom, led a group of his subordinates outside the city to encourage the farmers in their plowing. Duke Ling, meanwhile, just like village scamp playing truant from school or a rascally servant lad dodging his master, had decided to devote the next few days to another round of pleasure. Rising early, he repaired with his retainers to the Peach Garden. There the duke went into raptures at the sight of the peach trees adorned with blazing red and the emerald hued willows, among which orioles and swallows chirped and sported. Desiring to be entertained with stage performances, he told Tu'an Gu to summon a troupe of actors to the Crimson Cloud Tower. Now the tower was adjacent to the busiest street in

都是一个劲儿地摇头,说他"不像个国君"。

屠岸贾本来就是奸诈小人,见主君日夜沉溺于声色游乐,不仅不加规劝,反而想方设法,推波助澜。他在暗下里招集四方的能工巧匠,在桃园临街一侧又筑起一座三层高台,台上建了一座"绛霄楼",飞檐斗拱,直插云霄,雕梁画栋,丹楹玉阶。四周又有朱栏曲槛,凭栏四望,远近风光一览无余,绛邑城内的市井人群俱在眼前。灵公觉得非常有趣,越发乐不可支,竖起大拇指直夸屠岸贾忠诚能干,体贴国君。

这天,正值春光明媚之时,赵盾按照惯例,带着下属到城外各处奖劝农耕去了。灵公越发没了顾忌,好像讨厌读书的村童逃出了学堂,淘气顽皮的小厮摆脱了主人一般,打算着要痛痛快快乐他几天。一大早起来,便叫众人陪着,来到桃园。见满园桃红柳绿,处处莺歌燕舞,不觉又添了几分兴致,便命司寇屠岸贾召来几十名伶人,于绛霄楼上演出百戏杂技。这绛霄楼俯临都城绛邑一条最为繁华的街道,逢年过节自不用说,平日里也是行人摩肩接踵,如潮如堵,真是呵气成云,挥汗如雨。今日绛霄楼上百戏纷呈,自然引得大街小巷的行人驻足观看。一些闲着无事的老人、儿童,听说此事,也奔走相告,纷纷聚到楼下。屠岸贾见街上万众聚集,人头攒动,眼珠子一转,便想出了一个

the capital. Even on ordinary days, not to mention holidays, this street was always thronged with people, and when the news that performances were to be held in the Crimson Cloud Tower ran through the crowds, young and old flocked to the foot of the tower. As Tu'an Gu gazed down at the mass of bobbing heads, a dastardly thought suddenly occurred to him. Smiling obsequiously, he murmured to the duke, "Your Majesty, see there below! That mass of people who have gathered outside the Peach Garden to get a glimpse of the performances —— why, they are more numerous than the beasts in the wilds outside the capital!" Hearing this, Duke Ling, who took a fiendish delight in the sport of hunting, suddenly had exciting visions of deer and hares pursued and torn by hawks and hounds. "My dear commander," he burbled, "I have a wonderful idea! Let's pretend those people are animals, and each shoot arrows into the crowd. Hitting an eye will count as the top score, hitting the body will count as second place, and a miss calls for a fine of a jug of wine. How about it?" Tu'an Gu clapped his hands in approval, and laughed in delight. "A capital plan, Your Majesty!" He cried, and straightaway ordered his aides to bring bows and arrows. Duke Ling, scarcely able to contain his delight at this new game he had just thought up, said, "I'll shoot into the right of the mob, Commander," he cried, "and you shoot to the left. No slacking, now!" Tu'an Gu made a great show of bowing to his master. "Of course, Your Majesty!" he gushed.

As the two of them prepared for the contest, attendants brought refreshments and the prize wine jug. The duke and his chief bodyguard then began to take turns shooting arrows into the crowd of people below. Every time the cry, "A hit!" was raised from atop the terrace, an agonized scream rose from multitude.

At first, the throng at the foot of the terrace did not realize what was going on; most of the people assumed that the screams, mingled with the din made by the musicians on the terrace, were the customary cries of appreciation for the ongoing performance, and continued to press forward in their

坏主意,对灵公诣笑道:"主君快看,园外看戏的草民挨挨挤挤,熙熙攘攘,比西郊的野兽还要多呢!"灵公原本酷好打猎,听屠岸贾提起"野兽"二字,眼前便浮现出麋鹿野兔被鹰犬追赶、带伤奔逃的情景,心中大快,突发奇想,对屠岸贾说:"爱卿,我们今日何不以人为兽,各取弹弓击打街上人群,以角胜负,打中眼的为上,打中腰的为次,打不中的罚一大斗酒。"那屠岸贾听了,拍手叫绝,笑道:"主君好主意啊!"说毕,急忙唤卫士取来弹弓。灵公想出来一个玩乐的新花样,也不由得兴高采烈,手舞足蹈,当下与屠岸贾约定说:"寡人弹射右面的人群,爱卿弹射左面的观众,不得偷懒!"屠岸贾煞有介事地弯下腰道:"为臣遵命!"

君臣二人磨拳擦掌,开始比试。几名侍从站在一边,为君臣二人计数,还有的摆上果品,准备罚酒。一时间,弓如满月,弹如流星,灵公与屠岸贾开始轮番射击。每当台上一声高喊"看弹!"街上的人丛中便发出一声惨叫。

一开始,拥挤的人群还没有醒悟到发生了什么事,听到有人中弹后发出的叫声,还以为是在为台上的歌舞百戏叫好喝彩,一个劲儿地往前挤。等到有十几个人中弹受伤之后,人群才骚动起来,很多人惊叫呼喊,推搡着向四周逃开。有几名年老体弱的老人和孩子被惊

ignorance. Not until a dozen or more of them had fallen transfixed by arrows did the crowd begin to panic. Pushing and shoving, they stampeded in all directions, trampling underfoot children, the weak and the old, and ignoring their pitiful moans. This horrifying scene served only to send Duke Ling into further raptures, and, carried away by this new sport, he forgot about the contest as such, and called to his attendants, "Those of you who can use a bow, come and shoot a few arrows for me!"

The duke's lackeys scrambled to obey. In a twinkling, a hail of arrows whistled through the air, lodging in the skulls, bodies, eyes, mouths and ears of those unfortunate enough to be unable to get out of the way in time. The street below the terrace was turned into a bedlam of wails and pounding feet. Up on the terrace, Duke Ling howled with laughter, and slurped down a goblet full of wine. Casting the goblet from him, he guffawed, "What excellent sport! I've never had such a good time!"

From this time on, people avoided the street below the Crimson Cloud Tower, most preferring to make long detours rather than traverse that ill omened thoroughfare. This incident too planted bitter seeds of resentment against Duke Ling in the hearts of the populace of the capital. A satirical verse began to circulate:

Don't look at the tower on high.
Down from it deadly darts fly.
You'll go for a festival gay,
But groaning you'll come away.
But let us leave this grim scene, and seek out Minister Zhao Dun.

The minister was deeply worried at the antics of his ruler. Especially since the completion of the Crimson Cloud Tower, Duke Ling had abandoned all semblance of attending to state affairs. On the pretext of illness, he had stopped holding court; instead he spent night and day in revelry. What was worse, he was aided and abetted in his debauchery by Tu'an Gu, who stuck

慌的人群踩倒在地，哀呼求救。灵公见了，兴致倍增，觉得这种新游戏真是好玩极了，也顾不上计较比试的胜负，对左右下令道："会放弹的都来给寡人放弹！"

众人听令后不敢怠慢，一齐张弓拈弹，顿时，弹丸呼啸着像雨点儿一般纷纷落下。台下来不及逃开的百姓躲闪不迭，有被打破头的，有被击伤腰的，还有被弹瞎了眼睛，射掉了门牙，打破了耳朵的。一时间众人啼哭呼号，仓惶奔逃，令人目不忍睹。而灵公却在高楼上哈哈大笑，举杯狂饮，饮毕，将酒觚一丢，心花怒放道："有趣，有趣！寡人登台玩儿了多少次，从没有像今天这样畅快过！"

自此之后，绛霄楼下的街道上便车马稀少，行人绝迹。百姓们宁愿远远地绕路，也不从此处通过。心中对灵公产生了怨恨，还编出歌谣唱道：

莫看台，飞丸来。

出门笑且欣，归来哭且哀。

这是后话，暂且按下。

回头却说赵盾眼看着灵公近来的所作所为，不禁忧心如焚。自从建起绛霄楼，身为一国之君的灵公便将国事抛在一旁，托病不朝，日夜寻欢作乐，无所不为。加上屠岸贾与之形影不离，同恶相济，长此下

to the duke like a shadow. If things went on like this, what would become of the State of Jin? Zhao Dun was racked by anxiety. Seeing his master so distraught on this fine morning, his servant Zhao Yi urged the minister to take a walk in the back garden to try to ease his troubled mind.

Zhao Dun's residence was situated to the south of the royal palace, and was known as the Lower Palace. It had been built by the late Duke Wen for Zhao Dun's father, Zhao Shuai, as a reward for the latter's loyal services during Duke Wen's long exile. The mansion of the senior minister was inferior only to the duke's palace itself —— the Upper Palace —— in magnificence, with its lofty towers and elegant halls. The back garden was particularly charming, being endowed with crystal streams, ponds and rockeries. Zhao Dun had had little time to enjoy the garden's splendors, however, as he was a conscientious man, busy supervising government business, most of which had fallen on his shoulders since the duke had started to shun his responsibilities. On this day, he was feeling particularly vexed, and so his servant's suggestion was a welcome one. "Yes," he agreed. "Perhaps a stroll is just what I need."

Zhao Yi hurriedly made the arrangements, and the two of them went into the back garden, where they walked at leisure past pavilions and ponds, ornamented with quaint stones and creepers, until they came to the Piercing Clouds Pavilion. There they saw a wall made of red mud, and a cottage thatched with rice stalks. Over the wall hung the branches of peach trees, ablaze with fiery blossoms. Behind the cottage was a row of mulberry and willow trees, casting a mantle of green shade. Beside the trees was a well, with a well sweep and a pulley. On the left was a fenced-off vegetable garden, giving the area a genuinely rustic atmosphere. "Why don't you rest here for a while, sir?" urged Zhao Yi, with a winning smile. "It seems to be just the place for you to read and relax."

Zhao Dun sighed. "A few days of relaxation is exactly what I need. It's just that, these days...."

He cut short what he was going to say. Zhao Yi, knowing that some-

去,国家如何得了?想到此处,不由得双眉紧锁,愁容不展。家人赵义在一旁看到他心中不快,开口说道:"今日天气晴好,大人何不去后园走走,也好散心去闷。"

原来,赵氏所住的府邸座落在王宫南面,取坐北为君,坐南为臣之意,起名"下宫"。当年,晋文公新立,封赏随自己长期流亡在外的大臣,赵衰自然也在其中,官为上卿,所建住宅轩昂豪华,飞楼插空,轩阁穿云,后园中青溪泻玉,碧池生辉,湖山叠翠,绣栏凝彩,气象仅逊于国君居住的"上宫"。待得赵盾主持朝政,他为人谨严,忙于国事,很少去园中游赏。近日心里焦躁,又听赵义提起,便随口说道:"漫步一回也罢。"

赵义闻命,急忙张罗。主仆二人出亭过池,依石攀藤,来到"穿云阁"前,抬眼望去,见右面有一带红土泥墙,房上稻茎披覆。墙头数枝红桃枝桠横斜,探出墙外,喷火蒸霞一般。屋后一排桑榆,绿荫如盖,旁边一口水井,桔槔辘轳之类应有尽有。左侧两排青篱,内中分畦列畛,长着些绿茵茵的蔬菜,颇有几分田园风光,农家野趣。赵义笑道:"大人何时闲了,在此处读书赏乐,想来一定有些趣味。"

赵盾抬眼一望,叹了口气道:"老夫何曾不想清净几日呢,只是当今……"

不待说完,又止住了。赵义知主人心中有事,不

thing was preying on his master's mind, dared say nothing further. Zhao Dun paused for a moment, and then said, "Although this place was built by men's hands, it is extremely moving to gaze upon. Some day, when affairs of state are straightened out, I would like to retire to this cottage and live the life of a hermit." At this point, he suddenly let out a gasp, as if he had just remembered something important. "I recall I have a most urgent matter to attend to," he muttered. "If I had not come on a stroll in the garden today, and cast my eyes upon this rural scene, it would have slipped my mind completely."

Zhao Yi, who regularly attended his master at court and was thoroughly acquainted with his duties, suggested, "Perhaps, sir, you are referring to your annual excursion to encourage the farmers?"

"That's exactly it!" Zhao Dun cried. "As the saying goes, 'Food is everything to the people, and farming is the foundation of the state.' There is nothing of greater importance."

Now that the subject of encouraging the farmers had come up, a cloud of gloom overshadowed Zhao Dun's mind. Traditionally, at spring plowing time, generation after generation of rulers had gone to the suburbs in light carriages and accompanied by few retainers to bring comfort and encouragement to the farmers diligently working in the fields, and admonish the lazy ones. In this way, they showed how much importance was put on agriculture by the state. Dukes Wen and Xiang had been particularly scrupulous in carrying out this duty —— to the extent of grasping the plow handles themselves and cracking the whip over the ox to plow a symbolic furrow. In their days, there had always been bumper harvests of the five grains, the state had been at peace and the people had been content. When Duke Ling had come to the throne and been too young to understand such matters, Zhao Dun himself had carried out the formality of encouraging the farmers. But now that the Duke had come of age and should have taken on this responsibility, he did not give it a thought, but instead spent all day in the Peach Garden pursuing his giddy pleasures. Moreover, Zhao Dun recalled, in recent years, many of Jin's venerable statesmen and able ministers, dismayed at the duke's wayward life style and his utter disregard for

敢多言。赵盾停了一会儿，又道："此处虽系人力穿凿，却也入目动心，待日后国事清静，老夫倒有心在这几间茅屋里闲居，权当隐居山林。"说到这里，口中"呵"了一声，蓦然想起一件大事来，略一沉吟，续道："眼下有一件大事急需办理，若不是今日游园，见此田园风光，差点儿忘记了。"

赵义每日跟随赵盾上朝，对主人的心事了如指掌，当下问道："大人是在说一年一度的劝农吧。"

"正是。俗语曰：'民以食为天，国以农为本。'此乃第一件大事啊！"

说起劝农，赵盾心中又泛起一阵忧虑。原来，每到春耕时节，历朝历代的国君必定要轻车简从，到市郊去慰问在田间耕作的农夫，惩戒耽误农时的懒汉，以贯彻重视农业的政策。以前的晋文公、晋襄公，每到春季，都是亲自带人去郊外了解民情，抚慰农夫，鼓励百姓耕作。甚至有时还要象征性地手执犁耙，挥鞭赶牛，亲自劳作那么一下两下的。故而那些年五谷丰登，国泰民安。后来灵公即位，年幼无知，这一切便由自己代理。如今灵公已经成人，本应亲自出城劝农，可他却整天在桃园中嬉戏游乐，哪里记得起这件事？再一想，近几年来，国中一些元老大臣，见灵公行

right or wrong, and alarmed at the increasing numbers of venal and dastardly officials who were creeping into positions of power at the court, had one after the other retired from public life. Some kept their mouths shut, and quietly slunk away with their tails between their legs; others, overawed by Tu'an Gu's might and influence, sought safety by throwing in their lot with him. Although Zhao Dun was the most senior minister at court, he alone could not stop the rot that threatened to destroy the whole state.

As these distressing thoughts filled his mind, Zhao Dun could not suppress a long sigh. Suddenly he was no longer in the mood for viewing scenery. He ordered his servant to prepare his carriage for a drive to the suburbs to encourage the farmers.

Learning that her husband was intending to go out, Zhao Dun's wife did not try to stop him, as she knew full well his stubborn nature. Instead, she made haste to order his official robes brought and servants to attend to him. But Zhao Dun said, "Besides, encouraging the farmers, my purpose is to sound out the feelings of the people. But I am afraid that if I appear before them dressed in my official attire, they will be reluctant to speak their minds frankly."

"Do you mean, My Lord, that you wish to travel incognito this time?" his wife asked, and upon receiving an affirmative reply ordered her servant girl to bring plain robes.

Zhao Dun and his entourage, dressed in nondescript garb, left the city by the west gate, and headed for the suburbs. Their way was lined with peach and apricot trees in fiery-red bloom, and emerald-green reeds. The fields beyond them stretched as far as the eye could see, intersected by sparkling clear irrigation ditches. Partridges and cuckoos piped their sweet notes, and the whole of the countryside was vibrant with the vigor of spring. Zhao Dun found his heart lightening. He smiled, and said, "Since we have been blessed with such magnificent spring weather, excellent for plowing and planting, there is no excuse for slackening in the fields. If I find anyone not pulling his weight, I will come down hard on him. Mark my words."

Scarcely had he finished, when he espied a group of peasants carrying

事不端，是非不辨，朝中又有奸佞小人当道，有的隐退闲居，有的缄口不言，七零八落，溃不成军。还有些人见屠岸贾权大势重，炙手可热，竟然卖身投靠，依附巴结。以致朝中正不压邪，自己虽然全力支撑，毕竟大厦将倾，独木难支。

想到此处，赵盾禁不住长长地叹了一口气，再也无心赏玩景色，当下吩咐赵义预备车马，准备代灵公出城去劝农。

夫人得知丈夫又要出城，知道他的脾气，不敢劝阻，急忙命人取出官服伺候。赵盾道："老夫此去郊野，劝农之外，还想顺便查访民情。穿了官服，谁还敢说实话？"

"如此说来，老爷这次是要'微服私访'了。"夫人说着，又命丫环拿出一身便服。

赵盾一行人简装出发，由西门直达郊外，只见沿路桃杏绽红，菖蒲吐绿，田畴万里，清渠环绕，鹧鸪布谷，声声婉转，一派生机。赵盾心中渐渐轻松，笑道："如此大好春光，正是耕种良机，若有游手好闲、不用力劳作的，老夫定要惩处。"

话音方落，忽见几位农夫荷着农具，正要下田。仔细一瞧，其中有一个老妇人，衣衫褴褛，头发花白，

farming implements and entering a field. Among them was a white-haired old woman, shabbily dressed and with haggard, careworn face. Zhao Dun ordered his driver to stop the carriage, and, bowing humbly to the old woman, said, "Pardon me, but may I enquire as to your age, and the circumstances of your life?"

The old woman could see from Zhao Dun's entourage that he was a noble from the capital. She answered, "I am 65 years old, Your Honor. Last year, my only son died while on military service, and there is no one left at home to support me. So I have to work in the fields myself in order to keep body and soul together." As she said this, tears started from her eyes.

Zhao Dun found the old woman's words distressing. He reflected that the constant warfare between the feudal lords of the various rival state in recent years had caused the common people untold suffering. Just then, another peasant standing nearby, noticing the pensive expression on Zhao Dun's face, uttered a groan of sympathy and said, "Although we've had good harvests in the past few years, Your Lordship, the official taxes are crushing the life out of us."

So saying, he took out his lunch from a bamboo basket, and showed it to everyone. It consisted of a coarse bran cake together with a few scraps of wild vegetables.

Zhao Dun immediately understood the peasants' plight: The spring plowing and sowing season was one in which the winter stocks of grain had been used up, while the new harvest was still some months away. This realization tore at his heartstrings, and turning quickly to his attendants he ordered them to give the peasants some relief silver. As he drove away, Zhao Dun was too preoccupied with worry to pay any heed to the peasants' cries of gratitude and blessing. Nor did he notice any longer the sparkling water gurgling in the irrigation ditches or the warm breeze that caressed his cheeks. Suddenly, from high in the air he heard a cawing sound. Raising his head, Zhao Dun spied a chevron of wild geese winging towards the north. Looking to left and right, he discovered for the first time that the tops of the hills were

脸上绉纹纵横，神色凄凉。赵盾当下命车夫停车，俯身问道："老人家多大年岁了，日子过得可好？"

老妇人见了赵盾一行人的气派，心知是城里来的贵人，急忙答道："回禀大人，民妇六十五岁了，儿子前年出征战死，家中无人，老妇人只得自己下田耕种，借以糊口。"说着，早已滴下泪来。

赵盾闻言，心内酸楚。这些年来，列国纷争，诸侯混战，给百姓带来深重的苦难。站在一边的一名农夫见赵盾凝神不语，嘘唏开口道："这几年，虽然收成好些，可是官府的赋税却重多了，老百姓的日子反倒不如以前。"

说罢，拿出竹篮中的干粮给众人看，原来是一些掺和着野菜的糠饽饽。

赵盾心里明白，在此春耕季节，大部分农夫已经青黄不接，心里不由得好生难受，转身让随从留下一些赈济的银子，方才离去。众农夫都叩头相送，纷纷说些感戴恩德的话语。赵盾却因心中沉重，头也不回地去了。路边的渠水依然潺潺地流淌着，赵盾心事重重，一任暖风吹拂。忽听得空中一阵"呀呀"的鸣声，抬眼一看，却是两行大雁向北飞去。左右顾望，才发现山坡上光秃秃的，再没有往日的青苍翠碧，只留下一片半人高的树桩。赵盾心中明白这是因为近年来

bare of their usual greenery; all that remained of the forests that used to clothe them was stumps. This, he realized, was the result of the frenzy of building that had been going on in the capital.

Seven or eight days passed, and Zhao Dun's depression deepened. The field work was going well enough; the peasants were working diligently, and there were no signs of any slackers. Zhao Dun consoled himself that a bumper harvest was assured that year. Nevertheless, on the evening that he was driving back to the capital, as the sun was sinking in the west and the clip-clop of the horses' hooves lulled him into a reverie, his mind was haunted by images of the old peasant woman's despairing eyes, the repulsive bran cake from the bamboo basket, the sighing of the water in the irrigation ditches and the denuded mountain slopes. Over and over again, the question popped up in his mind, "How can I get Duke Ling to abandon his dissolute ways and return to the proper path of a ruler?"

His attendants were as morose as he was on the journey back, and uttered not a sound. So the entourage proceeded in silence, until they reached the eastern gate of the capital. There they saw a dark mass of humanity blocking the road. The carriage driver reined in his horses with a sharp cry. Taken unawares, Zhao Dun was thrown heavily forward.

"What's the matter?" he muttered angrily.

"Sir, there is a crowd of people kneeling in the road and blocking our progress," the driver replied.

Zhao Dun clambered down from the carriage, and saw that indeed there were people kneeling in the roadway, young and old, men and women, and with some white-whiskered seniors in the forefront. He perceived also that some of the crowd bore wounds, with bandaged eyes or limbs, bruised noses and swollen faces.

It was the very day upon which Duke Ling had shot arrows into the crowd below the Crimson Cloud Tower for sport. Some of the victims in fact had died of their injuries. While the people were giving vent to their rage and frustration, one elder had suggested that they take their grievance to Zhao

兴建亭台楼阁,将树木都砍光了。

走一程,叹一程,七八天转瞬逝去。赵盾心里沉甸甸的,幸喜各地百姓都在勤勉耕作,未曾有抛荒偷懒的,看来秋后丰收有望,还可以稍慰心怀。这日傍晚时分,车子已走在回城的路上,看看红日西坠,暮色渐起,马蹄声"哒哒"地响着,赵盾又陷入了沉思,几天来的所见所闻,沉郁在心间:老妇人凄惶的眼神,竹篮中难以下咽的糠菜饽饽,田间渠畔的叹息,山坡上的树桩……"如何才能劝说灵公弃恶从善?"

赵盾在心中反复思索,随从们都一言不发,车队在沉默中赶路。不知不觉,车子已到了东门外,却看到前方有黑压压的一片人群挡住了去路。车夫急忙喝止马匹,赵盾不防,身子向前一冲,不免心中不快,低声喝问道:

"出了什么事?"

车夫答道:"大人,路上跪着一群百姓,挡住了车马。"

赵盾闻言急忙下车,定睛细看,只见一群百姓跪在路中,男女老少都有,几位胡子花白的老者跪在前列。身后的人群中大都带伤,有用白布缠着眼睛的,有用布带吊着胳膊的,有的鼻青脸肿……

原来,灵公那日于绛霄楼上弹射行人取乐,无数百姓受伤,有几个伤势过重,流血不止,先后死去。众

Dun. "He's the only upright man at the court," the man said. "Let's beg him to curb the duke's wantonness."

This met with general approval, and the people marched straight to Minister Zhao's mansion. Learning that the minister had gone to the countryside to encourage the farmers, the petitioners then went to the eastern gate to await his return. They had been there for three long and bitter days when Zhao Dun's carriage finally hove into view. Immediately, a great wail arose from the people.

Zhao Dun was shocked to the marrow when he learned of Duke Ling's wickedness. "From ancient times," he said, unable to disguise his feelings of outrage and pain, "Enlightened rulers have shared their pleasures with the people. There have been, it is true, mediocre rulers who have indulged only themselves. But in all my sixty years on this Earth, I have never heard of a ruler who took pleasure in inflicting suffering on his subjects."

Abandoning all thought of going home that night, Zhao Dun ordered that relief silver be distributed among the suppliants and that the wounded be taken care of. He thereupon drove straight to the Peach Garden.

By this time, the whole city was enfolded in darkness, except for the Crimson Cloud Tower, which was ablaze with light, for in his pursuit of entertainment Duke Ling cared for neither night nor day. Gazing at the gaudy sight from afar, Zhao Dun said to himself, "I will confront the duke right there in the Peach Garden about this matter, and see what excuse he comes up with to justify his outrageous conduct."

His attendants had never seen their master so angry, and so not one of them dared to open his mouth all the way to the Peach Garden. When the carriage arrived there, the gate was locked tight, and there was no attendant to be seen. Zhao Dun was livid. He hammered on the gate with his fists, but all that was heard in return was the sound of stringed instruments wafted on the night breeze. Seeing that Zhao Dun was beside himself with rage, and fearing the consequences if he went as far as to break into the Peach Garden, the attendants sprang forward and pleaded with him, "Your Lordship, it is

人心中愤怒,却又无可奈何。一名老者道:"朝中只有赵大人光明磊落,我们去找他做主,请他主持公道。"

大家听了觉得有理,便一齐来到赵府门前,这才得知赵盾下乡劝农去了,于是又议定在城门外等待,已经在此苦候三日。

此时人群见到赵盾终于回城,未曾开口,先就哭成一片。赵盾连忙搀起众人,询问详细。当他听说是灵公在台上弹射行人,以致百姓中弹受伤,并有数人死去时,不禁面色剧变,怒道:"岂有此理!"顿了一顿,续道:"自古以来,开明的君主与民同乐,平庸的君主自己取乐。本官活了六十岁,还未曾见过拿百姓性命取乐的君主!"

说罢,家也不回了,命人拿些银钱散给众人,嘱咐他们好好养伤,自己带了随从驱车直向桃园而去。

此时,整个绛邑城已经处于暮色笼罩之下,赵盾等人远远就望见绛霄楼上烛火辉煌,一片光明,料想灵公正在楼上玩得昏天黑地,不辨时辰。赵盾气愤地道:"此去桃园当面质问主君,且看他如何推拖!"

众人从未见过赵盾如此恼怒,谁也不敢多言。转瞬间,车马在桃园门口停下,却见园门关得铁紧,外面也没有卫士。赵盾见状,越发气得眼里冒火,鼻内生烟。亲自上前用拳头将园门擂得山响,只听见里面

already late. Please come away. You will have the opportunity to chastise the duke tomorrow at the morning audience. "

Seeing that his furious rapping on the gate had brought nobody to open it, Zhao Dun resigned himself to going home for the night. He had scarcely entered his gate when he was informed that Minister Shi Ji had called on him.

Zhao Dun was well acquainted with the minister, who was renowned for his upright character at court. The two of them worked in perfect harmony on matters of state. So, Zhao Dun reasoned, if he has come to see me so late at night, it must be a matter of some importance. "Bring the minister to see me, " he ordered.

As soon as the two men were seated, Shi Ji came straight to the point. He gave Zhao Dun a succinct account of the day's atrocity, making a point of how incensed the common people were. "You really must persuade the duke to mend his ways, and devote himself heart and soul to his governmental duties, " he urged. Zhao Dun, did not reply for some time, but sat deep in thought. He was fully aware that getting Duke Ling to give up his life of dissipation would be an enormously difficult task. He finally breathed a long sigh, and said, "I should have known long ago that a day like this would come!" And before his eyes floated a scene from twenty years previously.

It had been a dark and stormy afternoon. Zhao Dun and other senior ministers were suddenly summoned to the palace, where Duke Xiang lay on his deathbed. The duke raised his eyelids with a great effort and gasped weakly, "Following in the proud footsteps of my father, I smote the Rong and Di barbarians time after time, and chastised the powerful State of Qin, never slackening in my zeal. But there is no prevailing against the will of Heaven, and now I am about to depart this life. The crown prince, Yi Gao (Duke Ling), is but a babe in arms; he is only two years old. My ministers, you must do your utmost to help him rule. Keep the peace with our neighbors, and preserve Jin's position as leader of the alliance of states. If you fail to do so, I will never be able to close my eyes when I have descended to the

传出一阵阵弦乐之声，却不见有人前来开门。众随从见赵盾怒火中烧，举止失措，怕他闯入园中惹出祸事来，便一齐上前劝道："此时已不早了，大人不如明早上朝，面见国君，相机进谏罢！"

赵盾将那园门擂了一阵，见无人出来，也只得先回府上。刚刚进门，便听得家人传讯说："大夫士季求见。"

赵盾素知士季大夫在朝中以正直著称，常与自己作枰鼓之应，今天深夜来访，必有要事，当即说道："快快请进。"

二人坐定，士季便直截了当，将灵公弹射行人取乐及绛邑城内百姓怨声载道的事说了一遍。然后道："此事必得先生出面，务要劝说主公改弦更张，从此专心国事，勤理朝政。"赵盾闻言呆了半晌，思量一番，心里明白若要灵公痛改前非，只怕比上天都难。想到这里，歔欷叹息道："唉！真是早知今日，何必当初！"眼前不由得浮现出二十年前的情景……

那是一个风雨如晦的下午，赵盾等人被晋襄公召进宫来。襄公病恹恹地躺在榻上，强睁双眼，有气无力地说道："寡人继承父辈功业，多次荡平戎狄，讨伐强秦，未曾稍挫锐气。无奈天命不佑，眼见得要与

Place of Nine Springs." With this, Duke Xiang relaxed his grip on this life, and returned to the netherworld.

That had been a time of turmoil for Jin. Two wars had been fought, with the State of Qin and the Rong and Di barbarians, respectively. Tension and hostility mounted daily, and the ministers over and over again discussed the problem of their leaderless state. Most of them were for putting a prince of mature years on the throne to be a focus of the people's loyalty and ensure overall stability. Some recommended Prince Yong, who at that time resided in the State of Qin; others were in favor of Prince Yue, who was living in the State of Chen. The result was endless bickering.

At last, Minister Shi Ji said, "The ancients had a saying: 'Elevate the good, and stability results; respect the elders, and things go smoothly; serve one's parents, and filial piety prevails; but for safety, maintain old ties of friendship.' Prince Yong is noble-minded, experienced and prudent. He is sure to win the hearts of the people. Besides, he is a kinsman of the ruler of Qin. By making him our duke, we will get rid of a lot of the enmity that has built up between our two states. That would be killing two birds with one stone. Now, as for Prince Yue, he resides at the court of Chen, which is a weak state and comparatively distant. He would not hold the reins of power long here, I fear."

Zhao Dun, as the most powerful minister, was in a quandary. On the one hand, he had to admit that what Shi Ji said made sense; but on the other, to appoint Prince Yong the new duke would be to betray the final wish of the late Duke Xiang that the infant prince rule. In the end, he sent envoys to Qin to invite Prince Yong to return and take the throne, at the same time making arrangements for the funeral of the late duke. On her way back from the funeral, Duke Xiang's widow, Mu Ying, with the young Yi Gao in her arms, confronted Zhao Dun. "What offense did the late duke commit?" she demanded. "And, what is more, what crime is this innocent babe, his lawful heir-apparent born of his proper wife, guilty of, that you should cast aside the royal flesh and blood, and seek a stranger in a foreign land to be the ruler of

诸卿长别。世子夷皋年方两岁，众卿当尽力辅佐，和好邻国，以保盟主之业。不然，寡人在九泉之下也难以瞑目呀！"一言未毕，襄公便撒手归天了。

当时，晋国正值多事之秋，相继与秦国及周边戎狄打了两次仗，关系日益紧张，怨仇越结越深。众大臣反复商讨，多数人主张拥立一位年长的公子为国君，以利于稳定局势，团结人心。有人推荐住在秦国的公子雍，有人推荐住在陈国的公子乐，因此产生争论，相持不下。

最后，士季大夫道："古人曰：'立善则固，事长则顺，奉爱则孝，结旧好则安。'公子雍心地善良，老成持重，定能深得民心。另外，他是秦国的外甥，拥立他可以消除与秦国的积怨，岂非一举两得！而公子乐客居陈国，陈国弱小而偏远，由公子乐来执政，恐怕不是长治久安之策。"

主持朝政的赵盾正在左右为难，听士季说得有理，遂下决心违反了襄公的遗愿，派人到秦国迎接公子雍回国为君，同时安排安葬襄公。襄公的夫人穆嬴及世子送葬归来，得知赵盾做主迎立公子雍为国君，当面指责赵盾道："先君何罪？他的嫡亲儿子又有何罪？为什么抛弃亲生的骨肉，而去外国求迎立新的国君呢？"

Jin?"

Zhao Dun replied, "This is a high matter of state. It is not my personal whim."

But Mu Ying was not to be put off so easily. After that, every morning when the court assembled she would appear, with the infant heir-apparent in her arms, and throw tearful tantrums. "This is the late duke's own son," she would shriek at the ministers. "Why have you ridden roughshod over him and chosen that Prince Yong to be the ruler of Jin in his place?" Her rantings put the court officials completely out of countenance. What was worse, after court was dismissed, she would hasten to Zhao Dun's mansion, and there she would remind the chief minister that her late husband, on his deathbed, had entrusted his son to Zhao. "If you put someone else on the throne, with the late duke's words still echoing in your ears and his corpse not yet cold, you will commit a grave act of betrayal. In that case, I and my child will have no recourse but to seek death!"

She said this with a conviction that made it seem that she was bent on self-destruction. This provided ammunition for those officials who had been in favor of enthroning Yi Gao in the first place, and they gave Zhao Dun no peace thereafter. One day, Mu Ying appeared before the harassed Zhao with her hair disheveled. Her eyes filled with venom, she screeched, "Zhao Dun, make no mistake about it. Until the new duke is installed, I, as the late duke's widow, have the power to dismiss you from office."

Zhao Dun shook in his shoes upon hearing this. If this were to happen, he fretted, not only would his father's achievements come to naught, but disaster would come upon his entire family, and the State of Jin would be plunged into chaos. He had no choice but to clench his teeth in resignation and make the decision to put Yi Gao on the throne. At the same time, he despatched a messenger to recall the mission he had already sent to Qin to invite Prince Yong to take the throne of Jin. In the meantime, he made arrangements for a lavish enthronement ceremony for Yi Gao. However, no sooner was all this completed than a commander arrived from the frontier to

赵盾回答说："这是国家大事，并非臣下一人的主张。"

谁知穆嬴夫人不甘罢休，每日上朝之时，都要抱着世子夷皋来大哭大闹，口口声声对众大臣说："这是先君的亲生儿子，为何要抛弃他而立公子雍为君？"搅得大臣们无法议政。散朝后，穆嬴又追到下宫，对赵盾啼泣不休，说："先君临终前，将世子托附于你，让你尽心辅佐。现在先君刚刚弃世，言犹在耳，骨肉未寒，若立他人，你就是不把先君放在眼里。若是不立世子，我们母子只求一死。"

说着，真个要寻死觅活。最初一些主张拥立世子的大臣也乘机天天与赵盾争论不休，弄得赵盾焦头烂额，心乱如麻。有一天，穆嬴夫人见一味哭求无济于事，索性破脸，披头散发，圆睁双眼，恶恨恨地对赵盾道："赵盾，你别不识好歹，眼下新君未立，我仍是先君的夫人，有权先将你这个上卿罢免！"

赵盾闻言大吃一惊，暗忖道：果真如此，不但父亲出生入死创下的功业就要付之东流，甚至会殃及全家，晋国也难免陷入混乱。于是一咬牙，决定立世子夷皋为君，派人上路去拦阻前往秦国迎接公子雍的人马。同时举行仪式，为夷皋举行登基盛典。不料群臣朝贺方毕，忽有边将来报："秦国派遣军队护送

announce that the State of Qin had sent an armed force to escort Prince Yong to Jin. This force had already reached a place called Hexia.

Zhao Dun was thrown into a panic. He thought to himself, "With Prince Yong as the ruler of Jin, our state would have friendly relations with Qin. If not, Qin will be our enemy. But Yi Gao is already seated on the throne, and it's too late to offer an apology to Qin. In fact, Qin would probably not only refuse to forgive us, but would use this as an excuse for mounting a military campaign against Jin. Truly, once one has mounted the tiger, one dare not alight!" Arriving at this point, Zhao Dun realized that the only way out of his dilemma was to launch a pre-emptive strike at Qin. He lost no time mobilizing the army against the advancing Qin troops.

The Qin ruler, meanwhile, Duke Kang, had been delighted at the news of Jin's invitation to Prince Yong. Rubbing his hands with delight, he had declared, "On two previous occasions the rulers of Jin have come from Qin. This time, Jin's ruler will also come from Qin!" Thereupon, he sent the Central Army, under Bai Yibing, to escort Prince Yong as far as Hexia, where it set up camp and waited for the expected Jin envoys.

But instead of envoys coming to welcome Prince Yong, the Jin army was advancing to make a surprise attack on the Qin forces. Arriving in the vicinity of Hexia, under cover of darkness the Jin troops sharpened their weapons, fed their horses, had one last meal, and hastened to attack, gagged so that no voice should alert the enemy. In the dead of night, just as the glittering stars of the Milky Way were slipping westward, a command rang out, drums and horns raised a frightful din, and the whole of the Jin army dashed headlong at the completely unprepared and sleeping Qin camp, howling their war cries. Bedlam erupted among the Qin troops. With time to neither saddle their horses nor snatch up arms, their troops scurried around in a panic, pursued by the ferocious Jin attackers who hacked them down relentlessly. Prince Yong perished in the carnage, and Commander Bai Yibing only just managed to escape with his life. Utterly routed, the remnants of the Qin forces limped homeward as best they could.

公子雍回国,已经到了河下。"

赵盾一听慌了手脚,暗想:"如果拥立公子雍,秦国就是晋国的宾客;不拥立公子雍,秦国就是晋国的敌人。此刻世子已经立为国君,再去向秦国道歉,只怕为时已晚,秦国不仅不会宽宥,反可借此为理由,发兵攻打晋国。真是骑虎难下!"想到这里,索性一不做,二不休,来了个先发制人,疾速派兵攻打秦国的军队。

当时秦国的国君是秦康公,他见晋国派人来接公子雍回国为国君,心中十分高兴,得意洋洋道:"秦国的先君曾经两次拥立晋国君主,今天我又送公子雍回国即位,看来晋国的国君只能出自秦国啊!"当下派中军主帅白乙丙率军护送公子雍归国,行至河下,便安营扎寨,放心等候晋国的使节前来迎接。

晋军心里明白自己一方属于背信弃义,无法与秦军公然对阵,便悄然行军,接近河下,在黄昏时砺兵秣马,饱食一顿,衔枚疾走,赶到秦营。其时银河灿烂,星斗西斜,恰好是三更时分。晋军将领一声令下,鼓角齐鸣,众军士高声呐喊,杀进秦营。秦军将士正在睡梦之中,毫无防备,忽听一片呐喊之声,犹如山崩地裂,不免惊惶失措,战马不及备鞍,兵士不及操戈,只在四下里乱窜,纷纷逃走。晋军奋力追杀,直到

This victory for Jin, while it removed the immediate danger from Qin, sowed the tragic seed of future chronic hostilities between the two states. But more of this later.

In the meantime, ever since he had installed Yi Gao as the ruler of Jin, Zhao Dun had devoted himself to assisting the new duke with the utmost devotion night and day. But Duke Ling did not at all turn out like a head of state should. He was interested only in feasting and entertainment, paying no heed to matters of government. There was little that Zhao Dun could do about this state of affairs, however: on the one hand, he was afraid that if he admonished the duke, other ministers would speak ill of him to curry favor with the latter, and on the other he feared that the rulers of other states would take advantage of internal discord in Jin to attack. All he could do was to try to handle all matters of state himself, which he found a great strain. As the years went by, Duke Ling's behavior became more and more outrageous; the government grew chaotic, and the plight of the common people grew more desperate by the day. All Zhao Dun's attempts at advice and censure fell on deaf ears, and he himself, weary and heartsick, from time to time found himself on the brink of despair. . . .

Disturbed by Zhao Dun's repeated sighs, Minister Shi Ji offered his friend a word of advice, "The duke's conduct is sure to bring disaster on our heads. As the prime minister, you have worked hard all your life. Now, in your later years, it is difficult for you to right these calamitous wrongs. Surely this is the time for you to make a bold decision to choose honorable retirement. That way, you would preserve the dignity of your family. Moreover, the duke is of an erratic temperament; I am afraid he may be inclined to do you some harm. And that is not all. That fellow Tu'an Gu is a wily rascal, and although at the moment he himself may be powerless to act against you, he has the duke's ear. There is no way you can influence the duke in these circumstances, and if Tu'an Gu gains the upper hand at court, do you expect that he will tolerate the presence of a loyal and upright prime

刳首之地，公子雍死于乱军之中，主帅白乙丙死战脱身，秦军被打得落花流水，狼狈回国。

然而，此次胜利，虽然解了晋国的燃眉之急，却埋下了晋秦两国争战不已的祸种，此是后话，暂且按下。

赵盾自册立夷皋为国君后，夙兴夜寐，忠心不二，全力辅佐。不料灵公毫无国君的样子，只知吃喝玩乐，不理国政。赵盾见状，几次想废旧立新，又抹不下面子，惟恐被朝中大臣褒贬，也怕诸侯各国乘机来进攻。只得自己越俎代庖，事事操心。近年来，灵公越发没了体统，眼见得国事蜩螗，民生日蹙，赵盾不得不拼死强谏，尽力维持，难免心力交瘁，不由得时时生出些后悔来。

士季大夫见赵盾连连叹息，又劝说道："看主君这个样子，迟早要酿出大祸。相国你辛苦一生，晚年也难逃辅佐不正之罪。倒不如及早抽身，急流勇退，还可保住清白家声。况且主君喜怒无常，弄不好相国的身家性命难保。再说屠岸贾那厮本是奸诈之徒，眼下虽说还不敢拿相国怎么样，但主君对他言无不从，今后尾大不掉，一朝得势，他岂能容得相国这样的忠直之士？"

minister like yourself?"

These words cause a shiver to run down Zhao Dun's spine. He mused, "All because I wavered on one occasion twenty years ago, when I made the mistake of putting Duke Ling on the throne, this present calamity has descended on the State of Jin and its people." A distressing sense of remorse clouded his mind, but he stiffened his back, and said, "Well, now that things have come to this pass, they can't get any worse. I have brought my troubles on myself, and I am determined to devote what few years I have left to serving my country, come what may!" As he said this, he could not hold back the tears that trickled from his eyes.

The sight of Duke Ling idling and carousing was like a knife twisting in the heart of the honest Shi Ji. He agonized over the fate of Jin. For Tu'an Gu and his cronies, Shi Ji had a deep and burning enmity. But, as a low-ranking official, his words carried little weight, and his frequent admonitions had no more effect on Duke Ling than the autumn breeze murmuring in his ears. Day after day, Shi Ji gazed on his fellow officials with cold and disdainful eyes. He saw some senior ministers afraid to speak out against abuses, and others cynically safeguarding their own positions with mild words and diplomatic manners. Only Zhao Dun preserved his integrity, daring to rebuke the fatuous ruler, who held him in some awe, to his face. As soon as he had heard of the duke's shooting at the people, egged on by Tu'an Gu, Shi Ji was outraged. In a state of extreme agitation and distress, as soon as he heard that Zhao Dun had returned from encouraging the farmers, he could not restrain himself from hurrying to see the latter and discuss a joint censure of Duke Ling. Now, seeing that Zhao Dun was prepared for a showdown with the duke for the sake of the state, heedless of his own safety, Shi Ji too gave way to tears.

And so it was that in the dead of night, hands clasped and gazing into each other's eyes, the two of them poured their hearts out to each other.

Zhao Dun muttered in distress, "What the duke has done this time is a heinous crime that even a dyed-in-the-wool tyrant would flinch from. If such atrocities are allowed to continue, how can the State of Jin escape its ruin?"

赵盾听了这话,禁不住打了一个冷战。可转念一想,二十年前,自己只因一念不坚,误立灵公,到如今殃及晋国黎民百姓,心中颇有愧疚之意,便挺直腰杆道:"一之为甚,岂可再乎!我赵盾是祸由自取,如今也顾不得许多,只有豁出一条老命,效忠国家。"说罢,滴下几点老泪来。

士季大夫本是耿直忠义之人,看见灵公所为,自然心如刀绞,为晋国的前途命运担忧,对屠岸贾等人更是嫉恶如仇,只因自己身为下卿,人微言轻,虽曾多次进言规劝,怎奈灵公只当做耳边风,全然不听。而自己平日里冷眼旁观,见众大臣或胆小怕事,隐忍不发;或明哲保身,虚与委蛇。只有赵盾还有几分耿直,敢于当面进谏,而灵公也畏惧他几分。近日得知灵公在屠岸贾唆使下弹射行人取乐,士季自然心中忿懑,坐立不安,今天得知赵盾劝农归来,便迫不及待地上门造访,想与赵盾商量一下,合力劝谏。现在见赵盾不顾自身安危,决心以死报国,心中甚是感动,也洒下了两行热泪。

二人四目相对,两手紧握。此时夜阑人静,正好促膝对坐,倾心而谈。

赵盾忧心忡忡道:"主君近日所为,实属造孽,就是无道昏君也未必做得出来,如此下去,晋国岂能不亡?"

His friend was more circumspect. "It seems to me," he said, "that although the duke is wild and outrageous, his follies are more those of youth and inexperience. An old saying goes: 'He who touches rouge will be stained red, and he who touches ink will be stained black.' If only we can keep the duke away from wicked people like Tu'an Gu and his cronies, and get him to turn over a new leaf, there may be hope for Jin yet."

Zhao Dun pondered these words, and had to admit to himself that there was reason in them. When he reflected on how he had rushed to the Peach Garden and hammered on the gate in a frenzy, it seemed to him that he had been acting somewhat rashly. He sighed, and with a bitter smile said, "There is sense in what you say. From now on we must act in concert. We must urge the duke to associate only with worthy officials, and avoid base courtiers —— and then perhaps the affairs of our state may take a turn for the better."

The rhythmical cadence of a night watchman's clapper disturbed their deliberations. Dawn was not far off, and so they parted to refresh their spirits with sleep for a short while before attending court, at which they were to bring the duke to book.

At first light, all the court officials lined up in two rows before the throne, military functionaries on the left, civilian ones on the right. After a while, Duke Ling sauntered in, together with a flock of attendants and flunkeys. As soon as he had plumped himself down on the throne, and before any of the officials could present a memorial, he dismissed the court with a wave of his hand. "I am not feeling my best today," he drawled. "If any of you has any business to bring to my attention, keep it for some other time." He then rose, and scurried out of the throne room.

The officials gazed at each other, speechless. Shaking their heads and sighing, they dispersed and went their ways. Zhao Dun and Shi Ji, who had gone virtually without sleep the whole night, sacrificed to their serious discussion and deliberation, to their dismay found that they would not have a chance to remonstrate with the duke after all. Distressed, they left the palace and wandered to a secluded place to discuss what to do next. But before they

士季分析道："依我所见，主君虽然荒唐暴虐，但其行为多属年幼无知之举。古语云：'近朱者赤，近墨者黑。'如果能使主君远离屠岸贾之类的奸诈小人，痛改前非，晋国或许还有希望。"

赵盾闻言，仔细想想，也觉得有理，回忆自己方才夜闯桃园的举动，不禁感到有点儿鲁莽。于是吁了一口气，苦笑道："士季大夫言之有理，从今往后，你我齐心合力，劝谏主君亲贤臣，远小人。国事自当出现转机。"

说话间，忽听得远处梆声悠扬，响了四下，已经是四更了。二人这才止住话头，分头躺了一会儿，养养精神，准备次日早朝进谏。

五更早朝，百官都已到齐，分列两班。灵公在一帮侍从的簇拥下来到大堂上，屁股刚刚坐定，不等众臣上前奏事，便摆摆手道："寡人今日身子不爽，众卿有事，改日再言吧！"说完起身就走，如风般去了。

百官瞠目结舌，一个个摇头叹气，纷纷散去。可怜赵盾、士季二人一夜无眠，商量好了一肚子的话，竟然没有机会说出来，实在于心不甘。二人心照不宣，出了宫门，来到一个僻静处停下，商量如何应付这样的局面。尚未开口，忽见两个内侍抬着一个竹筐，鬼鬼祟祟从宫殿的侧门走出来，一边走，一边东

had a chance to say anything, they spotted two palace servants sneaking out of a side door of the palace, carrying a large bamboo basket. As they proceeded, their eyes snaked left and right. Zhao Dun's suspicions were immediately roused, and he commanded the pair to halt. "Hey, what are you two up to?" he demanded. "And what have you got in that basket?"

The servants pretended not to hear, and attempted to scurry off round a corner. But both Zhao Dun and Shi Ji were suspicious by this time. Quick as a flash, they barred their way. The other two had no choice but to stop and put the basket on the ground.

Upon Zhao Dun's asking them again what was in the basket, the servants turned ghastly pale and gave no answer. Eventually, one of them stammered, "We dare not say, Your Honor. Please deign to look yourself."

Zhao Dun gazed at the basket. There was nothing unusual about it from the outside; it was an ordinary bamboo basket covered with cabbage leaves. But when he lifted the leaves, he was appalled to find that the basket contained the bloody pieces of a dismembered corpse. Recoiling in horror, he questioned the servants, "Who was this man, and who chopped him up like this?"

The servants dithered, mumbled and pretended not to know anything about the affair, until Zhao Dun, in a towering rage, threatened to have both their heads lopped off. Only then did the truth come out.

The previous evening, the guards in the eastern quarter of the capital had noticed the crowds of people who had gathered in the road waiting to pour out their complaints about the duke's devilish target practice to Zhao Dun on his return from encouraging the farmers. The news was straightaway brought to Duke Ling, in the midst of his usual debauch in the Peach Garden. Befuddled as he was, the duke knew quite well that Zhao Dun would lose no time in condemning him to his face right there in the Peach Garden. He was rescued from his dilemma by Tu'an Gu, who whispered in his ear advising him to have the gates of the Peach Garden locked, and all visitors barred from entry. "Otherwise, he could spoil our fun, Your Majesty," Tu'an Gu explained

张西望。赵盾心中生疑，暗想此中必有缘故，便大声喝道："你等二人鬼鬼祟祟地做什么？且将竹筐抬过来！"

那两名内侍佯作未闻，头也不抬，急急忙忙地绕道而行。赵盾越发疑心，与士季一同赶过去堵住去路，那两名内侍只好站定，将肩上的竹筐放在地上。赵盾问道："竹筐中究竟为何物？"

两名内侍已经吓得脸色煞白，抖抖索索地答道："大人既然问起，请自己来看，我等万万不敢说。"

赵盾见竹筐上面是一些菜叶，没有什么异状，用手拨开菜叶一看，只见血肉模糊，竟然是一堆被砍成碎块的人体。不禁大吃一惊，退了一步，转过脸来向两名内侍追问道："这是何人？被谁杀死而碎尸？"

起初两名内侍还支支吾吾，不肯说实话。赵盾大怒，喝道："再不从实说来，先将你二人斩首！"两名内侍见瞒不过去，只得战战兢兢地说出原委。

原来，头一天傍晚，绛邑东门的守卫见百姓拦住劝农归来的赵盾，哭诉灵公弹射行人之事，便飞报正在桃园内玩乐的灵公。灵公闻报，知道赵盾必然赶来进谏，不免有些慌张。屠岸贾在一旁献计道："主君可将园门紧闭，不放那赵盾进来，免得扫兴。"灵公心中正没主意，闻言大喜，急命卫士将园门关紧，不得将任何人放入。赵盾没有敲开园门，只得回府。但灵公

blandly. The duke gave the necessary orders without delay. The result, as we have see, was that Zhao Dun knocked on the gate in vain, and had to return home defeated for the time being. But somehow, the mood of the evening had been spoiled for Duke Ling. He was somewhat in awe of his senior minister, and he knew well that he faced a dressing down the next morning, when Zhao Dun would no doubt come stalking into the court to denounce his evil deed of that day. Before long, he called a halt to the revels, and with his entourage returned in a sullen mood to the palace. In the meantime, Tu'an Gu sent an urgent message to the palace kitchen to prepare the duke's usual late-night snack.

Now Duke Ling was inordinately fond of bear's paws, a gourmet dish, and this was what the palace chef was used to preparing for him every evening. However, on this occasion, as the duke had decided to go home early, the bear's paws were not properly cooked by the time he arrived. The royal waiter, trembling with fear, had no choice but to rush the dish to the duke just as it was.

Duke Ling was already in a foul mood when he raised a morsel of bear's paw to his lips, but when after chewing it a couple of times he found that it had the taste and consistency of cowhide, he flew into a towering rage. Flinging his elegant ivory chopsticks to the ground, he thundered at the cook, who was in attendance, "You insolent villain of a cook! How many heads have you got that you can risk having one chopped off for serving your sovereign uncooked bear's paws?"

The cook was beside himself with fear, and his knees knocked like clappers. He threw himself full length at the duke's feet, where he remained prostrate with his forehead beating the floor ceaselessly. At this, the duke became even more incensed. Grabbing the first missile that came to hand, which happened to be a heavy brass flagon, he flung it at the unfortunate cook's head. Blood and brains spurted from the smashed skull, and the cook died instantly. The horrified attendants stared, as speechless as wooden chickens. But the duke's wrath had not subsided yet. He drew his sword,

平素里对赵盾毕竟有所顾忌，眼前虽然躲了过去，但明日临朝听政，料想那赵盾必有一番规谏，真不知如何应付才好。又玩儿了一阵子，心中有事，不免意兴索然，带着人悻悻地回到宫中。

屠岸贾急忙传厨房预备夜宵。灵公一向酷嗜熊掌，厨师每晚必得准备。不料灵公今夜回来得早，熊掌正炖在锅中，尚未烂熟，无奈传膳的内侍一个劲儿地催促，厨师只得战战兢兢将熊掌端了上来。

灵公心中本来没有好气，举箸夹起一块熊掌放入口中，嚼了两下，好似牛皮，当下气得七窍生烟，将牙箸一掷，大声喝道："大胆厨师，你长着几个脑袋，竟敢将未熟的熊掌端给寡人！"

厨师本来心中惴惴，惧怕不已，此时见灵公大怒，早已吓得魂飞魄散，两条腿抖得如同筛糠一般，瘫在地上不住地叩头。灵公看了，更加气恼不已，顺手抓起几上的一个大铜爵，直向厨师掷了过去，不偏不倚，正中厨师的脑袋，顿时鲜血如注，脑浆迸流，一命归西了。一旁侍立的众人见状惊得瞠目结舌，呆若木鸡。灵公却还不解气，又拔出宝剑，亲自挥剑将厨师的尸体砍作数段，才气哼哼地回寝殿去了。

and proceeded to chop the corpse of the cook up into little pieces. Then he stalked off to his bedchamber, grunting with satisfaction.

As soon as he had disappeared, Tu'an Gu ordered the others, "Wait until after the morning's court has been dismissed, and there is no one around. Then take the remains of the body and bury them in some obscure place. Don't say a word to a soul about this. Any slip ups, and you'll pay for it with your lives!"

. . . .

On hearing the servants' story, Zhao Dun was filled with anger. Stamping his foot, he cried, "This wicked ruler, who treats human life as if it were no more than straw, will be the ruin of our state! I fear its demise is imminent. We must both go and take this tyrant to task. If he rebuffs us, we must commit suicide right there in the palace."

Shi Ji shook his head. "May I venture to say that this is not a suitable course of action? If the duke refuses to listen to us, there will be nobody else ready to admonish him. I think it would be better if I tackled him first, and then, if the duke remains adamant, you can then bring pressure to bear on him. Perhaps that would be better?"

Zhao Dun realized that the other's plan was a good one, so he let him enter the palace first, while he himself waited outside.

When a servant announced that Shi Ji requested an audience, Duke Ling knew quite well on what errand Shi Ji had come. But there was no fobbing off his visitor, so he sighed and ordered that Shi Ji be shown in. Shi Ji paced the long hall up to the throne, under the eye of the duke the whole time. He knelt, kowtowed the customary number of times, and began, "Your Majesty." But before he had a chance to continue, the duke, determined not to listen to a tiresome dressing down, and deciding that attack was the best form of defense, interrupted him, "You can save your breath, Minister. I know perfectly well that I am at fault. From now on, I have turned over a new leaf." With this, he turned to his attendants and ordered that the cook be given a solemn funeral, to appease his relatives.

屠岸贾吩咐众人道："你等务于明日早朝之后，趁内外无人时将尸体抬出野外埋了。谁也不准走漏风声，若有差错，小心性命！"

……

赵盾听罢，心中怒火升腾，跺脚道："主君无道，视人命如草芥，国家危亡，恐怕只在旦夕！你我二人此刻便去谏诤那昏君一番，如若无效，便死在殿前罢了！"

士季摇头道："鄙意以为不妥。我二人同去谏诤，万一主君不听，就无人再去谏诤了。不如下官先去劝谏，如果主君不从，大人再进宫面见主君力争，岂不更好？"

赵盾见士季说得有理，便由士季先入宫去，自己站在宫外等候。

灵公听内侍通报士季大夫求见，心中知道必是来指责自己轻率杀人，可又躲不过去，只得传士季入宫，远远望见士季走近跪下叩头，直起身子开口道："主君……"灵公实在不愿听士季絮聒不休，索性以守为攻，抢在前面说道："不劳大夫多说了，寡人已经知道过错，日后一定改正。"说罢，转过头去吩咐将厨师厚葬，抚恤其家人。

Hearing this, Shi Ji hastily kowtowed, and said, "Who is without fault, sire? But there is nothing more laudable than correcting one's transgressions. If Your Majesty really does turn over a new leaf, the state will surely prosper. Then, how happy will we your servants be!"

Thereupon he withdrew, and reported all that had happened to Zhao Dun, who commented, "If the duke is resolved to become a reformed character, this should be reflected in his actions from now on."

As they were talking, there arose a hubbub at the doorway of the palace, as orders were given for a carriage to be got ready to take Duke Ling to the Peach Garden. Zhao Dun's face stiffened with indignation. "A fine sort of repentance," he cried, "To be so soon plunging into frivolity once more!" Without more ado, he mounted his own carriage, and hurried off to the Peach Garden. He was waiting at the gate of the pleasure ground, determined to give the duke a good dressing down, when the royal party arrived.

The duke, meanwhile, was feeling very pleased with himself for having managed to get rid of Shi Ji with a shallow excuse, and was looking forward to a day of carefree pleasure with a bevy of beauties from his harem, when he perceived the stony-face Zhao Dun barring his way to the Peach Garden. There was nothing for it but to confront his accuser, and so, with a sickly grin, he said, "I have no business today, Minister, so I did not summon you. Perhaps you would care to join me in a little relaxation?"

Zhao Dun kowtowed before the duke's carriage. "Your unworthy servant," he said, "Ventures to have something to inform you of, Your Majesty. I hope you will have the magnanimity to indulge me. I have heard that a virtuous ruler uses music to gladden the hearts of the people, while a ruler who lacks virtue uses music only to gladden his own heart. From ancient times, it has been the practice of rulers to take their pleasure either within the palace with their courtesans and servants or abroad hunting and sightseeing. Never has it been heard that an upright ruler kills people for sport. Such atrocities as setting savage mastiffs on or shooting harmless passers-by and dismembering a cook for some trifling misdemeanor are unheard of even from

士季听灵公如此说,忙下拜道:"人谁无过,过而能改,是再好也没有的事了。主君如能改过,是社稷的福气,臣等幸甚! 国家幸甚! "

说毕退了出来,将方才情景细细说与赵盾。赵盾道:"主君如果真想改过,今后应该付诸行动才是。"

说话中间,却见宫门内外一阵忙乱,内侍们一片声地吩咐摆驾,要侍候灵公前往桃园。赵盾登时脸色铁青,怒气冲天道:"主君如此耽于游乐,哪里像个改过的样子! "说罢,登上车子,抢先赶往桃园,在园门外等待灵公,下决心要痛切谏诤一番。

且说灵公三言两语搪塞走了士季大夫,得意洋洋,心想今日又可痛痛快快地玩一天了,急命起驾,带了一大帮宫女侍从,径往桃园。不料赵盾已经守在园门外边,灵公无法回避,只得讪笑道:"寡人今日无事,不曾召卿,上卿敢是也想到桃园游览一番?"

赵盾在车前叩首道:"待死微臣,有言启奏,望主君宽容采纳。臣听说,有道之君,用音乐来使百姓快乐;无道之君,用音乐来使自己快乐。自古以来,国君的取乐方式不外乎宫室女色、打猎游乐而已。从古到今,还没有哪一个正派的国君用杀人来取乐。主君纵犬噬人,弹射行人,又因为小小的过失肢解厨师,凡此种种,无道之君也不曾做过,主君你却全都做了。

unrighteous rulers. But Your Majesty has been guilty of all these things! Human life is a gift from Heaven. If you spill blood so promiscuously the common people will rebel and the other feudal lords will invade our state, and then the disasters attendant upon the fall of the tyrants Jie of the Xia Dynasty and Zhou of the Shang Dynasty will befall Jin! It is because your humble servant cannot bear to sit by and watch the ruin of our country that I dare to risk death by speaking so bluntly. I beseech Your Majesty to turn your carriage around, return to the court and mend your ways by devoting yourself to affairs of state. No more frittering away day after day in petty pleasure-seeking, and no more taking of innocent lives! Only then will Jin be pulled back from the brink of disaster, and Your Majesty follow in the footsteps of the sage kings Yao and Shun. At such a time would I die without regret." Having said this, he kept kneeling in front of the duke's carriage.

Duke Ling, although he was muddle-headed and tyrannical, still had a spark of shrewdness left in him. Besides, he held Zhao Dun somewhat in awe. So when the latter reminded him of righteousness, a shiver of remorse touched his heart. But his heart was set on a day of carousing and cavorting, and nothing was further from his mind than court business. With a dismissive wave of a sleeve, he said, "Minister, you go back first, and leave me to one more day of relaxation. I promise you that after that I will heed your advice."

The sight of the duke, apparently in a state of abject contrition and whimpering like a child, dispelled the towering rage that had been bursting inside Zhao Dun's breast. The prime minister did not know whether to laugh or to frown. He felt like a negligent father facing his wayward son; indignation and affection, shame and regret struggled within him. Then, remembering his authority, he stood in front of the gate to the Peach Garden, resolutely barring the way for the duke.

Tu'an Gu had always resented the power that Zhao Dun wielded, his way of speaking out fearlessly, and especially that fact that he had many times denounced Tu'an Gu as a petty and evil man. He had long awaited an opportunity to trap the prime minister, but up until now none had presented

人命关天，滥杀如此，倘若百姓内叛，诸侯外侵，桀纣灭亡之祸将见于晋国。微臣今日不忍坐视晋国危亡，故冒死直言，恳请主君回车入朝，勤理朝政，痛改前非，不再整日游玩嬉戏，更不可滥杀无辜。如此晋国方能转危为安，主君亦可上追尧舜，微臣虽死无憾！"说罢，长跪不起。

灵公虽然颠顶暴戾，心中却不曾丧失灵智，况且对赵盾素来有所顾忌，听赵盾说得入情入理，心中也闪过一丝惭疚。无奈他早已游乐成性，实在无心朝事，当下以袖掩面道："上卿且先回去，容寡人再玩一日，以后全凭上卿做主。"

赵盾本来火冒三丈，怒气填膺。现在眼见灵公神态可怜兮兮，口吻犹如孩童，不禁感到又可笑又可气，犹如一个未曾尽职的父亲看着自己不成器的儿子，又气又爱，愧悔交加。于是索性倚老卖老，起身挡住园门，不放灵公进去。

屠岸贾一直嫉恨赵盾权大势重，正直敢言，不止一次指斥自己是奸恶小人，早就伺机陷害，只是没有机会下手，今日见赵盾当面让灵公下不来台，便在一旁阴阳怪气地插嘴道："相国拦门进谏，固然是一片好意，可是堂堂国君，车驾已至园门，如果听凭相国一言而返，岂不贻笑诸侯？况且相国协助国君治理国

itself. Today, however, perceiving that Zhao Dun had put Duke Ling in an embarrassing situation, Tu'an Gu butted in with insinuating words, "I am sure Your Honor has the best of intentions in presuming to block the gate and remonstrate with the duke. But you must take cognizance of our ruler's position. Here His Majesty is, already at the gate to the Peach Garden; if he were to heed your words, and turn back, how could he not become a laughing-stock among the rulers of the other states? Besides, your own duty to assist His Majesty to govern must occupy you with weighty matters of state. How is it that you allow yourself to be vexed over such a trifle as this?"

These words angered Zhao Dun. Drawing himself up to his full height and glaring at Tu'an Gu, he said, "The duke is young and inexperienced. He fritters away his time in idle pleasures. We, his ministers, have the duty guide him on the path of righteous conduct, not encourage him in his frivolity with base flattery! Do you not realize that this trifle, as you call it, is the sort of thing that could lead to the very downfall of our state?"

At this, Tu'an Gu gave a mirthless smile. "Oh, I see. So the prime minister is suggesting that His Majesty consult him about every little thing he wishes to do, I suppose! It is my humble opinion that the prime minister should calm down for the time being, and unblock the gateway. If the prime minister has any matter to bring up with His Majesty, it will surely not be too late to do so at tomorrow morning's court audience, will it?"

So saying, Tu'an Gu turned and gave Duke Ling a sly glance. This put new heart into the duke, who hastily interjected, "Yes, yes. That's right. I will summon you first thing tomorrow, Prime Minister!"

Zhao Dun had no choice but to stand aside and allow the duke and his entourage to enter the Peach Garden. His heart was full of rage and bitterness. As he glared at the retreating back of Tu'an Gu, he ground his teeth, and muttered to himself, "A blockhead of a ruler, and a doomed country — all the fault of that rascally official!"

家,有多少大事要办,何苦过问这些小事!"

赵盾听了,心中愤怒,立起身来,直瞪着屠岸贾,说道:"主君年少无知,耽于嬉戏游乐,我辈大臣正应谏诤劝止,岂能推波助澜,一味阿谀媚上!司寇说这是'小事',难道不知亡国败家,正是由这些小事引起!"

屠岸贾闻言,冷笑数声道:"如此说来,主君每天干些什么,还需向相国请示喽? 在下请相国还是暂行方便,让开园门。如果有所奏请,明日早朝也不迟呀!"

说罢,向着灵公丢了一个眼色。灵公心领神会,急忙插嘴道:"明日早朝,寡人一定召见上卿。"

赵盾不得已,只得将身子闪开,放灵公进桃园去了。心中却是无比忿恨,双眼瞪着屠岸贾的背影,咬牙切齿道:"君昏国亡,都是由此辈乱臣贼子所诱致!"

赵氏孤儿

Chapter Two
Chu Ni Dashes His Brains Out

With the connivance of Tu'an Gu, Duke Ling had managed to get back into the Peach Garden for another session of merrymaking. But Zhao Dun's intervention had dashed all his hopes of enjoying himself. The duke's temper became very sour indeed, until everything he looked at became loathsome to him. He stepped into garden, where the peaches and apricots were ripe in abundance, and the branches of the poplar and willow trees brushed the ground, as always. But this pleasant sight could not dispel the nameless burning in the duke's breast. He drew his sword and began to slash savagely at the grass and trees beside the path, leaving heaps of red and green ruin to mark his passage. Tu'an Gu at his side fanned the flames of the duke's anguish by saying, "Your Highness, please curb your wrath. If the prime minister should hear of this he would be sure to upbraid you for it."

These words, as they were meant to, goaded the duke into a paroxysm of fury, as they reminded him of how Zhao Dun had him in fetters. Just at that moment the duke and his retinue happened to arrive at a rockery beside a pond. The craggy stones were set off by fantastic plants and trailing creepers, some dangling from the top, and others wrapped around the foot of the ornamental stones, in a wispy fragrant green veil. The delicate artistry of the rockery did not please the duke's jaundiced eye, however. "What idiot put that pile together?" he bawled. "Green leaves have always, since time immemorial, been used to set off red flowers. How is it that this thing has green creepers and vines straggling all over it? Bring that damned gardener here to me at once!"

第二章　钮麂触槐

灵公得了屠岸贾帮腔，好歹算是进了桃园，可是一腔游兴，被赵盾扫了个净光，心中自然疙疙瘩瘩，满胸不快，见了什么都看不顺眼。进了园后，只见桃杏遮天，杨柳拂地，仍然是往日景色，却有一股无名之火横亘在胸中，手持利剑，对路边的草木大砍大杀，可怜红英绿叶，一片狼藉。屠岸贾又从旁煽风点火道："主君息怒，万一让相国知晓，岂不又是一场官司？"

灵公听了，越发闷气填胸，他本来就不满赵盾总是约束规劝自己，听了屠岸贾之言，愈加烦恼。上下一行人恰好走至一座湖石假山前，只见山石嶙峋，异态纷呈，上面仙萝异草，牵藤引蔓，或垂山顶，或穿山脚，有如翠带飘摇，又像青绳蟠屈；更兼香气馥郁，压过群芳。灵公无来由地迁怒于眼前的景色，厉声骂道："这山是哪个混蛋弄的？自古绿叶衬红花，怎么倒让这绿藤翠蔓爬了一山！岂有此理，还不快快给我打那该死的园公！"

With glee, Tu'an Gu perceived that his carefully timed words had had the desired effect. He lost no time sending soldiers to fetch the gardener, who was given a sound beating with clubs on the spot and thrown into the bushes, no one caring whether he was dead or alive. The duke let out a melancholy sigh. In truth he was beginning to feel somewhat better after this, and a trace of a smile could be detected on his face.

When the Peach Garden had been constructed, a channel had been chiseled to let in water, which gathered in a lotus pond in the southeast corner. In the height of summer, the pond was covered with bright red and green lotuses, a most delightful sight. The banks of the pond were lined with poplar, willow and locust trees, affording a deep and welcome shade from the sun. Within this arbor was a pavilion, with flying eaves and soaring corners. Inside were placed bamboo couches for the duke and his harem to sport upon. It was known as the "Pavilion of Joy". Now mid-spring was upon the place, and bright red fallen leaves floated upon the clear waters together with emerald lotuses. Fishes of many hues darted and glided in the ripples, now appearing, now vanishing. Duke Ling paced heavily to the edge of the pond. He summoned the courtesans he had brought with him, and began to embrace and fondle first this one and then that one. In the midst of his lascivious slobbering and groping, the duke suddenly noticed a pair of mandarin ducks nestling up to and feeding each other by the margin of the pond. An idea for a new type of amusement arose into his mind, and he chortled, "I think I'd like to have a bath with you, my dears, just like these mandarin ducks." Everyone was startled to hear this, especially Tu'an Gu. He hastened to advise the duke against such foolishness, "Your Majesty should not risk your precious health," he begged. "The pond water is far too chilly for Your Majesty's delicate constitution. Why not order one of your servants and a palace maid to have a bath together instead, and you can watch them from the bank. Wouldn't that be much more interesting?"

The duke was pleased with this suggestion. "All right," he said, "It shall be as you say."

屠岸贾见自己的谗言已经奏效，心中暗喜，急忙命卫士将园公找来，按倒在地，不由分说，狠狠打了四十大板，不管死活，扔到林中去了。灵公出了一口闷气，心中觉得畅快了些，脸上也有了笑意。

当日建造桃园时，凿石引水，在东南角上掘了一个莲池，盛夏时节，池中红荷翠盖，艳色怡人；池畔绿柳碧槐，浓荫蔽日。其间又盖起个华亭，飞檐翘角，内设竹榻锦帐，专供灵公与宫女们厮混，故名"快活亭"。眼下正是仲春，池水清澈，落红无数，溶溶荡荡。加上荷钱点碧，水藻浮青，又有五色小鱼，喋浪追波，上下浮沉，一闪一现，忽停忽游，十分有趣。灵公漫步来到池畔，早有宫女们妖姿媚态，迎了上来。灵公搂了这个，抱着那个，亲嘴摸乳，丑态百出。厮混中间，灵公忽见一对鸳鸯相依相偎，对浴岸边，看了一会儿，好不眼热，独出心裁，想起一个新鲜的玩法，开口道："寡人要与你等共效鸳鸯，在这池水中对浴一番。"众人一听，都惊呆了眼。屠岸贾也恐闹出事来，上前劝道："主君龙体要紧，这池水颇凉，不耐忍受。不如让侍从与宫女对浴，主君在岸上面观看，岂不更有趣些？"

灵公笑道："也好，寡人就听爱卿的。"

Duke Ling's lecherous nature knew no bounds, and he kept hundreds of courtesans for his own exclusive pleasure. One of these was particularly delicate and charming, with skin as soft and white as snow. By nature she was bewitchingly charming as a fox, and the infatuated duke's nickname for her was "Fox Lady". Her amorous exploits kept the duke in raptures. Now he ordered her and one of his close courtiers to imitate the mandarin ducks. The man knew well his master's evil nature, and dared not refuse to engage in this charade. So he doffed his garments and entered the water. But Fox Lady, pinning her hopes on the duke's previous affection for her, was loath to undress, anxious to escape the indignity. But a gruff command from the duke dashed any hope she had on that score. At once, his attendants rushed forward, howling like animals, stripped Fox Lady naked and hurled her into the pond. As she struggled in the water, she was grasped tightly by the courtier, and at the duke's direction the two were forced to imitate all the amorous cavortings of a pair of mandarin ducks. This sight caused Duke Ling extraordinary delight. He applauded heartily, and called out, "That's right, you're as good as a real pair of mandarin ducks!"

Although it was spring, the water in the pond was quite cold, and before the pair had been in it for half an hour, they were chilled to the marrow and quite purple in color, and were shivering from head to foot. But the duke showed no sign of tiring of the spectacle. Clapping his hands and laughing, he said, "You've shown me a proper spectacle today. I'll give you two a big reward tomorrow."

But Fox Lady could stand the cold no longer. "I'm freezing to death," she cried, and pushing away her companion, she struggled for the shore. But as soon as she placed her hands on the stone path surrounding the pond, Duke Ling's mood suddenly turned nasty, as he perceived that the entertainment was at an end. "Why, you ungrateful slut!" he cried. With that, and before anyone could stop him, the duke raised his sword and swung it down sav-

那灵公素日荒淫无度,宫女数以百计。内中有一个生得娇小玲珑,姿容俏丽,肌肤洁白细嫩,像是雪做的似的,且天生一副妖冶神态,狐狸精一般,直迷得灵公魂不守舍,对她爱怜非常,戏称为"狐姬"。这狐姬平日在灵公面前撒娇卖俏,无所不至。此时灵公心血来潮,指名要这狐姬与身边一个得宠的侍从同效鸳鸯。那位侍从知道灵公的性子,不敢违抗,心中暗暗叫苦,不得不脱掉衣服,下到水中。狐姬仗着灵公素日宠爱自己,还在一边忸忸怩怩,不肯脱衣。众侍从听得灵公一声吆喝,如狼似虎,上前按倒,将狐姬通身剥得一丝不挂,赤条条地抛进池里。狐姬还在水里挣扎,却已被那侍从紧紧抱住,按灵公之意,交胫贴股,吻腮抚面,做那鸳鸯之戏。灵公也不嫉妒,反倒觉得好玩儿,将两只手拍得山响,不住喊道:"好啊,将那真鸳鸯也比下去了。"

此时虽是春天,但毕竟还有几分凉意,池水侵肌入骨。不到两刻钟,水中的两个人便冻得肌肤发紫,浑身乱颤。灵公却只管拍手大笑,说:"今日寡人大开眼界,明日必定重赏你二人。"

狐姬实在忍受不住,一面大叫"冻死了!"一面奋力推开侍从,挣扎着扑腾到岸边,两只手扒在岩石上,想要爬出水来。灵公正看得有趣,见狐姬不肯表演下

agely, cleanly severing at a stroke the exquisite lily-white hands placed on the bank. Fox Lady slipped back into the pond, struggling in desperation as an ominous red stain darkened the limpid water.

The watchers on the bank were frozen with horror. One of the palace ladies, who had been jealous of the way Fox Lady had used her coquettish wiles to win the duke's favor, could not suppress a scream when she witness this brutality, and was poised for flight when the duke whirled round upon her.

"Oh, so you want to run away, do you, you bitch?" he snarled. And, without more ado, he ordered his bodyguards to chop off the unfortunate girl's legs.

This was done, following which a shocked silence fell upon the whole company on the margin of the pond, broken only by the moans of the dismembered girls as they thrashed about in their death agonies. The duke stretched lazily. "That's enough fun for one day," he yawned. "Now, up to the pavilion for some wine!"

Leaving the dying girls, the assemblage retired with the duke to the Crimson Cloud Tower. Watching them with glazed eyes was the courtier who had played the part of a male mandarin duck, his body rigid with cold. As the duke's retinue disappeared from view, so did he —— into his watery grave. Three lives had been snuffed out in an instant, all because of a whim of the evil Duke Ling.

The feasting and merriment in the Crimson Cloud Tower continued until it was time for the lamps to be lit. Duke Ling and Tu'an Gu exchanged toast after toast. Harem girls snuggled up to the duke, giggling and teasing. But the shadow of the frightful deeds of that morning hung over the rest of the duke's attendants, and they stood round in silence, hardly even daring to breath heavily. Outside the tower, the guards too stood like statues, too oppressed with horror to utter a sound, so that the hubbub in the tower was strangely pervaded with a hush redolent of death.

去，心中甚是恼怒，全然忘了素日恩爱，道："好你个贱人，竟敢不识抬举！"说时迟，那时快，众人不防，灵公早已操起宝剑砍了下去，可怜狐姬一双凝脂般的柔荑，刹那间被砍落在岸边，登时血流如注。狐姬滚落池中，在水里惨嚎挣扎，碧池内一片殷红。

岸上一班人见状，早已吓得魂飞天外，个个犹如木桩一般呆立不动。其中有一个宫女，自恃有几分姿色，平日见狐姬得宠，心内还有些嫉妒，忽见今日惨像，不由得大叫一声："啊呀！"转身就想逃走。

灵公闻声转头，见那宫女撒腿正欲逃跑，怒道："小贱人，你好胆大，居然想跑。"话音未落，又喝令卫士将那宫女两腿砍掉。

转眼之间，热闹的莲池岸畔肃如严冬，只能听见两名肢体残缺的宫女在婉转惨叫，灵公却伸了个懒腰，道："寡人也玩儿腻了，上楼喝酒去吧。"

众人闻言，也不顾两名宫女的死活，一齐簇拥着随灵公去了。池水中假扮鸳鸯的侍从早已冻得肢体麻木，目睹方才的惨状，又惊又怕，昏了过去，溺死在莲池中。可怜三条性命，转瞬之间丧于灵公之手。

不知不觉，已是点灯时分，宽敞的绛霄楼中，酒酣歌急。晋灵公和屠岸贾正在频频举杯，妖冶的卫姬千媚百娇地靠在灵公身上，嬉笑逗乐。可是众侍女慑于

Duke Ling's face flushed with wine, began to feel light-headed. There was a twinge of disquiet in his mind. Then rage started to bubble up inside him when he remembered the way that Zhao Dun had upbraided him over the death of the cook. But the thought of how powerful his prime minister was made him feel uneasy. Nonplused, he glanced at Tu'an Gu, and immediately perceived that his crony knew what he was thinking.

....

Tu'an Gu was the eldest grandson of Tu'an Yi, a general who had served Duke Hui of the State of Jin and who was a man of immense strength and courage. During a campaign against the State of Qin, Tu'an Yi wielded a huge iron halberd in a duel with the renowned Qin general Bai Yibing. The contest was a close one, as the earth rocked and the heavens resounded to the clash of the two champions. Tu'an Yi was struck by a treacherous arrow, and died on the spot. The Qin army, however, was routed, and fled taking the sorely wounded Bai Yibing with it. Safe in his home state, Bai vomited gallons of blood, and only recovered from his ordeal half a year later. But ever afterwards, whenever the name of Tu'an Yi was mentioned he was sure to turn pale and tremble.

Moved by Tu'an Yi's valor and his sacrifice in laying down his life for his country, Duke Hui bestowed lavish honors on his family, and made his son Tu'an Kui lord of a populous and productive estate. By the time Tu'an Gu was born, the Tu'an family was at the height of its prosperity. Tu'an Gu was also robust, and followed in the family tradition of studying the 18 martial arts. However, by nature he was degenerate, and perverted the qualities of heroism, loyalty and devotion which he had inherited from his forebears into treachery, viciousness and evil intent. With the demise in succession of Jin's senior ministers Luan Zhi, Xian Qieju, Xu Chen and Zhao Shuai, Tu'an Gu's star gradually rose at court. He had spent the previous several years intriguing to worm his way into the good graces of Duke

白日里灵公的暴虐，一个个肃然环立，大气也不敢
出。楼外的卫士同样一声不吭，犹如雕像一般。使得
绛霄楼内外于热闹之中透出一股肃杀之气。

几盏酒下肚，灵公脸上热了起来，心中翻江倒海
一般，不得安宁。一想起上午赵盾因厨师之死，当面
将自己大大斥责一番的情景，就不由得火冒三丈；转
而再想想赵盾的权势威信，又不由得阵阵不安。他抬
起头来看看屠岸贾，见那屠岸贾也正在若有所思。

……

屠岸贾本是晋国大将屠岸夷的长孙。晋惠公时，
屠岸夷力能举鼎，英勇无比。一次同秦国交战，屠岸
夷手执几十斤重的铁戟，与秦国名将白乙丙交手，直
打得天昏地暗，胜负难分。后来中了暗箭，死于沙场，
却使秦人闻风丧胆。听说白乙丙回国后，竟吐血数
斗，半年后才恢复元气，然而一提起屠岸夷，仍免不了
胆战心惊。

晋惠公体恤屠岸夷勇武，为国捐躯，下令旌表门
楣，并封其长子屠岸魁为千夫长，食二百石。到屠岸
贾时，屠岸家更为兴隆。屠岸贾也是力大无比，又随
父亲学了十八般武艺，只是生性奸诈，将祖辈的一身
英武之气、一腔忠心赤胆换作了阴险狠毒和满肚子的

Ling, until he could get the latter to do anything he wanted. As he came to realize how simple-minded the duke was, Tu'an Gu began to covet the throne for himself, but as he perceived that the time was not yet ripe, he refrained from acting on his ambition. As he mulled his plan of action, he came to recognize that Zhao Dun was the main stumbling block to his schemes, and decided that somehow the prime minister must be removed. But, unfortunately the good-for-nothing duke feared Zhao Dun, and seeing how Duke Ling had cowered beneath his prime minister's tongue lashing that morning, Tu'an Gu was convinced that only by getting rid of Zhao Dun first could he achieve mastery over the duke and then seize control of the whole State of Jin. At this point, he noticed that the duke had paused, his cup midway to his lips. Duke Ling seemed to be distracted by something, and Tu'an Gu knew that his mind was troubled by Zhao Dun. The wily Tu'an Gu then made a show of knitting his brows and sighing.

Duke Ling stared dully at Tu'an Gu's woebegone countenance for a while, and asked, "Minister, why are you not joining in the merriment? Sitting there sighing like that, you're spoiling my fun."

The other replied, "Who wouldn't want to join in the merriment, Your Majesty? It is just that I am worried for your sake, sire. I fear that after tonight there will be no more of these lavish entertainments."

The addle-brained duke fell into his minister's trap straightaway. "What do you mean?" he asked.

"Tomorrow, the prime minister will surely censure you, Your Majesty," Tu'an Gu explained. "Do you think he will ever allow you to come here again to enjoy yourself?"

The duke became crimson with fury, and was on the point of giving vent to his rage, but he thought he had better calm down. Tu'an Gu seized this opportunity to say, "Today he had the effrontery to try to prevent Your Majesty entering the Peach Garden, and tomorrow he will try to prevent you leaving the palace. I myself was the object of his censure today, and so I fear

鬼主意。等到晋国大臣栾枝、先且居、胥臣、赵衰等相继去世后，屠岸贾渐渐崭露头角。近年来，欺下瞒上，讨得灵公欢心，言听计从，随心所欲。后来见灵公头脑简单，竟然生出了觊觎君位的野心，只是见眼下时机还不成熟，暂时不敢发难。但思来想去，觉得赵盾终归是块绊脚石，必欲除之而后快。可恨灵公无能，竟怕赵盾三分。今天上午，又被赵盾当众指责了自己一番，看来要夺晋国天下，必先除去赵盾，而后才能摆布灵公，伺机行事。想到此处，转眼看见灵公停杯不饮，心神不宁，知道他必定是因赵盾而心中烦恼，便故意皱着眉头，假装长吁短叹。

灵公呆了半晌，见屠岸贾忽然面有忧色，便道："爱卿何不及时行乐，却屡屡叹息不止，岂不令寡人扫兴？"

屠岸贾道："及时行乐，何人不愿！只是微臣替主君担心，恐怕过了今夜，这快乐不能复得了。"

灵公本来是个头脑简单的无能之辈，立即堕入屠岸贾的圈套，不解地问道："这又为何？"

屠岸贾道："相国明日定然要有一番诤谏，岂能容得主君再来园中游玩？"

that I will no longer dare accompany Your Majesty on pleasure jaunts here."

Hearing this, Duke Ling turned purple with anger. "What on earth do you mean?" he spluttered. "It has always been the rule that ministers obey their rulers' commands. I've never heard of a ruler being under the thumb of one of his ministers. This Zhao Dun keeps popping up and lecturing me. I'll never have any peace while he is alive. Tomorrow I'll have him impeached and his head chopped off! Just see if I don't!"

Perceiving that his master was beside himself with rage, Tu'an Gu was secretly delighted, but he said soberly, "May I be so bold as to venture to say that Your Majesty is being somewhat rash. How can you have Zhao Dun executed openly? Apart from the fact that the common people of Jin would be outraged, Your Majesty's other ministers would never consent to it. Besides, I am afraid that when the rulers of the other states heard of it, they would raise a great cry about 'righting an injustice' and use this as an excuse to invade Jin. Then there would be uproar both at home and abroad. How could Your Majesty enjoy yourself at your ease in those circumstances? Besides, the Zhao clan is numerous and powerful, and Zhao Dun himself has served two rulers and acted as regent during Your Majesty's minority. The Zhaos might depose you and set up another ruler."

A pall of gloom descended on the duke as these words sank in. "Then there's nothing I can do about him, it seems," he muttered.

Tu'an Gu saw that the time was ripe for the next step in his scheme. He gave a dry cough, and whispered, "Your Majesty, I have a suggestion. But I don't know whether or not...."

The duke leaned forward eagerly, his eyes popping out as big as bronze bells. "Come on, tell me!" he ordered. "I'm all ears."

For the moment, Tu'an Gu said not a word, but gestured for the officials, servants and palace ladies to leave. Only when the two of them were alone did he bend towards the duke's ear. "Your humble servant has a retainer whose name is Chu Ni. He entered my employ to escape destitution and is devoted to me. If I order him to, he will sneak into Zhao Dun's

灵公闻言满面通红，便欲发作，转念一想，又蔫了下来。屠岸贾见状，趁热打铁道："他今日敢拦住园门，不让主君进园，明日就敢拦住宫门，不放主君出来。微臣今天也遭他训斥，从此再不敢随着主君来园中玩乐了。"

灵公听罢，愤然作色道："岂有此理！自古臣下听命于君主，从来没有听说过君主受制于臣下。赵盾不时来絮聒寡人，这老儿不死，寡人是不得安宁了。看我明日给他安个罪名，当堂斩了他！"

屠岸贾见灵公已被激怒，心中暗喜，口中却说道："主君错了，赵盾岂能当堂斩杀？别说晋国百姓不服，朝臣老将不从，就是诸侯列国听了，恐怕也会前来问罪。到时内外大乱，主君岂能安心玩乐？再说那赵家人多势众，赵盾又是两朝元老，托孤重臣，还要提防他废除主君，另立新君。"

灵公听了，好不心灰意懒，道："如此说来，寡人就无法收拾那老儿了。"

屠岸贾见火候已到，便干咳一声道："微臣倒有一个主意，只不知主君是否……"

灵公闻言，身子向前一倾，双眼睁得犹如铜铃一般，嚷道："爱卿快快讲来，寡人洗耳恭听。"

屠岸贾却闭口不说了，一挥手臂，令周围侍立的

mansion and assassinate Zhao without anybody being the wiser. Of course, it goes without saying that there will be no way that Your Majesty will be implicated. Would not that be a convenient way of removing this nail from Your Majesty's eye, this thorn from the royal flesh?"

Duke Ling was overjoyed. "I'll leave it all to you, Minister," he burbled. "And when the deed is accomplished, I will see that you are handsomely rewarded."

With the plot in place, the duke mounted his carriage, and returned to his quarters.

That night, Tu'an Gu secretly summoned Chu Ni to him. He told his hireling that Zhao Dun had been plotting against the duke, for he had his eyes on the throne. Chu Ni, who spent all his time on duty in Tu'an Gu's mansion, knew nothing of the goings-on at court or of state affairs, and his master's poisonous words stirred indignation within him against this treacherous prime minister known as Zhao Dun. When Tu'an Gu informed him that it was the will of the emperor himself that Zhao Dun be dealt with, Chu Ni assented readily. "I have for many years been the humble recipient of Your Lordship's bounty," he said. "And I have long been ready to lay down my life for you. I will go straightaway and make that rascally Zhao Dun perish under the knife, and rid our country of a subversive and overweening minister!"

Seeing that his sinister plot was working, Tu'an Gu was delighted, but his faced showed no sign of his pleasure, being clouded with feigned worry. "But Zhao Dun's mansion is closely guarded. There is no assurance that your bold attempt will succeed. Please reconsider."

But Chu Ni retorted indignantly, "My Lord, I am determined to carry out my resolve, both to rid our country of an evil man and to repay you for your kindness. Even if I die in the attempt I will have no regrets."

Tu'an Gu forthwith ordered wine to be brought, and shared three toasts with Chu Ni. The matter being settled, and dawn being not far off, the assassin bowed low to his master and took his leave, a dagger strapped to his

宫女侍从全部退下，这才附耳低言道："微臣家中有个门客，名叫钮麑，因家境贫寒，一向多承微臣照顾周济，愿效死力。若命他潜入赵盾府中，人不知，鬼不觉，将赵盾刺死，自然无人怀疑到主君头上。如此一来，主君不是就轻易地去掉了这个眼中钉肉中刺了吗？"

灵公听了，不胜欣喜，道："此事全靠爱卿，事成之后，寡人重重赏你。"

二人密议已定，灵公遂起驾回宫。

当天夜里，屠岸贾便暗暗将钮麑召到堂上，如此这般，编造了一套赵盾如何专权欺主的谎言，说了一遍。钮麑平时深居在屠岸贾府中，闭目塞听，朝政国事一概不知。听了屠岸贾的蛊惑，只当赵盾真是个奸人，心中便生出几分愤恨。屠岸贾又将灵公的旨意说了，钮麑当下承诺道："小人多年承主公厚待，早有效死之意，此去定让那赵盾奸贼毙命刀下，为国家除却欺主强臣。"

屠岸贾见奸计得售，心中大喜，脸上却装出忧虑的神情，说道："那赵盾奸贼深居下宫，防备严密，壮士此去吉凶莫测，还望三思。"

钮麑慷慨答道："小人此去，上则为国除贼，下则报答主公厚恩，虽死无憾。"

waist. Nimbly vaulting walls and scuttling over roofs, in no time at all he gained access to Zhao Dun's mansion.

The prime minister lived alone in secluded courtyard quarters. In the courtyard stood a Chinese scholartree one hundred years old. It was still vigorous, and its foliage was thick and luxuriant. As a result, it cast deep shadows. Chu Ni knew about this tree, and as soon as he had infiltrated the building, he made straight for the courtyard and hid in the branches of the scholartree. His plan was to wait for Zhao Dun to emerge ready to proceed to the regular early morning audience at court, and then perform the dire deed. The sound of a watchman's clapper told him that the night had advanced to the fourth watch. The glimmer of a candle informed him that Zhao Dun had arisen from his bed. Chu Ni slipped to the ground, and tiptoed to the window in which he saw the gleam. Through a chink in the lattice work he saw the figure of an official dressed in court robes seated bolt upright on the bed and holding a ceremonial tablet in both hands before him. A snow white beard hung from the man's chin, and his eyes were half closed. His whole bearing was one of solemnity and dignity. Zhao Dun was just as Tu'an Gu had described him. Chu Ni guessed that he had awoken early, and being afraid to fall asleep again and be late for court, he had donned his ceremonial garb, and was sitting there waiting for dawn.

Now Chu Ni was at heart an upright man. It was only because he had been the recipient of Tu'an Gu's bounty that he had listened to his insidious words, and ventured for on his murderous errand. But, seeing Zhao Dun sitting there in all serenity, it struck Chu Ni that he was the very image of a loyal minister, and unwittingly a feeling of admiration for the old man arose in his heart. He thought to himself, "This does not look like the villainous Zhao Dun who was described to me by my master. It seems that my master and the foolish Duke Ling have deceived me into making an attempt on the life of a loyal minister. That would be the sort of crime that I could not atone for even with one hundred deaths!" He thought for a while, and then concluded, "In my youth I studied the martial arts and the ways of chivalry. I

屠岸贾当下命人斟上酒来，钮麂连饮三觥，扎束停当，看看时辰已到三更，双手一拱，与屠岸贾告别，怀揣匕首，飞檐走壁，潜入下宫。

原来，赵盾平常总在下宫内一个小院独宿。院内有一株百年老槐，枝繁叶茂，树影婆娑。钮麂早已打听清楚，潜入下宫后直奔小院，隐身于槐树之上，想等赵盾起身上朝前寻机行事。耳听梆声响过，已是四更。眼见屋内烛光摇曳，料想赵盾已经起床。便跳下树来，轻手轻脚闪到窗前，从窗棂缝隙间定睛一瞧，只见屋内榻上一位官员朝衣朝冠，手捧象笏，端然正坐，颏下一缕花白胡子，双目微闭，神态凛然，看模样正是屠岸贾描绘的相国赵盾。钮麂心中猜想，赵盾一定是早早起身，准备上朝，见天色尚早，再睡又怕过了时间，故而装束整齐，坐以待旦。

钮麂本来也是忠直之士，只因受过屠岸贾的恩惠，又听了他的蛊惑，因此前来行刺。如今见赵盾如此勤勉恭敬，一脸正气，显而易见是一位忠臣，心中不由得暗暗敬服。因而想道："看来赵盾并非司寇所说的奸邪之辈，而灵公的荒唐，平时自己也隐约有所耳闻，莫不是他们骗着自己来刺杀忠臣，那样罪过可就大了，真是百死莫赎。"转念一想："自己少年学剑，行侠仗义，言出必诺，有恩必报，以忠信为立身之本，乃

learned to be true to my word and to repay kindnesses. Good faith and loyalty, I learned, were the principles a true man must live by. If I now kill by mistake an upright minister at his post of duty, that would be a treacherous act. On the other hand, if I disobey the order of my sovereign and my master, that would be an act of disloyalty. Either way, I would not be able to face the world again! The only way to save my conscience is to take my own life."

At this point, he made up his mind to commit suicide. But it occurred to him that if he simply did away with himself, Duke Ling and Tu'an Gu would find another way of harming Zhao Dun. So he had to do it in such a way as to put the prime minister on his guard. He thereupon stood a few paces from the tree, and facing Zhao Dun's bedroom, he called out, "My name is Chu Ni. Last night I received an order to assassinate you. However, impressed by your dignity, Prime Minister, I am unwilling to slay such a paragon of loyalty, and am resolved to fulfill my mission with my own death. But I fear that after my death others may come. Prime Minister, beware!"

With that, he bent at the waist and ran at the scholartree, splitting his skull and splattering blood and brains over its trunk. Hearing the noise, Zhao Dun and his household rushed out to see what the matter was, and stopped as if turned to stone when they beheld the gory scene. Later generations recited a verse about this event:

The assassin's blade was turned by Zhao Dun's dignity.

The virtue embracing killer found salvation at the tree.

After the first shock of the gruesome discovery had worn off, there was pandemonium in the Zhao mansion. After a while, Ti Miming, Zhao Dun's carriage bodyguard, burst through the panic stricken throng, and said to his master, "My Lord, it is better that you not attend court this morning, now that this incident has taken place!"

Zhao Dun replied, "Yesterday, the duke specifically charged me to appear before him this morning. It would be a breach of protocol to be absent.

堂堂男儿，正正丈夫。若今日误杀忠于职守的大臣，便是不忠；可接受国君主公之命而违背使命，又是不信。不忠不信，有何面目立于天地之间！惟有以死报之，方能不愧于心。"

想到此，决心寻个自尽。又觉得自己不明不白地死了，灵公和屠岸贾一定还会用别的办法加害于赵盾，应该让相国有个防备。于是退后几步，立于树下，对着屋内大声喊道："小人名叫鉏麑，今晚受命前来行刺。可小人见到相国的威仪，不愿伤害忠良，宁可一死以报命。我今死后，恐有后来者，相国还须谨防！"

说罢，侧身一头撞在老槐树上，当下脑浆迸裂，咽气身亡，飞溅的鲜血染得老槐树上斑斑点点。赵盾及家人闻声而出，看了这幅惨景，都是甚为感动。后人有诗专咏此事：

手携利刃暗藏埋，因见忠臣却悔来。

方知公道明如日，此夜义士自触槐。

赵府众人乱了一阵，每日随赵盾外出的车右卫士提弥明破众而出，对赵盾道："大人今日不可上朝，恐有其他变故。"

赵盾道："主君于昨日许我早朝召见，我若不去，便是无礼。况且死生有命，不必提心吊胆。"

Besides, life and death are ordained; there is no need to be over alarmed."

So saying, he gave orders for Chu Ni's corpse to be buried beneath the scholartree. He himself, shedding tears, bowed in reverence to the assassin's remains, mounted his carriage and left for the court.

Meanwhile, Duke Ling, confident that the evil scheme he had cooked up with Tu'an Gu had gone as planned, retired for the night and slept like a log. The following morning, as he mounted the throne to receive his ministers in audience, he was in an ebullient mood. He was looking forward to good news. But there, right before him, he saw Zhao Dun safe and sound! In his palpitating heart he cursed Chu Ni, but outwardly he managed to keep a rigid countenance as he allowed the prime minister to approach with his petition.

As soon as Chu Ni had left the previous evening, Tu'an Gu had despatched a trusted henchman to follow him. When the next day dawned and Chu Ni did not return, he was waiting with a sinking feeling for the spy's report. When the latter came running back with the account of the failed assassination attempt, and the suicide of Chu Ni, Tu'an Gu did not have the nerve to face Duke Ling. He excused himself from attendance at court that morning on the pretext of illness.

The fact that Zhao Dun was unharmed, coupled with Tu'an Gu's absence, sent palpitations of fear through Duke Ling. He became tongue tied and agitated. The fact was that someone had reported to Zhao Dun what the duke had done the previous day in the Peach Garden. With his face set as hard as granite, he heard the duke stammer that he should present his remonstrance, and then he said in a voice filled with wrath, "I have heard that Your Majesty cruelly punished a blameless park keeper yesterday in the Peach Garden. You then watched a disgusting display of 'mandarin ducks sporting in the water.' After that, you cut off the hands and legs of two palace ladies, finally causing the deaths of three people. Is all this true?"

Zhao Dun was seething with anger, and his strident voice caused Duke Ling's heart and liver to dissolve with fright. To make things worse, Tu'an

说毕,吩咐家人将鉏麑收敛,就埋在老槐树下,自己洒泪一揖,登车上朝去了。

再说灵公与屠岸贾安排好行刺赵盾的计策,一心以为好事必成。回到宫中,一夜睡得甚是安稳。次日早朝,怡然上堂,专候佳音。不料忽见赵盾随班行礼,安然无恙,活生生地站在自己面前。心中一阵惊悸,暗骂鉏麑无能,表面上却不好怎样,只得硬着头皮让赵盾上前奏事。

屠岸贾早在鉏麑动身之后,便派得力亲信暗中跟踪,监视鉏麑的一举一动。天已放亮,却不见鉏麑归来,已经心中打鼓。待得亲信气急败坏地跑回来,将鉏麑宁可触槐而死,也不愿对赵盾下手的事一五一十说了一遍,屠岸贾心中的沮丧怨恨可想而知。转念想到此事无法对灵公交待,只好托病不朝。

灵公见赵盾无恙,而屠岸贾却不见踪影,顿时没了主心骨,语无伦次,心不在焉。其时,早有人将灵公前一日在桃园的所作所为报告赵盾。赵盾脸色铁青,听到灵公让自己上前奏事,遂愤然道:"听说主君昨日在园内无故痛殴园公,还因观看'鸳鸯对浴'而砍断宫女手脚,致使三人丧命,可有此事?"

Gu was not present, and the other officials just stood there in grim silence. Not a single one stepped forward to defend their sovereign. The duke was at his wits' end. Finally, he jabbered, "I, er, I was just shooting at some birds, when I accidentally hit the park keeper by mistake...."

At this point, his voice faltered, and he made as if to scuttle off to his palace quarters. But Zhao Dun was too quick for him, striding forward and seizing the duke by the collar. The prime minister bowed, and in a voice full of pain said, "What Your Majesty has done even the tyrants Jie of the Xia Dynasty and Zhou of the Shang Dynasty would not have stooped to. If you do not mend your ways, I am afraid that the State of Jin is doomed!"

Duke Ling struggled, but could not free himself from Zhao Dun's iron grip. Panic seized him, and he broke out in torrents of sweat. A nervous murmuring arose from the assembled officials, aghast at the sight of Zhao Dun remonstrating with the duke at the risk of his life. Filled with awe and admiration, they eventually said, with one voice, "The prime minister is right. Please heed his words, Your Majesty!"

Duke Ling, realizing how deeply he had offended his officials, then tried to wriggle out of his predicament by saying, "I beg you not to say any more. I promise that from now on I will never enter the Peach Garden again. I will lock myself away and ponder my misdeeds. Moreover, I will hand over court affairs to the prime minister to handle."

And so, for the next few days Tu'an Gu kept away from the court, still pretending to be ill, and Duke Ling buried himself deep in his palace quarters. Much relieved, Zhao Dun ordered that the Peach Garden be locked, severely reduced the number of palace ladies, and forbade all performances of music and dancing. At the same time, he purged the ranks of officials, rewarding the honest and punishing the venal. He also stiffened the training of the army and beefed up the state's defenses. All this, together with encouraging the farmers and relieving the common people of their burdens kept Zhao Dun busy night and day, leaving him little time to eat or sleep. But he was content to see the State of Jin increasing in prosperity before his very eyes.

灵公见赵盾满面怒色，语气冷峻，心中先就胆怯几分，加上屠岸贾不在眼前，而众大臣肃然静立，也没有一个人上前为自己说话，越发没了主意，只得支支吾吾道："寡人射鸟时误伤了园公……"

话才说了半句，已经语不成调，声音发颤，于是拔脚想要逃回后宫。赵盾跨步上前扯住灵公的衣襟，叩头苦谏道：

"主君所为，实乃夏桀、商纣所不曾为也。若不能改正，臣恐晋国将步其后尘！"

灵公脱身不得，又急又怕，汗下如雨。众大臣见赵盾冒死直谏，字字掷地有声，都敬服不已，于是齐声劝道：

"相国之言句句在理，望主君采纳。"

灵公深知众怒难犯，只得满口答应道："你等不必多言，寡人往后再也不去桃园玩乐了，从今日起闭门思过，朝政听任相国处置。"

从此以后，屠岸贾装病在家，灵公深处寝宫，着实安宁了几日。赵盾心中喜欢，命人闭锁桃园，裁减宫女，禁绝歌舞。同时清肃吏治，奖廉惩贪，整军练武，加强国防，奖励农耕，赈济百姓，真是日理万机，忙得废寝忘食，眼见着晋国又有了兴旺的气象。

However, his carriage bodyguard Ti Miming was extremely worried that his master's hectic round of state affairs was undermining his health. Ti was a man of integrity, who was honest and straightforward in his dealings with others. He was intensely loyal to his friends, abhorred wickedness and had tremendous physical strength. He had long served Zhao Dun with the utmost fidelity. In recent years, he had watched with growing disquiet how Tu'an Gu had been becoming ever more outrageous in his plotting, cruel deeds and wild ambition. He perceived that Tu'an Gu posed a danger to his master. He had guessed immediately that Tu'an Gu had been behind the botched assassination attempt, and the latter's skulking at home ever since only confirmed his suspicion.

One day, Zhao Dun came home early from the court. Ti Miming had made up his mind to tell his master of his foreboding, and broached the subject in his usual blunt and honest manner, "My Lord, the duke is dimwitted, but Tu'an Gu is crafty and scheming. You really must be on your guard!"

Zhao Dun, however, had his mind on governmental matters, and as everything had been going smoothly recently he paid little heed to the warning. Smiling, he said, "Ti, you worry too much! The duke is determined to become a reformed character. And, as for Tu'an Gu, well, it's difficult to clap with only one hand, you know. So what can he do, eh?"

Ti Miming saw that preoccupation with affairs of state had pushed all thoughts of his personal safety to the back of the prime minister's mind. He realized that it incumbent upon himself to keep a high state of vigilance and guard his master at all times.

Meanwhile, Duke Ling, who had been used to living in a giddy whirl of pleasure, was finding life cooped up in his silent chambers with only his thoughts for company unbearably tedious. Some ten days had passed, and he was on the brink of collapse. Needless to say, his crony Tu'an Gu never showed his face; the only people he saw were Zhao Dun and the rest of his court officials, who came round every day preaching at him to forsake the

　　且说赵盾忙于国事，不顾自身，一旁却急坏了车右卫士提弥明。此人性恪耿直，与人相处肝胆相照，为知己两肋插刀；且嫉恶如仇，力大无穷，多年来忠心耿耿，跟随赵盾。近年来见屠岸贾虚伪狡诈，渐生野心，兼且心地阴险，手段毒辣，常为主人暗中捏着一把汗。那日钮麂前来行刺，触槐而死，推究情理，必是屠岸贾所遣。又听说屠岸贾自此称病不朝，越发证实了自己的想法。

　　这一天，赵盾下朝回家，时候还早，提弥明便瞅空将自己的猜测和盘告知赵盾，又提醒道："主君昏暗不明，屠岸贾狡诈阴险，大人务要多多提防！"

　　赵盾一心只在朝政上，近日诸事顺利，不觉有些大意，当下大笑道："车右不必多虑，主君已经下决心改过，屠岸贾孤掌难鸣，又能有什么作为！"

　　提弥明心知赵盾一心只惦着朝政国事，将自身的安危丢在脑后，当下不宜多言，只得自己提高警惕，昼夜小心防备。

　　那灵公玩乐惯了，在寝宫里拘了十几日，静极思动，早已快要憋出病来。只是见屠岸贾不露面，自己单枪匹马，赵盾等一班大臣又每日里劝自己摒弃小人，杜绝游乐，几次想要出去散散心，也实在难以启

company of petty men and eschew pleasure. He often thought of going out to relieve his boredom, but he never dared to open his mouth on the subject.

It was the height of the summer. The flowers were blooming and the grass formed a thick carpet in the duke's private courtyard. Flocks of orioles flitted here and there. After breakfast one morning, the duke dismissed all his attendants and sat listless and alone in the Pavilion of Celestial Attainment in the courtyard. Before long, drowsiness overcame him, and he slumped over the table in a doze.

Through a haze he heard a muffled voice, "You have a wicked heart, Your Majesty," it said. "You chopped off your favorite's hands and left her to suffer agonies. You cast her off heedlessly, and now that she is gone, she will never return."

An icy blast seemed to buffet the duke's face, and his eyes opened wide. He saw Fox Lady standing in front of him, holding out the bleeding stumps of her arms and with tears rolling down her cheeks. Duke Ling looked closely at her. Her fine eyebrows, sparkling eyes and peach like complexion were even more bewitching than ever. But her face wore an expression of the deepest sorrow, and her stare was full of tragedy and hatred. Terrified at this apparition, the duke croaked, "But, aren't you dead? How did you come here, to this place?"

Fox Lady wailed, "I died an undeserved death, and so cannot rest. I have come to condemn you." So saying, she thrust the gory stumps of her arms forward and threw herself at the duke. The latter shrieked in horror . . . and woke up bathed in cold sweat. He glanced around, and saw that the sun was still shining as brightly as ever. It had been a bad dream, that was all. But the memory of it lingered, and sent icy shivers all over his body. After sitting staring gloomily into space for a long time, Duke Ling suddenly felt that he couldn't stand his seclusion any longer. Come what may, he had to get out of this dreadful place. He sent for Tu'an Gu.

齿。

此时已是盛夏季节，寝宫内的花园里花繁草长，群莺乱飞。这天早膳之后，灵公摒退左右，独坐园中"仙极阁"内发呆，百无聊赖，一阵倦意袭来，不觉依案而眠。

朦胧之际，听得有人说道："主君你好狠心啊，那日剁去臣妾双手，令臣妾痛入骨髓，主君却丢下臣妾不管不顾，一去不返。"

灵公只觉得一阵冷风扑面，睁开双眼，见狐姬拖着两条鲜血淋漓的胳膊，泪流满面地站在面前。细细看那狐姬，只见她蛾眉凤眼，杏脸桃腮，较往日更加妖冶艳丽，却带着一脸戚容，目光哀怨。灵公大惊道："你不是死了么？如何进了寝宫，来到此处？"

狐姬哭道："臣妾无罪而死，心中不平，前来与主君讲理。"说着，举着鲜血淋漓的双手，扑入灵公怀中。灵公吓得一声惨叫，蓦地从梦中醒来，打了一个冷颤，睁眼一看，阳光灿烂，原来是一个噩梦。定神回想梦中情景，身上犹然一阵阵发冷。呆坐了半晌，实在忍不下去了，横下一条心来，命人传司寇屠岸贾进宫。

Ever since the failure of his scheme to assassinate Zhao Dun, Tu'an Gu had been brooding over more sinister schemes. Still under the pretext of illness, he had been lying low at home and watching how the situation developed. When he heard that Duke Ling had succumbed to pressure from Zhao Dun to turn over a new leaf, and that Shi Ji and the other officials were backing Zhao Dun in his efforts to put the government in order and improve the situation in the country, he realized that if this continued, his dream of some day seizing the throne for himself would burst like a bubble. Moreover, he might be hard put to preserve his own life!

So when the summons came from the duke, he leaped with joy, ordered his carriage to be brought and dashed off to the palace. He congratulated himself on slipping away without being seen.

Seeing Tu'an Gu again, Duke Ling was as delighted as if he had been visited by an auspicious phoenix bringing good tidings. "My dear minister," he cried, "I've been dying of boredom since you absented yourself day after day."

While Tu'an Gu was pouring out profuse greetings to the duke, he was slyly taking stock of the other's countenance. He was struck by how lonely and dispirited the duke looked, and guessed that this was the result of the pleasure-loving duke's enforced stay in his now dreary quarters. Immediately Tu'an Gu had an idea for reversing their misfortunes. He thereupon seated himself and assumed the expression of a loyal servant who is distressed by his master's trouble. "Since ancient times," he said, "What has always made a ruler respected and honored has been his ability to enjoy the full pleasures of life. But now Your Majesty's bells and drums hang mute, singing and dancing are banished, the palace halls stand empty and the Peach Garden is locked. Gloom pervades Your Majesty's quarters. Lacking diversion, and with time lying heavy on your hands, I am afraid that Your Majesty will fall prey to illness!"

This little speech cheered the duke up. Immediately he felt that Tu'an Gu was a man who really understood what his feelings were. He exclaimed,

屠岸贾自那日派遣钼麂行刺赵盾不遂，心怀鬼胎，便称病不朝，蜗居府中，静观事态。听说灵公答应赵盾痛改前非，不再行乐，士季等一班大臣与赵盾齐心协力，共同整饬朝纲，眼见得朝中气象一新。果真如此下去，不但自己篡夺晋国江山的如意算盘成了泡影，只怕连身家性命也难保了。

如此整日在家中胡思乱想，忽听灵公传唤，喜出望外，立即备了车马，赶到上宫，幸喜无人撞见。

灵公一见屠岸贾，仿佛得了个凤凰，道："爱卿连日不来，寡人都快要闷死了。"

屠岸贾慌忙施礼，抬眼偷窥灵公的神色，见他一脸落寞，神情无聊，便知道这位游玩惯了的国君连日闷在寝宫，早已静极思动。屠岸贾心中便有了主意，于是一边落座，一边装出一副主忧臣死的忠诚面孔，叹息道："自古人主之所以尊贵，就在于能够尽享人生声色之乐。如今主君钟鼓空悬，歌舞不兴，宫室虚设，园门紧锁，只是闷在寝宫内，且不说何乐之有，时候长了，怕是还要憋出病来。"

灵公闻言大喜，一时间不禁生出知己之感，急忙道："寡人请爱卿来正是为此，爱卿可速速为寡人出个主意。"

"My dear minister, that is exactly why I summoned you. Quickly, I beg, think of a way out of this dilemma for me!"

Perceiving that his plan was working right from the start, Tu'an Gu hastened to add, "Since Your Majesty is temporarily confined to the palace, why not order a search to be made far and wide to fill these echoing chambers with the most beautiful girls in the land? They can be trained to sing and dance, and you can have a wonderful time!"

Upon hearing this, the duke immediately lost every scruple he had ever had about keeping his promise to Zhao Dun and his other officials. He chortled with glee: "My dear minister, that is exactly what I want! Please take care of the matter right away. Search high and low city girls, country girls, whatever, so long as they're pretty. Bring me as many as you can find. I expect you to report back in three days."

Tu'an Gu had never expected that, just when he thought that he was at the end of his tether, such a glorious road to salvation would suddenly open up. Galvanized with energy and excitement, he lost no time issuing an imperial decree, and mustering men and horses. This retinue scoured the capital, going from door to door and dragging off all the most comely maidens and putting the whole populace in a panic. After a few days, quite a few girls had been seized, but none that were really "fit for a king". To make up the numbers, Tu'an Gu had to force himself to abduct some girls who were only so-so at the most.

On the way back with his prizes to the duke, the despondent Tu'an Gu, together with his retinue, was passing through the eastern suburbs of Jiangyi, when he noticed by the side of the road a particularly stately large courtyard house, over the gate of which were the words, "Happy Abode". It was apparently the residence of some official. Tu'an Gu was filled with curiosity, and he examined the place carefully. He could see that the courtyard was not extensive, but it was exquisitely arranged. A row of large buildings faced the gate, and there were side rooms to the east and west. The main building was discreetly tucked away behind, adorned with crimson balustrades and em-

屠岸贾见开口便赢得灵公欢心，知道计策奏效，便接着道：

"主君既然暂时不能出宫，何不广求绝色女子，充实内宫，教习歌舞，以备娱乐呢？"

灵公闻言，早将答应赵盾等人的话头一笔勾销，欢喜道："爱卿此言正中寡人之意，爱卿可速去办理，无论城里郊外，只要是绝色的女子，不论多少，就与寡人拘来。三日内前来复命。"

屠岸贾没想到山穷水尽之时，不期柳暗花明，重见生路，自然分外尽力。当下打出奉旨行事的招牌，带着人马，在绛邑城中挨门逐户，搜罗漂亮女子，直搅得京城百姓鸡犬不宁。忙了几日，虽然得了几个女子，却都不是很中意，充其量只能算是中等的人才，不禁发愁无法向灵公交待。

这天，屠岸贾带着一帮随从来到绛邑东郊，忽见路侧一个院落，气象轩峻，门楣上大书"怡园"二字，显见得是个官宦人家。心中好奇，便抬眼细细查看。只见院内虽不十分宽敞，却也小巧别致。正面一溜大厅，东西两边又有厢房。后面重楼隐秀，朱栏绣幕，隐隐是一座花园，乔松秀柏，奇石名葩，掩映着几座玲珑的亭阁。院内红男绿女，穿梭往来。

broidered curtains, and in front of it was a sequestered courtyard with tall pines and elegant cypresses, grotesque rocks and rare plants. Nestling among them were dainty pavilions. In the main courtyard, young male and female servants flitted back and forth.

After he had taken all this in, Tu'an Gu made inquiries in the neighborhood, and learned that the house had belonged to a rich merchant, who had died three years previously, leaving a widow and an infant son, as well as a huge fortune. The household continued the merchant's lavish lifestyle, and had an army of servants.

Tu'an Gu was particularly surprised to learn that the widow, although she was nearly thirty years old, was surpassingly graceful and charming. Her sparkling eyes, in particular, were supposed to be able to bewitch men at a glance, and so the local rakes had given her the nickname Laiji, meaning "Bedroom Eyes". Widowhood had left Laiji restless. Besides, she had with her a favorite maid named Qiuhong, who was pretty and flirtatious. Qiuhong was partial to love intrigues, and acted as a go-between for her mistress. The two of them had a tacit understanding, and often engaged in outside liaisons together.

Learning all this, Tu'an Gu had an idea, and he marched straight up to the gate as if he were a visitor. The gate was opened by a smart and pretty serving maid. As soon as she saw that the caller was a high court official, she hurriedly ushered him and his attendants into the main hall. Before long, Laiji herself came to greet them, wearing her most elaborate gown and adornments. At first glance, Tu'an Gu thought that he had set eyes on an angel who had descended to Earth. He had seen Duke Ling's extensive harem of beauties, but not one of them compared to Laiji in sheer attractiveness. His eyes started from their sockets, and his mouth gaped wide open. Laiji dropped a curtsey, and said, "Sir, we are unaccustomed to such distinguished company here in the wilds. Please forgive the lack of proper courtesy."

Her voice was as sweet as the echoing twitter of young orioles in a mountain gorge, or like fledgling swallows returning to their nest; not like a

屠岸贾看罢，便着人四处打听，得知这院子原是一位富商的宅院，三年前，主人逝世，抛下孀妻并一个年幼的儿子，还遗下泼天似的一副家产。故而家中依旧起居豪奢，养着成群的丫环小厮，仆从如云。

更奇的是这女主人虽然年近三十，却是风韵犹胜当年，生得妖冶迷人，尤其是那双惯会瞧人的眼睛，光华灼灼，勾魂摄魄，令男子一见难忘，故丈夫戏称之为"睐姬"。睐姬寡居之后，不甚安分，加上身边有个婢女，叫做秋红，长得伶俐风骚，颇通情事，擅于为主母引线搭桥。主仆二人心照不宣，常与外面勾勾搭搭，做些风流韵事。

屠岸贾摸清了底细，心里便有了把握，遂亲自上门去拜访。只见开门的是一个艳色丫环，生得修短合度，丽质天成。听说是司寇大人光临，不敢怠慢，忙将屠岸贾等人接到大厅上。不一会儿，女主人睐姬盛妆而出，屠岸贾一看，果然犹如天仙下凡，灵公身边成百的姬妾，上千的宫女，却无人有这份成熟的风韵，一时间惊得目瞪口呆。睐姬袅袅婷婷敛衽施礼道："贱妾久居乡野，不意司寇大人光降，有失远迎，还望见谅。"

那声音婉转动听，犹如新莺出谷，又似乳燕归巢，

woman approaching middle age at all. The longer Tu'an Gu ogled her, open-mouthed, the more difficult he found it to think of something to say. Finally, he blurted, "I ... er ... I was out hunting when I ... er ... I ... you know ... just happened to be passing. I took the liberty to approach your gate in order to rest for a while. Please forgive the intrusion."

Laiji smiled, and said, "You are most welcome, sir, most welcome indeed. You honor my humble home." As she said this, she signaled her servants to fetch tea.

Tu'an Gu continued, "It is said that the landscape in your mansion's rear courtyard is superb. May one be so bold as to ask to glimpse it?"

Laiji beamed. "I was just about to ask you to be so kind as to deign to view it. Please allow me to change my clothes, and then I will accompany Your Honor."

So saying, she curtseyed once more, and was escorted by her maid into the inner quarters. Shortly afterwards, she returned. She had shed her outer robe, and was clad only in flimsy garments, under which her body gleamed like pear blossoms in the moonlight and plum flowers in the snow. At the sight of her magnificent figure, Tu'an Gu could not help gasping out loud and swallowing painfully. He followed Laiji into the rear courtyard, to a square pond by an artificial hill. The pond was just over three meters across, the water was a limpid blue, and the pebbles on the bottom, among which fish darted, could clearly be seen. Flowers and grass presented a riot of color on the banks, and gave off a heady perfume. Laiji had already arranged for wine and delicacies to be made available in the courtyard to entertain the guests. This was just what Tu'an Gu needed after his tiring days kidnapping maidens, and he sat himself down in the refreshment pavilion, by the pond. Laiji encouraged her guests to drink wine, and after a few rounds she and Tu'an Gu began to lose all sense of decorum. Tu'an Gu stared at Laiji as if spellbound, while she in turn cast coquettish glances at him. It was not long before Tu'an Gu was befuddled with drink as well as besotted with his beautiful companion.

全然不像半老徐娘。屠岸贾越发惊诧，张口结舌，不知如何说明来意，嗫嚅半晌，方说道："本官外出打猎，路过此处，冒昧登门歇足，望恕唐突。"

眛姬启齿道："岂敢，岂敢！大人玉趾下临，寒舍生辉。"

说话中间，早有侍女捧上茶来。屠岸贾笑道："听说府上后园景致幽雅，可否一睹为快？"

眛姬闻言，答道："正要请大人赏鉴，且容贱妾进内更衣，再陪大人入内。"

说毕，敛衽一礼，扶着丫环进内去了。片刻后出来，只见她卸下外面服饰，露出一身淡妆，犹如月下梨花，雪中梅蕊，别是一番雅致。屠岸贾见了，情不自禁，"咕噜"咽了一口唾沫。当下跟着眛姬径往园内，见假山边一方水池，池宽不及一丈，水清如碧，游鱼细石，直视无碍，池畔遍植花草，姹紫嫣红，幽香阵阵，直透鼻关。女主人早已命人备下酒馔菜肴，款待贵宾。屠岸贾求之不得，假意客套两句，就于池边花亭上入席。眛姬举杯相陪，与屠岸贾等一起饮起酒来。几盏酒下肚，二人早已忘记了廉耻，屠岸贾这里目不转睛，眛姬那里流波送盼，真正酒入快肠，屠岸贾不知不觉已烂醉如泥。

When his head cleared, Tu'an Gu found himself in bed snuggling up to his hostess. Suddenly remembering the mission he had been sent on, he leapt out of bed, flung on his clothes and bade a hasty farewell to Laiji. Whipping his horse furiously, he galloped straight to the palace. There, he described his discovery of the fascinating widow to Duke Ling, taking care, of course, to omit the details of his own sampling of Laiji's charms.

The duke was doubtful. "But, isn't she a bit old?" he inquired. "I mean, she must be fading by this time, mustn't she? As they say, 'like a peach blossom in late spring,' hmm?"

"I have gazed on her beauty with my very own eyes, Your Majesty," Tu'an Gu rejoined. "It is truly beyond description. Not only that, Your Majesty; they say that her skill at the arts of the boudoir would make a man think that she was an 18-year-old virgin!"

Duke Ling beamed. "Well, then, bring her to me, quickly!" he cried.

But Tu'an Gu balked at this. "Ah, well, Your Majesty," he said, hesitatingly. "Bringing her here would be easy enough. It's just that I am afraid of what the prime minister might say. You know that he is dead set against Your Majesty enjoying himself!"

This mention of Zhao Dun punctured Duke Ling's ebullience, and he looked crestfallen. Tu'an Gu, however, had an ace up his sleeve. "The Happy Abode is located outside the capital, sire," he explained. And although it can't compare with the Peach Garden, it is quite scenic. Now, recently, the prime minister has been preoccupied with government affairs, and if Your Majesty were to say that you has not been feeling well of late, and wishes to partake of the fresh country air. I am sure that the prime minister will not object. You can go straight to the Happy Abode and have a rendezvous with the frisky widow. Isn't that the best way to do it?"

醒来的时候，却躺在女主人怀中。他忽然想起身负的使命，立即披衣起身，别过睐姬，打马径直入宫，将睐姬细细说与灵公，只瞒过了自己与睐姬同饮共枕一节。

灵公听了，疑疑惑惑道："此女年岁已长，恰如暮春桃花，未免改色了吧？"

屠岸贾道："微臣亲见那睐姬妖冶艳丽，风韵尤胜。又听说其谙熟房中之术，与人交合之时，有如十七八岁的处女，妙不可言。"

灵公笑道："既然如此，还不快快给寡人拘来！"

屠岸贾眨眨眼道：

"召睐姬入宫不费吹灰之力，只是怕相国知道，岂能容主君快活？"

提起赵盾，灵公不由得垂头丧气，无计可施。屠岸贾遂献计道：

"那怡园在绛邑城外，虽说比不上桃园，却也有几分景致。近来相国忙于朝政，若主君只说近日身子不爽，要去郊外散心，料相国也不会阻拦。主君自去怡园与睐姬相会，岂不更有趣些？"

This suggestion sent Duke Ling into raptures. He clasped his hands and explained, "What a brilliant idea! Tomorrow, we'll go together to the Happy Abode. How about that?" As he said this, he grinned with an almost simian glee.

And so, the next day, according to plan, at the morning audience the duke complained to Zhao Dun of feeling somewhat under the weather of late. He added that he felt like taking a short jaunt out to the suburbs to get a breath of fresh air, with Tu'an Gu as his escort. Neither Zhao Dun nor any of the other court officials suspected what the wily duke really had in mind, so the pair set off without more ado.

The whole way, Duke Ling never stopped looking about him, fidgeting and shuffling his feet in agitation and excitement. He was as light headed as a bird that has just been let out of its cage or a fish taken from a pond and returned to the river.

When they arrived at the Happy Abode, and Laiji was informed that the duke himself had come calling, she gushed with effusions of welcome. Duke Ling, for his part, was transported with delight when he saw that Tu'an Gu had not exaggerated the lady's appeal. Unlike his companion, the duke was not a person to beat about the bush. Utterly entranced, he jabbered, "Madame, as I gaze upon your beauty, the 3,000 damsels in my harem suddenly become as repulsive as dross to me!"

During the subsequent welcoming banquet, Laiji plied the duke with wine. The potent brew quickly went to the duke's head, and it was not long before he was sitting rigid in a drunken daze. Tu'an Gu thereupon discreetly slipped away, and Laiji went to bathe and await the duke's summons.

When Duke Ling came to his senses, the first thing that he saw was the maidservant Qiuhong standing before him, holding a bowl of soup. Through his bleary eyes, the lascivious duke noticed how pretty she was; in fact, she looked somewhat like his late favorite Fox Lady. As if by instinct, he made a grab for her. But the girl was too quick for the befuddled oaf. Dodging nimbly to one side, she said, with a tinkling laugh, "Your Majesty, I think

灵公闻言拊掌笑道："爱卿真正高明的计策,明日你我君臣二人便去那怡园可好?"说话中间,露出一脸猴急的模样。

次日依计而行,灵公在早朝时向赵盾提出身子不爽,想去郊外散心,只要屠岸司寇一人陪着即可。赵盾等大臣果然没有劝阻。

君臣二人当下出宫,一路行来,灵公左张右望,手舞足蹈,大有飞鸟出笼、池鱼归渊之感,好生快活。不觉已到怡园。

睐姬听说国君上门,越发盛情招待。灵公喜之不尽,见那睐姬果然如屠岸贾所言,也不再拐弯抹角,色迷迷地瞅着睐姬道:

"寡人见了你,再看那宫中三千粉黛,竟都是些粪土了。"

饮宴之间,睐姬频频劝酒,灵公几杯热酒下肚,肚内火辣辣的,倚酒卖醉,瘫在榻上不肯起来。屠岸贾早已躲至别处,睐姬则入内沐浴,等待召幸。

待灵公酒醒,只见丫环秋红端着一碗汤站在眼前,细细看来,艳色逼人,大有狐姬之态,禁不住伸出手来拉拉扯扯。秋红躲了过去,嫣然一笑道:"主君请先喝了这醒酒汤。"

you had better drink this hangover soup first."

Realizing that she was neither Fox Lady nor Laiji, the duke took the bowl. The very first sip filled his mouth with a deliciously sweet and sour fragrance. The liquid then produced within him an overwhelming sense of well being as it seeped into his innards. "What kind of soup is this, and who made it?" he asked.

"This soup, Your Majesty, is a special tonic for those who have over indulged in wine," the girl replied. "It is called sour plum soup."

"Well, my dear," rejoined the duke, "You can certainly make a very fine soup. But I wonder if you can do something else for me. Could you be my go-between in a very serious matter?"

Qiuhong replied archly, "I am but a servant here, Your Majesty, and busy all the time with household chores. Would you be referring to some specific person by any chance?"

"To tell you the truth, my dear, it was your mistress I came here specially to see."

"Oh, Your Majesty," Qiuhong cried. "My mistress is far too plain and humble in status to be worthy of your exalted notice, I'm sure."

Fascinated by the girl's wiles, the duke pulled her towards him, and started to fondle her, saying, "Well, never mind about your mistress, then; it's you I want now."

By this time, dusk had set in. Qiuhong, bearing a candle, led Duke Ling through winding corridors into the inner quarters of the mansion. There, Laiji had arranged brocaded coverlets and embroidered pillows for the expected tryst. Even before Qiuhong had a chance to retire, Laiji had flung her arms around the duke. She heaved him behind the bed curtains, where they both undressed and began to cavort on the bed. In the dim light of the lamp, Duke Ling observed that Laiji did indeed have tender skin like a virgin's. In addition, her store of lascivious tricks and blandishments made him feel that he wanted to melt into her body. He congratulated himself on meeting with

灵公见睬姬不在跟前，接过碗来喝了一口，只觉得酸甜可口，爽心沁脾，遂问道："这汤是什么汤？谁做的？"

秋红答道："此汤专为醒酒之用，叫做酸梅汤。是小女子为主君熬制的。"

灵公笑问："你能做梅汤，可能为寡人作个大媒吗？"

秋红答道："小女子自当奔走，只不知主君要的是何人？"

灵公笑道："寡人此行专为你家主母而来。"

秋红道："只恐我家主母蒲柳贱质，难当主君青顾。"

灵公见她妖冶迷人，一把拉了过来，搂在怀里狎戏，一面道："别说你家主母，寡人连你也一块儿要了。"

此时已是黄昏时分，秋红掌灯导引，曲曲弯弯，引着灵公直入内室。睬姬早已整备锦衾绣枕，不等秋红退下，便拥了灵公入帏，解衣共寝。灵公在灯下看那睬姬果然是肌肤柔嫩，犹如处子，更兼百般的淫态浪语，自己仿佛就要化在她身上，遂自以为不世之奇遇也。

this sublime opportunity.

From this time on, there was no softening of Duke Ling's vicious and sadistic nature, and his lecherous appetites grew apace. Every few days he would find some excuse to rush off to the Happy Abode with Tu'an Gu, and, as time went on, these expeditions, and the goings on they entailed, gradually became the scandal of the capital.

Zhao Dun and the other court officials, meanwhile, were having their own suspicions about the duke and his mysterious disappearances. At the morning court audiences he was weary and inattentive, and on two occasions excused himself altogether on grounds of illness. When questioned about their master's comings and goings, his attendants were afraid to speak the truth. When the prime minister himself questioned them, Tu'an Gu suavely interrupted, and successfully obscured the issue.

One morning, as the officials were assembled for the court audience, the duke arrived in his carriage, as if from a journey. The officials' first thought was that he had been out hunting the day before and had spent the night away from the palace. Such behavior in itself deserved a reprimand, but Duke Ling simply brushed aside their anxious enquiries with a few brusque words, and with an airy wave of his hand dismissed the court, saying, "Unless you have some important business to broach, you may all retire. I have something to discuss with Tu'an Gu."

The officials had no choice but to withdraw, but as they did so they made an implicit pact between them to wait just outside the door listening to what was said inside the court chamber.

Thinking that he was quite alone with his crony, Duke Ling threw all inhibitions to the winds. Turning to Tu'an Gu with a smile, he said, "My dear minister, rest assured that I will reward you handsomely for finding for me that tasty morsel."

With a fawning smirk, the other replied, "A servant's duty is to lighten, if he can, his master's burden. How would I dare to covet such a thing

自此之后，灵公暴戾之性未减，而淫迷之心日增，隔三岔五，便要寻一个理由，与屠岸贾同往怡园鬼混。时候一长，京城内沸沸扬扬，传得妇孺皆知。

赵盾等人几次见灵公早朝时神情怠惰，意态慵懒，甚至有两次托病不朝，心中不禁有些怀疑。询问宫中侍从，都不敢明说，直接向灵公问起，却被屠岸贾抢着截过话头，遮掩过去。

这天又是早朝时分，众大臣等候在朝堂外，却见灵公驾车从外面回来，料想是野宿于外。赵盾等瞧得真切，自然又是一番劝谏。灵公虚与委蛇，应付了几句，挥挥手道：

"如无大事，众卿可先退下。寡人今日与屠岸司寇有话要说。"

赵盾等人只得退出，却相约守候在门外，只将耳朵竖起来听着里面的动静。

这里灵公以为众人退下，没了顾忌，对屠岸贾笑道："爱卿为寡人物色了这个可意儿的美人，寡人当厚厚奖赏。"

屠岸贾媚笑一声道："为臣自当为主君分忧，何敢奢望奖赏？"

as a reward?"

"Be that as it may, " said the duke, still smiling, "I was thinking more along the lines of you sharing your master's pleasure —— tasting the morsel, if you see what I mean. Now wouldn't that be a far better reward than things like gold, silver and jewels?"

Hearing this, the face of the guilty conscienced Tu'an Gu turned a bright crimson. But, glancing at his master, he realized that he could speak freely about what had taken place between himself and Laiji. Again, he assumed an obsequious smile. "I hope Your Majesty will not be angry, " he said in an oily voice, "But your humble servant has already sampled the morsel, to make sure that it was fit for Your Majesty's palate. I dared not risk its being displeasing to you. "

Duke Ling roared with laughter. "I thought so!" he said. "Yes, Minister, you were quite right to do so. "

Tu'an Gu joined in his master's merriment. The duke went on, "So, you were swifter than your master in grabbing that delightful dainty. And what token did she present to you?"

As he said this, he produced from his waistband a blood-red handkerchief, and waved it in front of Tu'an Gu's nose. The latter gaped with glee. "I have a present from the same lady, " he said, "But it does not compare with that granted to Your Majesty. " Whereupon, he produced a perfumed pouch on which was embroidered a pair of mandarin ducks. The duke guffawed, "It seems that you and I have both received love tokens. I propose that the two of us go to the Happy Abode tomorrow and enjoy ourselves with our hostess all together in the same bed. "

Their salacious conversation continued in this vein, becoming coarser and cruder as their voices gained in stridency. They were unaware that every disgraceful word was being overheard by the officials who were hovering outside in the ante-chamber. At last, Zhao Dun could endure it no longer. He stamped his foot and groaned. Then, straightening his robes and holding his

灵公笑道："也罢。爱卿不如与寡人同乐，也与那美人做些勾当，尝此美味，可要胜过金银珠宝多多。"

屠岸贾闻言，脸上不由泛红，但再看灵公的模样，料想将前事说了也无妨，便笑道："敢请主君止怒，微臣先已尝过了美味。微臣以为好似主君要吃什么东西，微臣先尝一尝，若味道不美，岂敢进献！"

灵公哈哈大笑道："原来如此，爱卿说得有理。"

屠岸贾也是捧腹大笑。灵公又问："爱卿虽然捷足先登，替寡人尝了美味，那美人可曾赠送了你什么东西么？"

说着，沾沾自喜地从腰间抽出一条血红的汗巾，拿给屠岸贾看。屠岸贾也眉飞色舞道："微臣这里也有一个美人赠送的物件，只是与主君的相比就差得太远了。"说着取出一个香袋，上面绣着一对鸳鸯。灵公见了，笑道："你我君臣二人都有美人赠送的表记，不如明日共去怡园与那美人来个连床大会，一定有趣。"

两人污言秽语，不堪入耳，说到得意处，不禁忘形，声音越来越大。却不防被候在门外的赵盾都听在耳中，顿时气得顿足长叹，当下整襟执笏，入门直进，众大臣都随在身后。灵公忽见赵盾等人去而复回，吓

tablet of office rigidly in front of him, the prime minister marched back into the court, followed by the rest of the state officials. The duke nearly jumped out of his skin when he saw them suddenly reappear. The prime minister did not stand on ceremony, but came straight to the point. "Your servant has heard," he intoned, "That a certain decorum should be maintained between a ruler and his ministers; also that propriety demands strict separation of the sexes. If a ruler casts aside all sense of purity and shame, then it is easy for unchaste women to disorder the state. Now, right here in the hallowed seat of government of the State of Jin, we find the sovereign and his servant abetting each other in lewd pursuits. Such undermining of proper conduct and morality will surely lead to rampant lechery, disorder, chaos and the ruin of Jin!"

Duke Ling reddened and paled in turn at this verbal onslaught. Thoroughly disconcerted, he stammered an excuse: "Oh Prime Minister, it was just a slip on my part ... an aberration, nothing more, I assure you. From now on, I will definitely start to live a regular life, just as a proper ruler ought to."

Zhao Dun, assuming that the duke had recognized that his behavior was unacceptable, felt loath to berate him further. Instead, he turned to Tu'an Gu, and said, "When a ruler's actions are righteous, his servants should encourage him in such courses. But when a ruler's actions are base, his servants have a duty to bar him from continuing in his degeneration. Who should bear this responsibility more than you, Tu'an Gu —— you who are His Majesty's chief bodyguard? Yet you even go so far as to lure your master into debauchery, exulting in your wickedness right here in the very seat of sovereignty! If the nobility and gentry were to learn of this, it would shake the very foundations of the state. Aren't you deeply ashamed?"

Tu'an Gu could say nothing to defend himself, but stood with bent head, gnashing his teeth, like a whipped cur. Fuming with righteous indignation, Zhao Dun turned on his heel, and swept out of the court chamber, the rest of the officials close behind him.

The duke and Tu'an Gu gazed at each other for a while through nar-

了一跳。赵盾也不再客套,开门见山道:"臣闻君臣有序,男女有别。如国君无廉耻之化,则国中有失节之妇。现在晋国君臣竟然在朝堂上淫词滥调,互相标榜,真是廉耻丧尽,体统尽失。无序则乱,无别则淫,乱而且淫,实乃亡国之道啊!"

灵公闻言,脸上红一阵,白一阵,汗下涔涔,赧颜道:"寡人偶一为之,日后定当改正。"

赵盾听灵公已经认错,不好逼迫过甚,转过脸来看着屠岸贾道:"国君有好的行为,臣下应当鼓励;国君有不好的行为,臣下应当劝阻。现在你身为晋国司寇,自己做那淫乱之事,又用这些诱惑主君,还在朝堂公然宣扬,倘若让国内士民知道,成何体统?你难道不为此而感到羞耻吗?"

屠岸贾无言以对,只得咬牙低头装死狗。赵盾见状,怒气冲冲地与众大臣走了。

灵公与屠岸贾面面相觑,不知如何是好。过了一会儿,屠岸贾故意道:"从今往后,主君不可再去怡园,免得受相国责备。"

说罢,偷眼看着灵公。灵公怅然道:"爱卿可还去那怡园吗?"

屠岸贾道:"相国是因为微臣带着主君去那怡园,

rowed eyelids, at a complete loss what to do. Then, Tu'an Gu said, weighing his words carefully, "From now on, Your Majesty, I think you had better keep away from the Happy Abode, in order to avoid the wrath of the prime minister."

With this, he glanced slyly at the duke, who said in a voice full of chagrin, "I suppose there's nothing to stop you chasing off to the Happy Abode, is there?"

Tu'an Gu's ambiguous reply was, "The prime minister, sire, blames your servant for leading you astray, I am afraid. But, so long as I no longer escort Your Majesty, the prime minister will not care where I go."

This sly barb found its mark, and Duke Ling exploded in fury. "I don't care if that doddering old fool Zhao Dun doesn't like it," he yelled, "I positively refuse to be deprived of the delights of the Happy Abode, so there!"

Tu'an Gu saw that the time was ripe for adding fuel to the flames. Simulating distress at his master's resolution, he said, "Oh, Your Majesty, that would be most unwise! The prime minister would never countenance it. I implore Your Majesty not to provoke Zhao Dun into coming here again with his harsh words!"

Duke Ling was hopelessly addicted to debauchery, and the idea of eschewing the pleasures of the flesh was inconceivable to him. Hatred for Zhao Dun seethed within him. Grinding his teeth, he growled, "That sharp tongue of Zhao Dun's grates on my nerves. If only I could stop it wagging! Do you, minister, have any idea as to how that might be accomplished?"

There was venom in Tu'an Gu's reply. "The only way to stop Zhao Dun's mouth is with his death."

This sinister note was echoed by Duke Ling, "Right. When he is a dead man, let's see if he can keep interfering with my pleasure!" The two then put their heads together, and plotted the disposal of Zhao Dun.

因而责骂微臣。如果微臣不再陪着主君前往，自然可以独自前去。"

灵公被屠岸贾一激，愤然作色道："寡人宁可得罪那赵盾老儿，怎么舍得不去怡园，与那美人儿同乐呢？"

屠岸贾见时机成熟，便再加上一把火，佯作惧色道："主君还是不要再去了吧，否则相国岂肯善罢甘休！主君又无法让那赵盾不来絮叨。"

灵公沉溺女色，难以自拔，哪里肯轻易放弃？不禁对赵盾恨之入骨，咬牙切齿道："赵盾那老儿长着一张利嘴，实在令人讨厌。寡人恨不得让他再也开不得口，爱卿可有什么良策？"

屠岸贾恶狠狠地道："要想那赵盾不开口，除非他是个死人。"

灵公闻言，也是恶狠狠地道："对，就让他做个死人，看他如何再来阻拦寡人行乐！"当下君臣二人将头凑在一起，密议如何除去赵盾。

赵氏孤儿

Chapter Three
The Slaughter of a Family

Duke Ling and Tu'an Gu felt hatred towards Zhao Dun when he betrayed them. They had plotted how to get rid of Zhao and resume their carefree and debauched lifestyle.

Tu'an Gu brooded for a while, and then he said, "I have a plan, Your Majesty. I know how to get rid of Zhao Dun with no risk to yourself at all."

"What is it? Quick, tell me!" cried the duke eagerly.

Tu'an Gu bent towards his master's ear. "You must think of a pretext for inviting Zhao Dun to a banquet at the palace. Have a dozen armed men waiting in ambush. Then, when the wine cups have gone round a few times, ask him to show you the sword he wears at his waist. He will have no choice but to draw it in order to show it to you. At that point, I will shout, 'Zhao Dun is threatening the duke with his sword. Help, save our master!' The men-at-arms will then spring from their hiding place, seize Zhao Dun and execute him on the spot. Everybody will then think that Zhao Dun was plotting an insurrection, and brought his death upon himself, and you, Your Majesty, will escape censure for his slaughter. Nobody will be able to protest. What do you think of this plan?"

Duke Ling clapped his hands in delight. "Splendid! Splendid!" he cried. "My dear minister, please put your plan into execution as speedily as possible!"

The other then added, "But to make sure that nothing goes wrong, I need to borrow Your Majesty's Terrible Hound."

At this point, we must explain about the Terrible Hound.

第三章　满门抄斩

灵公与屠岸贾君臣二人在朝堂上淫词滥语，互相标榜，被赵盾一阵指责，心中怀恨，密谋如何除掉赵盾，也好恣意寻欢作乐。

屠岸贾苦思冥想了一会儿，说道："臣有一计，可杀那赵盾老儿，万无一失。"

灵公急不可耐地问道："卿有何计？快快讲来！"

屠岸贾附耳低言道：

"主君可找个理由召赵盾到宫中饮酒，预先在墙后埋伏十名甲士，等酒过三巡之后，主君便向赵盾索要佩剑观看，赵盾一定捧剑呈上。此时微臣即刻高喊：'赵盾拨剑于主君之前，欲行不轨，左右快出来救驾！'伏甲齐出，缚而斩之。朝野必盛传赵盾是欲行不轨，自寻诛戮，主君可免滥杀大臣之罪名，内外都无话可说。此计如何？"

灵公拍手道："妙哉！妙哉！爱卿可从速依计而行。"

屠岸贾又道："为防不测，还需借用主君神獒。"

这神獒系何物？还得从头说起。

A few months previously, the Western Rong tribe had sent a fierce dog to Duke Ling as tribute. It was a huge mastiff with bright red bristles, giving it the appearance of a glowing piece of coal. Its handler explained, "This dog is utterly loyal to its master. It has an uncanny sense of people's intentions, and is good at discerning both upright and wicked natures. If any of your entourage is plotting against you, Your Majesty, this dog will sniff the villain out."

Duke Ling was very pleased with this gift. "Excellent!," he commented. "In the ancient days of the sage emperors Yao and Shun, there was said to be a magical animal with an unerring sense for identifying evil. Who would have thought that the State of Jin during my reign would have an animal with supernatural powers too? Haha! Let's see who dares to plot against me now!"

Duke Ling was as pleased with this beast as if he had received a precious jewel. He doted on the dog, appointed a full-time keeper for it and even gave it an official rank. He stopped holding court in the court chamber, and made the officials wait on him in his quarters. He paraded the dog before them, and if anything in their reports or petitions displeased him he would order the dog to bite the luckless man. The Terrible Hound was so powerful and savage that a single bite was enough to leave the victim lifeless. As a result, everyone in the royal household, whether a minister, clerk, servant, member of the harem or palace maid, was kept in state of constant terror. When the duke went out hunting, he ordered the dog keeper to bring the Terrible Hound along on a golden chain. The citizens of the capital too, would flee in terror when they saw the duke with the Terrible Hound at his side. Zhao Dun several times upbraided the duke about this, but his words just went in one ear and out the other. The prime minister would then sigh and say, "He alienates his people for the sake of an animal! Apart from being fierce, what use is the creature?"

Now the duke was always fond of novelty, and soon tired of familiar

数月之前，西戎国向灵公进贡了一只猛犬，身高三尺，毛色纯赤，犹如烧红的炭块。使者历数此犬的本领，道："这狗能解人意，忠于主人。且善辨忠奸，主君身边若有藏奸使坏的小人，它都能嗅了出来。"

灵公闻言大喜，道："好啊，当初尧舜之时，有獬豸触奸；不想如今我晋国也有此神獒，看哪个臣子再敢欺瞒寡人？"

灵公自得了这神獒，如获至宝，专门指定一名内侍喂养，唤做"獒奴"。灵公爱乌及屋，还封其为中大夫。自此灵公不去大堂上朝，却让众大臣到内宫奏事，时时将神獒带在身边，稍不如意，便喝令神獒噬人。这神獒不噬人还罢，若露齿噬人，则凶狠异常，非到被噬者血肉模糊，当场毙命不止。所以宫中大臣、内侍、宫女，个个见了神獒战战兢兢。灵公外出打猎，也令獒奴用金索牵着神獒跟随，不离左右，京城百姓见了无不毛骨悚然，避之惟恐不及。赵盾多次劝谏，灵公只当作耳边风。赵盾叹息道："舍人而取犬，虽猛何用啊！"

好在灵公生性喜新厌旧，过了数月，另有所爱，也就对神獒冷淡下来。只派獒奴在后园喂养，自己已经快要忘掉它了。如今屠岸贾索要神獒，况且是为了

things. And so, before long, he grew bored with the Terrible Hound too. He dispatched it and its keeper to a rear courtyard, and he himself more or less forgot all about it. But now that Tu'an Gu had requested a loan of the animal in order to rid him of the bane of his life, Zhao Dun, he was only too willing to comply. "Of course! Just tell its keeper to take it to your mansion. But how will the beast recognize Zhao Dun, and know that it is supposed to bite him?"

Tu'an Gu's reply was a mysterious one. "I don't want to bother you with the details, Your Majesty, but I have a way to overcome that little difficulty."

The duke, relieved, asked, "When will you accomplish what I most desire in all the world?"

"Please be patient for a few days, Your Majesty," replied Tu'an Gu. "When I have everything arranged, I guarantee the plan will work perfectly."

Duke Ling was content to let him have his way.

The Tu'an family was an illustrious one in Jin, and had produced several generations of famous generals for the state. It was this reflected glory that had secured for Tu'an Gu the position of chief of the duke's bodyguard. He lived in a sumptuous mansion with extensive grounds and crowds of servants. Like all scions of the Tu'an family, Tu'an Gu had trained in martial arts as a youth, and in the parklands of his estate there was a drill ground, with archery targets and apparatus for practicing various weapons exercises.

Tu'an Gu had the Terrible Hound shut up in an empty room, and gave instructions that it was to be given no food or water for several days and nights. Then, a straw figure dressed in court robes and holding a tablet of office before it was set up on the drill ground. When seen from a distance, the figure was a close likeness of Zhao Dun. When these preparations had been completed, the following morning Tu'an Gu ordered that the Terrible Hound be released.

The ravenous beast darted out of the room where it had been kept, like a mad thing. It looked around, desperate to find something to eat. It soon

除掉自己的心腹之患，自然没有不给之理。当下道："这有何难？让獒奴带着神獒一起去你府上就是，只是那畜牲怎么能认准赵盾老儿，择人而噬？"

屠岸贾神秘兮兮地说："这个就不劳主君费神了，微臣自有计较。"

灵公乐得省心，只问道："何时才能遂了寡人的心愿？"

屠岸贾道："主君还须耐心等待几日，待微臣准备停当，方能万无一失。"

灵公也只得任他行事。

屠岸家也算得上是晋国的旺族，历代出过几位名将。屠岸贾凭借祖宗积荫，官至司寇，住着一座阔绰的府邸，府中自然多有楼阁园林，仆从如云。由于屠岸家出身将门，子弟代代习武，府中除了花园之外，又有一片武场，设着箭靶，刀戟林立，专供练武之用。

屠岸贾带着神獒回到府中，将神獒关进一间空房里，几天几夜不饮不喂。而后又派人于武场上扎了一个草人，身穿紫袍，腰束锦带，手持象笏，脚蹬乌靴，妆束打扮酷似赵盾，远远看去，难辨真假。

待草人立定，屠岸贾于次日早晨命獒奴将神獒放出，那畜牲饿了数日，饥不择食，从空房内扑出来，

espied in the middle of the drill ground what looked to it like a living man. With the speed of an arrow, it bounded towards it, uttering a low growl. At a signal from its keeper, it leapt through the air and pounced on the straw figure, and began to rend it savagely with its mighty fangs. Tu'an Gu had instructed that the entrails of a sheep be placed inside the figure, so that the smell of blood from the entrails should madden the animal. In no time at all the straw figure had been torn to shreds, and the Terrible Hound had gulped down the entrails.

The dog keeper was unaware of Tu'an Gu's real intention, but he dared not be slack in carrying out his master's orders, and so this charade was repeated four or five times. Thus, the Terrible Hound came to associate the sight of a figure in the prime minister's court robes with a delicious meal. No longer did it await its keeper's signal, but as soon as it was let out of the room it opened its cavernous jaws and straightaway fell upon the straw figure, tearing it to shreds and feasting on its innards.

But Tu'an Gu was still not satisfied. Early one morning, he had the dog brought to the front of the palace gate. As soon as the Terrible Hound saw Zhao Dun passing by it bared its teeth and claws, and if it had not been restrained by its chain, it would have attacked the prime minister there and then. Tu'an Gu then knew that the time was ripe to put his dastardly scheme into practice. He sent the dog keeper and the Terrible Hound back to his mansion, while he himself went into the palace to report to the duke. "Your servant has completed the necessary arrangements," he said. "Your Majesty may summon Zhao Dun to a banquet tomorrow, and I guarantee that from thenceforth you will be able to enjoy yourself to your heart's content. That interfering dotard will trouble Your Majesty no more." He laughed loudly in anticipation of his success.

Ever since he had consulted Tu'an Gu on how to get rid of the prime minister, Duke Ling had worried from time to time that news of the plot might leak out, and Zhao Dun might take countermeasures and over throw him. At the same

犹如疯了一般，四处寻食。忽见空地上立着一个生人，便箭也似地扑上前去，两只前爪搭在地上，低声咆哮。獒奴对着神獒做了一个手势，神獒当即凌空窜起，将草人扑倒，拼命撕咬。屠岸贾早已命人在草人腹中放了一副羊下水，神獒闻到血腥味，更是不肯放过，三口两口将草人撕碎，掏出羊下水来，狼吞虎咽，饱餐一顿。

獒奴并不明白屠岸贾的真实意图，只是不敢怠慢了司寇，照着屠岸贾的要求，精心训练。如此三番五次，那神獒得了几次甜头，便认定紫衣人就是自己的美味佳肴，每次从空屋中放出，不须獒奴指点，径直张开血盆大口，对着草人直扑过去，将那草人撕得稀烂，掏出肠肚来吞下肚去。

屠岸贾还不放心，择了一日早朝时分，命獒奴牵着神獒伏于宫门之外。那神獒见赵盾过来，当下张牙舞爪，沉声吠叫，若非铁链系着，早已扑了过去。屠岸贾看在眼里，心中暗喜，将獒奴打发回府，自己入宫拜见灵公，奏道："主君可于明日召赵盾侍饮，微臣已将一切安排妥当，可保大事必成，从此主君便可任意游乐，再也不须担心那赵盾老儿了。"说罢，哈哈大笑。

灵公自从与屠岸贾商定密计，要找借口杀死赵

time, he was looking forward to putting Zhao Dun out of the way for good and resuming his carefree debauched life style. So, agitated in both directions, he felt as though he were sitting on needles, and time dragged by slowly. Now everything was ready. The following day, as the morning audience came to a close and Zhao Dun was withdrawing, Duke Ling suddenly addressed him, "I have been blessed with the unstinting assistance of you worthy and loyal servant. You have advised me on numerous occasions, and caused me to mend my careless ways and concentrate on governmental affairs. As a result, the state is prospering as never before, and the common people live and work in contentment. This is all owing to your wholehearted carrying out of your official duties. Today I have prepared a little reception in my quarters for your refreshment, and I hope you will attend."

Zhao Dun was a loyal subject and a good-natured person at heart. Seeing what he took for an expression of gratitude and sincerity on the duke's face, he was pleased. He bowed to the duke, and said, "Your servant's duty is to devote his utmost energies to the service of the state, diligently attend to governmental affairs and assist Your Majesty. Having received the royal summons, your servant begs leave to retire and attend to some pressing affairs first."

Thereupon, he left the court chamber, and after having given some instructions concerning urgent matters to his subordinates, prepared to return to join the banquet. Ti Miming, bowing low, impeded his progress, saying, "Your Honor, the duke has always been tyrannous and vicious. Although recently he has shown himself somewhat milder in disposition, it will be difficult for him to change his base nature. Now, even though he has invited Your Honor to a banquet, I feel that there is something fishy about it. I fear that he is hatching some dastardly plot. I beg Your Honor to make some excuse for not attending this so-called banquet."

The prime minister's attendants, too, agreed with Ti, and all added their pleas to Ti's that Zhao Dun avoid the banquet. But the latter dismissed

盾，心中不时惊悸，生怕机密泄露，被赵盾先行发难，又盼着计策成功，从此可以肆意游玩。两下里受着煎熬，真是如坐针毡，度日如年。现在屠岸贾已经将一切安排妥当，万无一失，岂有不喜之理？次日早朝，赵盾等大臣奏事已毕，正待退下，灵公开口道："寡人得爱卿全力辅佐，屡进忠言，方能改弦更张，倾心朝政。而今眼见得国家气象一新，百姓安居乐业，全是上卿忠心为国所致。寡人今日于内宫聊备薄酒，与上卿同乐，还望上卿不要推辞。"

赵盾天性忠良，并无防人之心，见灵公有改过的表现，心中甚是欢喜，起身施礼道："微臣理应为国家效力，勤理朝政，辅佐主君。既蒙主君宠召，且容微臣退下将要紧的事情安排一下，而后即刻入宫。"

出得宫来，赵盾当场将几件急需办理的事情交待给下属，自己则掉头准备入宫赴宴。提弥明上前一步拦住去路，躬身道："主君一向荒淫暴虐，近日虽有所收敛，本性毕竟难改。今日突然召大人饮宴，事有蹊跷。依小人看来，恐怕其中另有奸计，大人此去凶多吉少，还是推辞不去的好。"

赵府众人听他说得有理，也都纷纷劝止赵盾。赵盾摆摆手道："我得蒙主君召饮，倘若拒绝不往，那就

their anxieties with a wave of his hand. "It would be an act of disrespect to refuse to accept my sovereign's invitation. Moreover, this is especially so now that the duke has been sequestered in the palace for several days, mulling state affairs. How can I decline, when he expressed the wish to have me at his side to advise him at any time?"

So saying, he turned to enter the palace. Ti Miming, still uneasy, followed close behind. As the two approached the duke's quarters, they noticed that guards armed with pikes lined both sides of the staircase to the duke's quarters, standing stiffly to attention. Ti Miming, alarmed, stepped in front of his master, and whispered, "It is most unusual to have armed guards on duty at such a time. Please, sir, return to your home for the moment. Tomorrow you can make your excuses." But Zhao Dun was not to be put off like this. Loudly, he ordered Ti Miming out of the way, and walked straight ahead. Ti Miming had no choice but to obey. He was right behind Zhao Dun, until they reached the stairs to the duke's quarters, when the guard in front of the door boomed, "His Majesty summoned only the prime minister into his presence. No others may enter!"

Ti Miming watched like a hawk from the foot of the stairs as Zhao Dun ascended.

The ambushers, meanwhile, were concealed in the rear of the duke's quarters, and the Terrible Hound was held on a leash by its keeper on one side of the banqueting chamber.

Seeing Zhao Dun enter, Duke Ling rose to greet him and escorted him to a seat with the utmost courtesy and kindness. Even Tu'an Gu showed himself to be unusually affable and attentive, showering the prime minister with flattering words. The three of them shared a table; the duke was in the middle, with Zhao Dun on his right and Tu'an Gu on his left. Servants hastened up with wine and delicacies. The duke took the lead in offering toasts, and the three of them drank merrily as they chatted. Before he had noticed, Zhao Dun had downed three large beakers of wine. His head began

是臣下的过错。何况主君近日来安居内宫，关心国事，正要我等辅佐，时刻规谏，岂能推辞？"

说罢，回身入宫。提弥明毕竟放心不下，便紧随在赵盾身后。二人来至寝宫门前，只见两排卫士荷戟肃立，戒备森严。提弥明见情形有异，抢上一步拦在赵盾身前，低声道："今日内宫戒备森严，有异往日，请大人暂且回府，明日再做计较。"怎奈赵盾执意前往，大声喝叱提弥明退下，自己径直前行。提弥明无奈，只得紧紧跟随，寸步不离。守在寝宫门前的卫士见了，大声喝道："主君单独召见相国，闲杂人等一律不得入内。"

提弥明闻言只得止步，立于石阶下面，一双眼睛却直盯着殿上，不敢有丝毫懈怠。

此时寝宫之后早已伏下甲士，獒奴则带着神獒立在殿内一侧。

灵公见赵盾来到，亲自上前迎接，赐座免礼，格外宽厚。屠岸贾也表现得十分殷勤，说了一番奉承的话语。当下灵公居中，赵盾居右，屠岸贾居左，君臣三人各据一张几案，排成一个"品"字形。侍者捧上酒馔，灵公首先举觥相邀，君臣三人遂欢然对饮起来。赵盾平时酒量不宏，今日灵公与屠岸贾有意将他灌

to feel fuzzy, and, as if through a thick haze, he heard Duke Ling say, "Prime Minister, I have heard that you carry a most precious sword of exceptional sharpness. My I be allowed to examine it?"

Many years before this, when Zhao Shuai had accompanied Duke Wen of Jin in exile, they had sojourned among the Di nomads of the northwest. It happened that the Di captured two girls during a campaign against another tribe and brought them back as prisoners. They were exceedingly beautiful and gorgeously dressed. One was named Shukwei and the other, Jikwei. Now the khan of the Di tribesmen recognized Duke Wen as a man of extraordinary character, and someone who was destined to accomplish great things, so he gave Jikwei in marriage to the duke, and Shukwei to Zhao Shuai. The son Shukwei bore to Zhao Shuai was Zhao Dun. Later, as Duke Wen and his entourage were about to depart from the land of the Di, it was impossible for Zhao Shuai to take his wife and son with him. He said to her, "Wait here for me for three years. If you do not see me returning by that time, you may freely remarry."

Holding Zhao Dun to her breast, and with tears streaming down her cheeks, Shukwei said, "I have born this child as the scion of the Zhao family; how could I marry another man? I have made up my mind to wait for you, no matter how long it takes."

So saying, she presented Zhao Shuai with a precious sword. The sword had been an heirloom for generations among Shukwei's people. It glittered with a cold sheen, and was so sharp that it could slice through iron as if it were mud. Shukwei continued, "Some day, when your master has regained his rightful place, a ruler of Jin, and has accomplished mighty deeds, I beg that you will send for me and the child, so that the boy can inherit this sword."

From that time on, Zhao Shuai had worn the sword at his waist at all times. Seven years later, when Duke Wen had regained his throne he made

醉，口中说些闲话，暗地里轮番劝酒。赵盾全无防备，不一会儿连尽三大觥，当时酒力涌上头来，直觉得晕晕乎乎。朦胧之中，听得灵公说道："寡人听说上卿所佩宝剑，乃天下利刃也。今日可否让寡人观赏一番，也好开开眼界？"

原来，赵衰当年随晋文公流亡之时，曾在狄国停留。正值狄国讨伐异族，俘获了两名女子，一个名叔隗，一个名季隗，都生得艳丽天成，花枝招展。狄君见晋文公生具异相，料将来必成大事，便作主将季隗、叔隗分别嫁给了晋文公和赵衰。赵衰娶了叔隗，生下一个儿子，便是赵盾。待到文公等人将要离开狄国时，无法带着妻儿同行，赵衰于临行前吩咐叔隗道："你可等我三年，如到时仍不见我归来，自行改嫁就是。"

叔隗怀里抱着赵盾，泪流满面道："我已经为主公生下此子，就是赵家的人了，怎么能随意改嫁呢？我决意等主公回来，决不变心。"

说罢，送给赵衰一把宝剑，那剑本是叔隗族中世代相传的利器，寒光闪闪，削铁如泥，同时说道："他日主公若能回到晋国，成就大业，务要接我们母子回去，由儿子来继承这把宝剑。"

Zhao Shuai a senior minister and married his daughter, Junji, to him. Junji bore Zhao Shuai three sons —— Zhao Tong, Zhao Kuo and Zhao Ying. Despite being born into privilege as a member of the royal family, Junji was virtuous, wise and faithful by nature. Moreover, she was unassuming and modest. Conscious of the fact that Zhao Shuai had a previous wife and a son, Junji sent for them to be brought to Jin, where Zhao Dun inherited his father's post. On his deathbed, Zhao Shuai called Zhao Dun to his side, and said, "The Duke of Jin has bestowed incalculable benefits on the Zhao family. After my death, it will be your duty to serve our sovereign with the utmost loyalty, while at the same time driving out wickedness, to protect the land of Jin." With this, he handed the sword to Zhao Dun. From then on, the latter was reminded of his father's admonition whenever he strapped it on.

Hearing Duke Ling's request, Zhao Dun struggled to his feet, tipsy with wine, and started to draw the sword.

Watching from afar, Ti Miming was horrified, but there was no way he could intervene to prevent his master falling into the trap. All he could do was raise a warning cry.

Hearing Ti Miming's voice, Zhao Dun immediately realized the danger, and his heart turned cold. But it was too late, Tu'an Gu seized the moment to shout, "Zhao Dun has drawn his sword! There is some treacherous plot afoot to harm the duke! Quick, to the rescue of His Majesty!"

The words were scarcely out of his mouth when the men-at-arms who had been concealed in ambush rushed into the banqueting hall, brandishing swords and pikes, and surrounded Zhao Dun. Seeing this from the foot of the stairs, Ti Miming was possessed with but one thought —— that he must save his master at all costs. So, seizing a halberd, he sprang up the stairs and into the banqueting chamber. Fending off the attackers with his weapon, he pulled Zhao Dun towards the door.

　　自此之后，赵衰一直将此剑佩在身边。七年后，晋文公归国即位，封赵衰为上卿，又把自己的女儿嫁给他，人称君姬氏，先后生下赵同、赵括、赵婴三个儿子。君姬氏虽然出身公门，为人却贤惠忠厚，颇有逊让之德。她派人将赵盾母子接回晋国，并由赵盾承袭了父亲的官爵。赵衰临终前，将赵盾叫到榻前，道："先主君对赵家恩重如山，我死后，你务要忠心耿耿，上辅君主，下除奸佞，力保晋国江山。"说罢，将宝剑赐给赵盾。赵盾从此时刻将宝剑佩在身上，铭记父亲的教诲。

　　此时赵盾因酒力涌上头来，听了灵公的话，不及细想，便站起身来待要解下宝剑呈上。提弥明远远看见，心急如焚，大声喊道："臣侍君宴，礼不过三爵，相国为何于酒后在国君面前拔剑？"

　　赵盾闻言，心中一凛，恍然大悟，可惜为时已晚。屠岸贾及时发难，大声喝道："赵盾在堂上拔剑，欲加害于主君，图谋不轨。左右快快救驾！"

　　话音未落，预先埋伏好的甲士闻声蜂拥而出，手执剑戟，将赵盾团团围住。提弥明在阶下望见，救主心切，持戈冲上大殿，一手执戈与卫士相搏，一手拉着赵盾向外就走。

As the ambushers reeled from the surprise and impact of Ti Miming's ferocious sally, Tu'an Gu ordered the dog handler to unleash the Terrible Hound. The beast had been starved of all nourishment for two days, and at the sight of Zhao Dun, whom it associated with the straw man and his delectable innards, entering the hall had uttered a low and menacing growl, and it had been all its handler could do to restrain it. Now that it had been freed it didn't wait for any order from its master but bounded as if in flight towards Zhao Dun, who had just reached the door of the hall. Perceiving the Terrible Hound bearing down on him, Zhao Dun was terrified, and tried to dodge behind a pillar. But the ravenous beast was not to be cheated of its prey; in the twinkling of an eye it had pinned the prime minister to the ground.

Ti Miming, however, was just as speedy in coming to the rescue. With his eyes bulging from his head in fury and his hair standing straight on end, Ti Miming let out a roar, "You hellhound, how dare you harm my master!?"

And he seized the dog by the back legs, swung the huge animal in the air and dashed its brains out on the adamantine floor. Panting in its death agony, the Terrible Hound was past all evil doing, but just to make sure, Ti Miming seized the animal by the head, gave a tremendous wrench, and broke its neck, whereupon it expired on the spot. The throng of banqueters was struck dumb with awe at the sight of this feat of strength. As for Duke Ling, he was petrified with fear where he sat. Then, trembling like an aspen leaf, he determined to flee to the rear of the palace, but his limbs would not obey the royal summons. But Tu'an Gu, who was, after all, a soldier by training and had seen slaughter on the battlefield, had remained calm throughout the commotion and had the presence of mind to bellow an order, "Guards, seize that miscreant at once!"

As if waking from a dream, the men-at-arms dashed forward to grapple with Ti Miming. The latter, knowing that he was outnumbered and that he

屠岸贾见提弥明横里杀出，勇猛难当，众卫士一时抵挡不住，便急命獒奴将神獒放开。那畜牲被饿了两天，方才见了赵盾，与草人装束一般无二，便将他当做美味的食物，挣扎着低声咆哮。若非獒奴死命拉住，早已扑上前去。此刻束缚忽去，不等主子指点，"嗖"一下冲了出去，奔跃如飞，在宫门前追上了赵盾。赵盾见这畜牲凶猛异常，惊得环柱而逃，哪里又是这猛畜的对手，眨眼间被扑倒在地，眼见就要丧生于犬吻之下。说时迟，那时快，提弥明见状怒气勃发，眼眶迸裂，头发上指，大声喝道："恶畜胆敢伤我主人！"

说着，冲上前去，双手一把攫住神獒的两只后腿，大喝一声，将那条近百斤重的猛犬举到半空，猛地摔在坚硬的地面上。只听"啪"的一声，神獒落地，脑袋破裂，气息奄奄，再也无法逞凶。提弥明犹然不肯罢手，健步上前，提起神獒的脑袋用力一拧，众人看时，神獒早已脖颈断裂，当场毙命。众人见提弥明如此神勇，当时都惊得呆了。灵公何曾见过这种场面，早已吓得瘫在座椅上筛糠，想着起身逃回后宫，怎奈两腿不听使唤，站都站不起来。屠岸贾毕竟是个武夫，也曾在战场上经历过厮杀的场面，倒还能镇定自若，高声喝道："众卫士速速将这犯上作乱的贼子擒下！"

would be lucky to escape with his life if he stood his ground, hustled Zhao Dun outside the palace and urged him to flee, assuring his master that he would be right behind him.

As Zhao Dun tottered off, Ti Miming turned to bar the progress of Tu'an Gu's men. After a fierce battle, the outnumbered Ti Miming fell dead, covered in wounds. His enormous strength and supreme loyalty to his master inspired later generations to compose ballads about him, which were sung from generation to generation. He was likened to Jing Ke, the heroic assassin of the king of Qin. But this was later.

Thanks to Ti Miming's self-sacrificing act in delaying his pursuers, Zhao Dun managed to stumble out of the palace gate unscathed. As he reached his carriage, he saw his driver lying dead beside it. Moreover, two of the four horses had vanished, and the carriage was lying on its side with one of its two wheels missing. Zhao Dun looked around anxiously, but there was no sign of the attendants who had accompanied him to the palace. A cold shiver ran down the prime minister's spine, as he realized what a desperate predicament he was in. He turned, and saw a husky soldier running towards him. Zhao Dun, straightened his back, faced his executioner and awaited his inevitable end.

But the soldier ignored Zhao Dun for the moment, and turned his attention to the broken carriage. He lifted it upright with one hand, saying in a low voice to Zhao Dun, "Prime Minister, never fear! I have come to repay a small favor by helping you out of your difficulty. Please make haste and mount the carriage."

Zhao Dun was flabbergasted, but he realized that this was no time to start asking questions, and so he scrambled into the carriage. The stranger yelled at the horses to break into a gallop, while he himself supported the side of the carriage with the missing wheel on his shoulder and started to run. As the carriage rattled off through the city and out of the city gate, Zhao Dun, who had begun to recover from his fright, looked carefully at his savior. The

众甲士这才如梦方醒，冲上前去与提弥明搏斗。提弥明深知众寡不敌，今日绝无幸免，上前一手将赵盾拉起，道："大人快走，小人来殿后。"

赵盾踉跄着向宫门外奔去，提弥明转身拦住去路，与众甲士拼死力战，终因寡不敌众，浑身上下都被鲜血染的赤红，最后力尽身亡。因他力大无比，忠心护主，后人将他的故事编成曲词，代代传唱，名垂青史，犹如那刺秦王的荆轲一般，此是后话。

赵盾赖提弥明抵挡甲士，得以脱身逃出宫外，正欲上车，却见车夫死在一边，驾车的四匹马只剩下两匹，两只车轮也不见了一只。车子歪倒在一边，无法行驶。左右张望，随自己上朝的家人也都不见踪影，一时惊惶无计，出了一身冷汗。回头一看，只见一名相貌魁梧的甲士奔了过来，自知难免于死，索性立足不动，静以待毙。

谁知那奔来的甲士竟然一手将车子扶正，低声道："相国莫怕，小人特来报一饭之恩，救相国脱难。相国请快快上车。"

赵盾心中疑惑，当时情形紧急，也无法细问，先一步登上车子。那甲士用单肩扛起倾斜的车子，一声吆喝，竟然用自己的双腿替代一侧的车轮，策马奔驰

man's shoulder by this time was rubbed raw and drenched with blood. A flicker of recognition stirred within Zhao Dun as he took account of the other's thick eyebrows, large eyes and robust frame. He wondered where he had seen the man before. When the carriage was well clear of the capital, and there had been no sign of pursuit for a long time, the stranger stopped for a rest. Zhao Dun stepped out of the carriage, straightened his dress, gave a low bow and addressed the soldier thus, "May I ask your name, sir, and why you have risked your life to save me, with whom you have no acquaintance?"

The other, who stood by the roadside panting heavily after his herculean exertions, hastened to raise the prime minister upright from his obeisance. He in turn made a bow to Zhao Dun, saying, "I suppose, Prime Minister, that you must have forgotten the starving man under the mulberry tree five years ago?"

Upon hearing these words, the mind of Zhao Dun was taken back five years. . . .

It was in the summer, and the day was unbearably hot. Zhao Dun and his entourage were on their way back from a hunting trip to Mount Jiuyuan, when they came upon a delightful spot. With the mountains and stately trees as the background, the place was carpeted with wild flowers. Beside the road stood a mulberry tree. Its trunk was extraordinarily thick, and it was adorned with luxuriant branches and leaves, and crowned with green. Zhao Dun alighted from his carriage to rest for a while in the emerald shade. As he did so, he noticed a hulking figure stretched on the ground under the mulberry tree. Although the man's body was sturdy, his face was bony and pinched. His mouth was wide open, and he lay quite still. At first, Zhao Dun was alarmed at the thought that this fellow might be a villain of some kind. He instructed his attendants to find out who he was. They ascertained that the man was starving. He was devoid of strength, and his eyes were dull and lacklustre.

起来，车子如飞一般出了城门。赵盾惊魂甫定，只见那驱车的甲士肩上磨得鲜血淋漓，再一细看，见他浓眉大眼，身材魁梧，有几分似曾相识，仿佛在何处见过。再行一程，离那绛邑城已远，后面也未见到有甲士追来，二人方歇息下来。赵盾抬腿下车，略整衣冠，向那甲士躬身一揖，问道："敢问壮士姓名？你与老夫素昧平生，为何要舍命搭救老夫？"

那甲士肩扛车轴奔驰，一路下来，早已累得脱力，瘫在地上大声喘息。此刻见赵盾施礼询问，急忙勉强站起身，还了一礼，说道："相国莫非忘了五年前桑树下的饿夫了吗？"

赵盾闻言，五年前的一件往事蓦地兜上心来……

那是一个夏季，天气炎热难当。赵盾带着从人去九原山打猎回来，行至一处，见景色幽美，远山佳木交碧，近野奇花织锦，路旁有一棵大桑树，树身粗达数围，枝叶扶疏，绿冠如盖。赵盾便欲在树荫下歇息片刻，下车走近，却见树下躺着一个大汉，身材虽然高大，脸上却瘦骨嶙峋，一张嘴巴张得大大的，一动不动。赵盾起初怀疑这大汉是个歹人，命从人上前询问，却发现那大汉已饿了多日，有气无力，眼见得不

When Zhao Dun asked him how he had come to be in that emaciated condition, the man replied, "My name is Ling Zhe. Three years ago, I traveled to the State of Wei to study, and am now on my way back. My pack is completely empty; not a morsel of food or a drop of drink have passed my lips for three days. I had thought to pick some of these mulberries to assuage my hunger, but I was afraid that the owner of the tree might take me for a thief. Rather than bring such disgrace upon myself, I decided to lie under the tree with my mouth open, on the off-chance that some of the fruit might fall into it. If no mulberries did fall, then I was resolved to die of hunger rather than be tainted with the foul name of thief."

Zhao Dun was touched by the man's story. He exclaimed with a sigh, "What a truly upright gentleman!" He then gave orders to his attendants to give some of the food and wine they had with them to Ling Zhe. When they did so, strange to relate, Ling Zhe did not immediately devour the victuals, but first took out a small bamboo basket, and put half of what he had been offered in it. That done, he ate the rest with great gusto.

Curious, Zhao Dun inquired, "Sir, the food and drink just now provided for you were scarce enough to allay the hunger and thirst of a man who has been starving for several days. Yet you actually put some aside. Why was that?"

Ling Zhe replied, "Your Honor, I have at home my old mother. She lives near the West Gate of Jiangyi, only a few *li* from here. During the three years I have been away, she has no doubt been living a hard life. So I put some of the food and drink Your Honor kindly offered to one side to give to her to appease her hunger."

Zhao Dun uttered several deep sighs of admiration upon hearing this, and said, "Sir, you are not only a man of righteousness, but a filial son the like of whom is rarely seen!" He thereupon turned to his attendants, and told them to give Ling Zhe some more food to take to his mother. Later, a verse was written about this incident, as follows:

能活了。赵盾问道:"壮士因何饿成这般模样?"

那大汉答道:"小人名叫灵辄,三年前去卫地游学。如今学成归来,囊空如洗,已有三日水米未曾沾牙。本想摘几棵桑椹充饥,又恐主人将我当作盗贼,白白招来耻辱。只好躺在树下,张大嘴巴等着。如果桑椹熟透落下,掉到嘴里,我便吃了;如果掉不到嘴里,我宁可饿死,也不愿落个盗贼的恶名!"

赵盾听罢,心中惊叹道:"这汉子真乃义士。"当下吩咐左右,将携带的酒食取出来拿给灵辄。谁知那灵辄得了酒食,却不急着吃,而是从身边取出一只小竹筐,将酒食分了一半放入筐中,这才狼吞虎咽地将剩下的酒食吃了个一干二净。

赵盾觉得奇怪,又问道:"义士饥饿数日,这点儿酒食不足一饱,为何不全都吃了呢?"

灵辄答道:"小人家有老母,住在绛邑西门外,离此只有几里地。我外出三年,老母必定度日艰难,小人要将大人所赐的食物带给老母充饥。"

赵盾闻言连连感叹道:"义士不但高义感人,也是世间少见的孝子啊!"当下命从人又取出一些酒食,送给灵辄的母亲。后人有诗道:

Returning from a rural ride, he rested as the sun set.

Simple fare, a swig of wine revived the starving stranger.

At this point in his reverie, Zhao Dun came to himself again. He scrutinized Ling Zhe closely, and found that sure enough he was the man under the mulberry tree. Filled with compassion, he said, "I hope, sir, your aged mother at home is well."

Ling Zhe replied, "After receiving Your Honor's bounty on that day, I returned home. Alas, I found that my mother had already passed away. I had no choice but to offer Your Honor's gift as a sacrificial offering at her grave. Later, I was summoned to a post at the capital as a guard in the duke's palace. When it came to my attention that Tu'an Gu meant to harm Your Honor, I eavesdropped from time to time. It must have been Heaven's determination to save the life of a good man that guided you into my hands today!"

As the two stood there talking, the rumble of chariots and the pounding of horses' hooves were heard, and before long Zhao Chuan and a company of followers galloped up.

As soon as news of the commotion at the palace had reached the Zhao mansion, the company had hastened to the spot. There they beheld the bodies of Ti Miming and the driver, but there was no sign of Zhao Dun or his carriage. Making inquiries, they learned that a burly fellow had pushed the carriage out of the city, so they set off in hot pursuit. Zhao Dun told his brother all that had happened. Zhao Chuan said, "Elder Brother, it seems that this rascally Tu'an Gu has a deep enmity for you. On top of that, the duke is muddle headed, and doesn't know right from wrong. I think you should take shelter somewhere for a few days and then decide what to do."

Thereupon, Ling Zhe chimed in with, "Sir, you are absolutely right. I beg to be allowed to escort the prime minister deep into the mountains, to some safe place."

Zhao Dun was loath to abandon affairs of state, but as he seemed to have

为乘春令劝农耕,巡遍郊野日未晡。

壶浆箪食因谁下,要济山间一饿夫。

想到这里,赵盾细看灵辄,果然是当日桑树下的大汉,心中不觉感慨万千,遂问道:"义士家中老母可好?"

灵辄答道:"小人受大人一饭之恩,回到家中,不料老母已经下世,只得用相国所赐酒食去坟上祭奠一番。然后来到京城应招,充任宫中卫士。因见屠岸贾欲加害恩人,便于暗中时时探听。今日正遇在小人手里,也是上天有眼,要保全好人呀!"

二人正说话时,忽听得车声如雷,蹄声急骤,只见赵穿等人驾车赶到。

原来,赵府忽听上宫中发生变故,众人当即赶到宫门前,只见到提弥明和车夫的尸体,却不见赵盾和车子的踪影,四下打听,得知一名壮士驱车出城去了,遂带着人马急急赶来。赵盾与赵穿兄弟相见,将方才之事诉说一番。赵穿道:"兄长与那屠岸贼怨隙已深,主君又昏庸无道,不明是非。不如先去别处躲避几日,再作打算。"

灵辄也道:"大人正当如此,小人愿随大人隐居深山。"

赵盾心中抛不下国事,可眼前又无可奈何,只好

no choice in the circumstances, he reluctantly acquiesced. So, instead of going home, he mounted Zhao Chuan's carriage, which Ling Zhe then drove away. As the verse goes:

Zhao Dun was in desperate straits; his carriage was missing a wheel.

But just in time, Ling Zhe came up, and repaid the gift of a meal.

Having ordered his guards to finish off Ti Miming, Tu'an Gu went in pursuit of Zhao Dun. But when he saw that the rest of the Zhao clan had reached the prime minister before him, he turned back to report to Duke Ling.

He found the dull witted duke in high spirits. Although the plot to kill Zhao Dun had not succeeded, Duke Ling thought that as his importunate prime minister had been driven far away from the palace he would be no longer bothered by him. He chuckled, "Now that I've got rid of that nail in my eye, that thorn in my flesh, let's see who dares to play the busybody with me now!"

His officials, who had witnessed Zhao Dun's hairbreadth escape from assassination, stood as mute as frozen crickets. From then on, none of them dared say a word concerning the duke's behavior. The duke himself was as carefree as a lark, forgot all about governmental affairs, sent for Laiji and took her and a large contingent of palace ladies and guards to the Peach Garden, where he indulged himself in feasting, entertainment and all imaginable pleasures from morning till night.

Tu'an Gu, meanwhile, took himself off home. He was uneasy about the way the whole business had gone.

He woke up after a noontide nap, and wandered alone into his back courtyard. He pondered on how his plans had gone awry, The sudden appearance of Ti Miming had spoiled his scheme to get the Terrible Hound to do away with Zhao Dun. And then there was that fellow Ling Zhe. Where had he suddenly sprung from? Tu'an Gu was troubled; it boded ill, he thought. Then an alarming scenario came into his head, what if Zhao Dun fled to another state, and there brooded on how to return and get his revenge? In the meantime, Zhao's son was married to Duke Ling's daughter; in fact, the

答应。当下也不回家,换乘了赵穿的车子,依旧让灵辄驾驭,逃往别处去了。正是:

紫衣逃难出宫门,驷马华车摘一轮。

却是灵辄强扶归,报得山间一饭恩。

屠岸贾指挥众卫士杀死提弥明,然后去追赶赵盾。半路上见赵家已有接应,便折了回来,向灵公复命。

灵公本来没有什么头脑,虽然除去赵盾的计划没有彻底成功,却也将他远远地赶跑了,心中大喜,哈哈大笑道:"寡人总算去了这眼中钉、肉中刺,以后看哪个还敢多管闲事?"

众大臣见相国赵盾险遭毒手,一个个噤若寒蝉,再也不敢对灵公的举动说三道四。灵公好不欢喜,真个胸怀舒畅,快不可言,索性不问朝政,派人接了睐姬,带着一大群宫女卫士长住在桃园,朝歌暮乐起来。

屠岸贾回到家中,心里却感到空空荡荡,很不踏实。

这日午睡醒来,独自来到后园,想起那些天安排计策,训练神獒,实指望除去赵盾老贼,不料中途杀出个提弥明和灵辄来,将一场好戏搅黄了,心中好生懊恼。又想道:"那赵盾倘若逃到别国,自然要想法回

Zhao clan was represented all over the country, from the court down. There were a lot of them, and if they rose in sympathy with Zhao Dun returning at the head of another ruler's army —— it didn't bear thinking about! He himself had had so many clashes with Zhao Dun that they were now mortal foes. If Zhao Dun got the upper hand again, he would be finished!

At this point, Tu'an Gu was gripped with terror, as only a person with a guilty conscience can be. But he forced himself to analyze the situation rationally, "At the moment," he said to himself, "Zhao Dun is on the run. The dragon is headless, and so I have no rival at court. Why not seize the opportunity to strike now, clear away all my enemies, root and branch, and get rid of the source of future danger?"

Thus resolved, the very next morning after breakfast Tu'an Gu hastened to the Peach Garden and demanded an audience with Duke Ling. The duke had spent the previous night frolicking with Laiji and the palace ladies. When Tu'an Gu called he was fast asleep with his arms round Laiji. But Tu'an Gu had always been on easy terms with the duke, so the duke's chamberlain did not hesitate to wake his master, who, when he heard who the visitor was, rubbed his bleary eyes and ordered that he be admitted.

Tu'an Gu marched straight into Duke Ling's bedroom. He made a perfunctory bow, and uttered a deep sigh.

"What's the matter, minister?" cried Duke Ling.

Tu'an Gu gave a mirthless laugh. "Your servant, sire," he said, "has something weighing on his mind. Surely you can't have forgotten that for many years Zhao Dun handled government affairs, and was plotting to seize the throne when the time was ripe. He has fled now, but where has he fled to —— perhaps to the State of Qin, or the State of Chu? If so, then he intends to borrow forces with which to wreak his revenge, and raise supporters among local ruffians here to attack the capital. The Zhao clan is well represented at court, and it has powerful forces at its disposal. If they rise up in concert with an attack from outside our borders, you and I, Your Majesty, will be slaughtered out of hand."

国报仇。而眼下他的儿子是当朝驸马，兄弟子侄布满朝野，人多势众。万一那赵盾带了诸侯的军队来报仇，里应外合，岂不是易如反掌。自己多次与他做对，已成死敌，到时他哪里肯轻易放过？"

想到此处，不禁毛骨悚然，正是作贼心虚。转念一想："眼下赵盾逃亡在外，朝中群龙无首，何不趁此时来个先下手为强，斩草除根，杜绝后患？"

主意拿定，次日早膳后即前往桃园请见灵公。灵公昨晚与眯姬及众宫女宣淫终夜，此时还在抱着眯姬高卧酣睡。内侍忽报司寇屠岸大人请见，灵公睡眼惺忪，随口道："让他进来。"

屠岸贾平时与灵公并不严守那君臣名分，昂然直入灵公的寝处。施礼已毕，屠岸贾长叹一声。

灵公道："爱卿为何叹息？"

屠岸贾苦笑道："微臣心中有事。主君难道忘了，那赵盾多年把持朝政，早有篡夺之心，此番逃走，不是投奔秦、楚，借兵报仇；就是招募乡勇，攻打绛邑。赵氏族人满布朝中，又拥有重兵，如果来个里应外合，只怕你我君臣二人死无葬身之地啊！"

灵公听了，觉得有理，不禁害怕起来，急急问道："爱卿有何良策，能为寡人去此隐忧，好于此生此世

The duke was appalled. "Quick, minister," he urged, "Think of a good plan to remove this dreadful danger from me, so that I can go on enjoying life without a care in the world!"

Tu'an Gu gestured to Laiji to retire, and feigning a worried frown, said, "All my previous plans have come to naught, I am afraid, Your Majesty, and so I dare not speak incautiously. But, you are a man of wisdom, sire. In this matter I beg you to take decisive action."

The addle-brained duke had no idea what his minister was talking about. "My Dear Minister," he pleaded, "You are full of ideas. Please suggest a good one for me."

Seeing that Duke Ling was confused as to his intention, Tu'an Gu chose his words with care, slowly spelling out his scheme, "Now that Zhao Dun has fled, Your Majesty, the dragon is headless, so to speak. In order to get rid of the sources of future troubles, I suggest you decree the execution of the whole Zhao clan, all three hundred of them, high and low."

Now although the duke resented Zhao Dun for his irksome admonitions and for interfering in his pleasures, he did not harbor any deep-seated hatred of the man. He was well aware that Zhao Dun had served his father as well as himself, and had a reputation for loyalty to the country. Duke Ling balked at the idea of committing so monstrous a deed as wiping out his whole clan. To overcome the duke's scruples, Tu'an Gu reinforced his argument. "I know that I deserve death for suggesting such a thing, Your Majesty, but if Zhao Dun returns with an armed force and conquers the capital, he will certainly depose you, and set himself up as ruler. And in that case, even if you manage to escape with your life you will surely be banished to some remote region where life will not be worth living. Every time I think of the fate which awaits Your Majesty, my heart breaks into little pieces and I cannot restrain my tears!" As he spoke, he squeezed two tears from his eyes. The alarming picture painted by Tu'an Gu sent the duke into a state of complete stupefaction, in the midst of which the only thought that came into his head was that he must protect his life at all costs. He blurted out, "Well, if that is

长乐无忧?"

屠岸贾挥手命睐姬退下,装模做样蹙眉道:"微臣前番出了几个主意,都未曾得手。如今也不敢乱说,主君英明,还祈果断处置。"

灵公本来是个糊涂虫,叫屠岸贾一说,越发没有主张,只道:"爱卿足智多谋,快替寡人想个良策。"

屠岸贾拿腔捏调,直到见灵公慌了手脚,这才慢条斯理道:"如今赵盾出逃,下宫内群龙无首,主君何不下令将赵家良贱三百余口满门抄斩,以绝后患呢?"

灵公平日虽嫌赵盾屡屡谏阻自己尽兴玩乐,毕竟没有深仇大恨,何况赵盾是两朝老臣,忠心为国,如今要诛杀其全家,一时间却也下不了这个毒手,难免露出几分犹豫。屠岸贾急欲置赵氏于死地,见灵公还在犹豫,索性以退为进道:"微臣死不足惜,只是那赵盾若是杀回绛邑,必定废掉主君,篡国自立。到那时主君纵然得保性命,也必定被打入冷宫,生不如死。微臣每一念及,不免为主君心碎堕泪。"说着假惺惺地落下两滴眼泪来。灵公听了屠岸贾一番言语,唬得六神无主,想想毕竟自己性命要紧,便道:"既然如此,此事就责成爱卿速去办理,务要消除后患。"

屠岸贾得了灵公之命,二人又秘密商议了半天,

the case, you must see that it is done at once, Minister. Your duty is to see that all future harm to me is averted!"

After conferring with the duke for a long while on the details of the massacre, Tu'an Gu went home in a buoyant mood. Just before dawn the following morning, he ordered some 1,000 of his guards to assemble. Under the personal command of Tu'an Gu, they surrounded the Zhao family's mansion, cutting off all avenues of escape.

Following the flight of Zhao Dun, the whole of the Zhao clan had been thrown into gloom and despair. They cursed the doltish duke bitterly, but they never suspected that he would move against them, much less consent to the massacre of the entire clan. And so, when the sudden assault on the mansion came, all 300 of the Zhaos were fast asleep and completely unprepared to defend themselves. Zhao Chuan and his attendants were startled from their slumbers to see soldiers armed to the teeth smashing their way into the mansion and hewing down all they encountered, young and old. In no time at all, the Zhao mansion was turned into a shrieking pandemonium, and corpses littered the floors. Zhao Chuan and his attendants were military men, and their first reaction was to draw their swords and rally everyone left alive to counter-attack. But they were doomed from the start. One after the other, Zhao Chuan, Zhao Tong, Zhao Kuo and Zhao Ying fell dead. Leaderless, the handful of survivors fled in all directions, only to be slaughtered by Tu'an Gu's men. Within less than an hour, the massacre was complete —— the whole 300 member Zhao clan, high and low, had been butchered. Dawn found the Zhao mansion heaped with corpses and swimming with blood. Not a living soul was left alive inside its walls.

When the court officials, both civil and military, and the common people of the capital heard the shocking news, not a soul dared to utter a word about it, but everyone walked with downcast eyes, completely crushed in spirit by the bloodthirsty tyranny of Duke Ling and Tu'an Gu.

Worried that some member of the Zhao clan might have slipped through the net and survived to cause him trouble in the future, Tu'an Gu sent men to

这才兴兴头头回到家中。次日四更时分,传令集合卫士上千人,由屠岸贾亲自带领,分作四路,突然将下宫围了个水泄不通。

自从赵盾出逃,赵氏一家人整日里忿懑不平,痛骂灵公昏君,却做梦也想不到屠岸贾心黑手毒,竟然撺掇着灵公抄斩赵氏满门。这天夜里,赵氏阖家上下三百余口都在睡梦之中,被突袭的甲士杀了个猝不及防。待得赵穿等人惊醒起身,只见成群的兵士披甲操戈,破门而入,不管老幼,逢人便砍。整个下宫人哭马嘶,鸡飞狗跳,乱成一团,眨眼间尸体狼藉,倒下一片。赵穿等人都是武将,当即持剑率领家人拼死搏斗,无奈众寡不敌,赵穿、赵同、赵括、赵婴等人先后被杀,赵氏家人群龙无首,四散奔逃,却被四面围住的甲士尽皆杀死。不上一个时辰,这场血腥的屠杀便告结束,赵氏一家三百余口人,不分良贱,都成了刀下之鬼。待到天亮,下宫内只见尸山血海,再无一个活人。

朝中文武及京城百姓惊闻下宫遭屠,慑于灵公和屠岸贾的淫威,道路以目,无人敢言。

屠岸贾犹恐赵氏家人有漏网之鱼,贻患将来,又派人一一查验尸体,务要斩草除根。结果发现只有驸马赵朔因为昨晚与公主宿于宫中,未曾遭难。

search through the piles of bodies one by one and dispatch anyone whom they might find still alive. In this way, he came to learn that Zhao Shuo, the duke's brother-in-law had escaped the assault on the Zhao mansion because he had been with the princess in the duke's palace the previous night.

Zhao Shuo was Zhao Dun's son. He held a high rank at court, and had married Duke Ling's younger sister. They were a loving couple who lived in wedded bliss. At this time, the princess was expecting a child soon.

Learning that Zhao Shuo was still alive, Tu'an Gu was so alarmed that he broke out in a cold sweat. Zhao Shuo would be sure to seek revenge for the enormity visited on his family, Tu'an Gu thought to himself. Not only that, but the duke himself might protect his close relative by marriage, and then Tu'an Gu would never be safe. At this point, he gave a hideous cackle and ground his teeth fiercely. "Zhao Shuo, Zhao Shuo," he hissed, "You might have escaped my grasp this time. But you certainly will not the next time!"

He turned the matter over and over in his mind. He had to act quickly, before a complaint was lodged with Duke Ling. Tu'an Gu immediately led a dozen men-at-arms to Zhao Shuo's quarters.

Zhao Shuo had heard of the massacre early that morning. Burning with outrage and fury, he snatched up his sword and was ready to seek out Tu'an Gu there and then. But the princess restrained him, saying, "How can you face Tu'an Gu's men alone? They are as fierce as ravening wolves or tigers. Moreover, that villainous Tu'an has poison in his heart. It is very likely that he is coming here to slay you at this very moment! You must flee for your life. In the eastern mountains you can foment an uprising and get your revenge."

At this moment, Tu'an Gu and his henchmen burst in. At the sight of them, Zhao Shuo's eyes blazed with fire, and he was on the point of lunging at the intruders, when Tu'an Gu waved a hand in deprecation. "Sir, please calm yourself. Your servant has come to deliver an order from the duke." So saying, he adopted a grave expression and intoned as follows, "The treach-

那赵朔是赵盾之子，官任都尉，娶的正是灵公之姊，乃当朝驸马，算来还是灵公的姊夫。赵朔自与公主成婚后，二人恩爱异常，公主现在已经怀孕数月，不日即是分娩之期。

屠岸贾得知赵朔幸免于难，不禁大吃一惊，冷汗涔涔而下。暗想那赵朔与自己有灭门之恨，将来岂能不思报仇？可他现在身为驸马，如果报告灵公，万一灵公看在姊弟情分上将赵朔饶过不杀，必然成为自己的一大遗患。想到这儿，屠岸贾不由得冷笑一声，恶狠狠地咬牙切齿道："赵朔啊，赵朔！只怕今日我饶过你，你也不肯放过我呀！"

思来想去，只有一不做，二不休，假传圣旨，马上带人将赵朔处死，到时生米已成熟饭，纵然公主向灵公哭诉，也是为时已晚。事不宜迟，夜长梦多，屠岸贾立即带了几十名甲士，径往驸马府中。

这日一早，赵朔惊闻下宫之变，悲愤交加，当即拔剑要找屠岸贾拼命。公主在一旁忍悲劝道："夫君只有一人，怎能与那如狼似虎的大队卫士抗衡？何况屠岸贾一向心狠手辣，恐怕马上就会来杀夫君。夫君不如快快逃走，留得性命，以图东山再起，报仇雪恨。"

二人正在说话之间，早见屠岸贾带着一群甲士

erous minister Zhao Dun, having plotted insurrection and fearing punishment, has fled. Zhao Shuo colluded with his father in his wickedness. As Zhao Shuo is kin to the royal person by marriage, he is excused by the rules of protocol from undergoing public execution, and is hereby granted leave to commit suicide. The princess must return to the royal palace to await a decision on her fate. Let this order be carried out without fail. "

On hearing this, Zhao Shuo and his wife beat their foreheads and wailed in agony. Tu'an Gu interrupted their grief with words of uncertain import, "When the sovereign commands it, it is his servant's duty to die. Sir, it is an honor to die by one's own hand in such a case." Thereupon, he laid a dagger, a goblet of poisoned wine and a rope on a table.

Zhao Shuo was beside himself with rage and sorrow. Wiping away his tears, he cried, "For generations, we Zhaos have been paragons of loyalty in the service of our lords. And now we have descended to this!" So saying, he snatched up the goblet and drank its contents.

The princess turned pale with fear at the sight. She made a feeble attempt to snatch the goblet from her husband's hand, but she was too late. He had drained the poisoned wine to the dregs. The poison soon began its work. Zhao Shuo fell to the ground and rolled over and over in agony, his four limbs thrashing wildly. His face was a steely gray, and large beads of sweat streamed from it. Before long, a thick black spot appeared between his eyebrows, he fought desperately for breath. Watching this tragic scene, the princess, distraught with grief, threw herself upon her husband, wailing, "My dearest, if you die, I will have no reason to go on living. Please do not depart this world just yet, but wait for me to accompany you!" She then seized the dagger, and made as if to plunge it into her breast.

Zhao Shuo, despite being at his last gasp, was still aware of what was going on around him. He wrested the dagger from his wife's hand, and pleaded in a low voice, "Princess, you must not die! You are bearing the

闯了进来。赵朔见了，两眼几乎要喷出火来，就要上前拼命。屠岸贾却摆摆手道："驸马稍安毋躁，本官特来传谕主君之命。"说罢，正色高声道："贼臣赵盾，图谋不轨，惧罪潜逃。赵朔身为驸马，不思精忠报国，反与贼臣勾结。念其身为外戚，不予显戮，赐令自尽。公主且回上宫听命，不得有误。"

赵朔夫妻闻言，抱头大哭，心碎肠断。屠岸贾在一旁阴阳怪气道："君令臣死，臣不得不死。驸马好自为之。"说毕，将一把短刀、一觥毒酒并一根绳索放在几上。

赵朔悲愤莫名，抹了一把泪道："我赵家数代忠心耿耿，辅佐主君，不意落得如此下场！"说罢，端起毒酒来一饮而尽。

公主一见，大惊失色，待要夺下赵朔手中的铜觥，毒酒早已被赵朔饮得涓滴不剩。转眼间药性发作，赵朔疼得在地上滚来滚去，四肢抽搐，脸色铁青，豆大的汗珠成串地滴下来，不大一阵功夫，眉间便显出一股浓黑的青气，眼见着入气少出气多。公主在一旁看着，不禁柔肠万断，心痛欲裂，扑在赵朔身上大哭道："夫君若死，贱妾也不想活了。夫君且慢些儿走，等贱妾赶来同行。"说着就起身抓起短刀，意欲自尽。

heartbeat of the Zhaos within you. Heaven has eyes, and if you give birth to a boy, he will inherit the duty of gaining revenge for the massacre at the Zhao mansion!"

With these words, he turned his eyes to Heaven, and fell back. His legs shook with convulsions, and after a little while he was dead. The heartbroken princess hugged his corpse and wailed piteously. Tu'an Gu, on the other hand, felt that a great weight had been lifted from his mind, and after mouthing a few empty words of condolence to the princess, secretly dispatched men to surround Zhao Shuo's quarters and keep it under tight surveillance. He himself then strode off, with a light heart, to report to Duke Ling.

赵朔此时虽然气息奄奄,所幸神智清醒,挣扎着夺下公主手中的短刀,附在耳边说道:"公主,死不得! 你腹中怀着赵家的血脉,老天有眼,若生下一个男孩,赵氏的血海深仇可就全靠他了!"

说罢,仰天摔倒,双腿抽搐,顿时气绝身亡。公主抚尸痛哭,悲痛欲绝。屠岸贾见赵朔死了,心中一块大石落地,假意安慰了公主几句,暗中派人将驸马府紧紧围住,密切监视。自己则踌躇满志,打道入宫,向灵公报讯去了。

Chapter Four
Cheng Ying Saves a Child

After Tu'an Gu got Duke Ling to order the massacre of the Zhao clan, and he himself deceived Zhao Shuo into committing suicide, he gathered the reins of power in his own hands. While making sure that everything was arranged to keep the duke fully occupied with merrymaking, leaving him no time to take any notice of governmental affairs, he set about forming a powerful faction, at the same time eliminating those who were not of like mind. This was all done to pave the way for usurping the throne. When Commander-in-Chief of Jin died of illness, Tu'an Gu, without asking Duke Ling's permission, took over his authority, and thus controlled both the civil and military power of the State of Jin. Tu'an Gu was now in a position of unassailable authority. Yet, dizzy with success as he was, he still had one worry: The princess carried within her spawn of the Zhaos! If he allowed the whelp to grow up, he would be unleashing a deadly enemy against himself. However, he did not dare move against the princess yet, as she was after all the duke's sister. He decided therefore to use the pretext of ensuring the princess' safety and station some of his most trusted men around her. Nobody else would be allowed near her, and when the baby was born it would be spirited away and killed.

As the princess' time grew near, Tu'an Gu arranged for a constant stream of gifts and ordered his men to enter the princess' quarters every day on the pretext of checking on her condition and escorting the presents. Then, as soon as the baby was born they would be in a position to snatch it away.

第四章 程婴救孤

　　且说屠岸贾自从怂恿灵公下令将赵氏满门剿灭，矫诏赐死赵朔，便独揽大权，把持朝政。一面广收犬马女色，哄着灵公专心玩乐，不问国事；一面紧锣密鼓，培植党羽，残害异己，为篡国窃权铺平道路。未几晋国司马病死，屠岸贾也不奏明灵公，索性一人兼任二职，将军政大权都揽在自己手中，真正大权在握，炙手可热。但得意忘形之余，也常有几分惴惴不安，想起公主腹内怀着赵氏血脉，倘若容其长大成人，必成自己的死敌。可是公主身为灵公之姊，又不敢对其逼迫过甚，只好借保护公主之名，派心腹将领和卫士将驸马府严密把守起来，不准闲人出入，打算等到那婴儿出生，便抢过来杀死，以绝后患。

　　这几日，屠岸贾估算着公主即将临盆，便吩咐手下每日里假借探视送物，频频窥视，只等婴儿落地，便强行抢走。

The princess had been brought up in the royal palace. She had been pampered and spoiled, and finally she had been married to the man of her dreams. But now, a terrible calamity had befallen her: Her husband's clan had been massacred, and her husband himself had drunk poison and expired before her very eyes. The princess had been devastated by the enormity of these events, and spent every waking hour in tears. One afternoon, as she was sitting alone by a window, she noticed that the sun was growing pale, and fallen leaves were being whirled by the wind. She felt a chill in her heart. Again, the tears started to fall. Suddenly, she heard the patter of cold raindrops. Raising her head, she looked out into the courtyard, to see that a thin mist had collected there. The rain was by this time falling in sheets, reminding her of her own pent up grief. Depression and despair welled up inside her when she thought of how the 300 members of the Zhao clan had met their unnatural end. There had been no news from her father-in-law, Zhao Dun, since he had fled the capital several months previously. She recalled that her husband, just before he died, had urged her to brave the humiliation that was in store, and make sure that she gave birth to their child, so that the Zhao clan would have posterity. Now she was about to give birth; who knew whether the child would be a boy or a girl? Tears cascaded down her cheeks as she realized that Tu'an Gu had her chambers tightly guarded by his men, and he would never allow the child to live if it should be a boy. As dusk gathered, the rain abated somewhat, and the princess ordered her maid to bring her a light coverlet, and lay down fully clothed.

Suddenly, the door of her room opened, and her husband entered, with disheveled hair and covered in blood. The princess tried to sit up to welcome him, but found that she could not move. Zhao Shuo approached, lightly stroked her swollen abdomen, and said, "My dear, if you give birth to a boy, you must call him 'Zhao the Orphan.' Nurture him carefully and raise him to manhood, so that he can wreak vengeance for the Zhao clan."

The princess was overcome with distress. She wanted to say something to her husband, but no coherent words would pass her lips. As she mumbled

程·婴·救·孤

那公主自幼长在宫中，众星捧月，娇生惯养，又嫁了一个如意夫君，恩爱非常。没想到祸从天来，夫君家里一门灭绝，驸马饮药自尽，死在自己面前。从此胆颤心惊，思夫悲子，整日以泪洗面。这天午后，公主独坐窗前，见窗外日色暗淡，落叶飘零，心中好不凄清，禁不住滴下泪来。忽一会儿，淅淅沥沥，又下起了一阵冷雨，抬眼看去，院内薄雾蒙蒙，雨脚如麻，正是雨滴愁肠，公主越发愁绪满腹，忧虑重重。想赵家一门三百余口，死于非命；公公逃出绛邑已有数月，全无消息；而夫君临死前要自己忍辱偷生，为赵家留下一脉血胤。如今眼看着自己要分娩了，谁知是男是女。况且府外被屠岸贾派人把得铁紧，就是生下一个男孩，又岂能逃出他的手心？想到这里，早又泪流满面。挨至黄昏时分，雨歇人静，叫宫女为自己盖了一层薄被，和衣躺下。

恍恍惚惚间，突然见丈夫披发沥血，推门进来。公主要起身迎接，却怎么也动弹不得。丈夫走上前来，轻抚自己凸起的腹部，道："公主若是生下一个男孩，就起名'赵氏孤儿'。一定要设法将他抚养成人，好为我赵家一门报仇雪恨！"

公主心中焦急，想和丈夫说几句话，偏偏却半个字也吐不出来，只是哽哽咽咽。倏忽间，丈夫没了踪影，

and moaned, Zhao Shuo vanished from her sight. In terror, she leapt to her feet, and rushed out of the door. There was no sign of her husband, but the sound of lamenting was heard. Staring wildly around her, the princess spied a multitude of people —— some headless, some without feet, some with gaping chest wounds, some with their entrails spilling outside their bodies. They cried with one voice, "We are the ghosts of the 300 murdered members of the Zhao clan, calling for redress. Princess, you must take good care of yourself, and raise your child to be a man who will avenge our bloody slaughter!"

The princess was about to reply, when she heard a shout of command. In the twinkling of an eye, Tu'an Gu and a crowd of guards burst in, bearing sharp implements. Without more ado, they pinned the princess to the floor, with the intention of ripping open her belly and taking the child. As they did so, she heard Tu'an Gu gloat, "I tell you that I will exterminate the Zhao clan once and for all. Its seeds will never sprout again!"

A sharp pain tearing through her abdomen caused the princess to shriek in agony, but through the mist of pain she heard a voice. "Princess, wake up, wake up!"

The princess rolled over, and sat up. The room was dimly lit by the guttering remains of a candle. Her most trusted maid stood by her bedside. It had been a nightmare. But her screams had been real enough. A pain in her stomach caused her to cry out again. Then there was another, and then another. Her maid knew that the princess' time had come. "I'll fetch the midwife," she said.

But the princess urged her in a whisper, "Make not a sound! If that monster Tu'an Gu finds out that I am about to give birth, he will make sure the child does not survive!"

The maid understood the situation perfectly well, and lost no time preparing what was needed. Huge beads of sweat poured from the princess' forehead as the birth pangs tore through her. But, afraid lest anyone hear her, she clenched her teeth and smothered her groans. She had to endure this

公主心中大急，拼命起身，追出门外，不见丈夫，却又听得一阵哭诉之声，回头一看，满地都是人，或无头，或缺腿，或是胸前一个血洞，或是肚肠流在外面，齐声说道："我等是赵氏三百余口的冤魂，求公主善自保重，将小主人抚养成人，也好为我们报这血海深仇！"

公主闻言，正欲答应，却又听得一阵呐喊之声，眨眼之间，见屠岸贾带着一群卫士，如狼似虎闯了进来，手持利刃，不由分说，将公主按倒，就要剖腹取婴。那屠岸贾口中还道："我叫你赵家根尽苗绝，萌芽不发！"

公主只觉腹部锐痛，不由急得放声痛哭，忽听宫女叫道："公主醒醒，公主醒醒！"

公主蓦地翻身坐起，只见屋内残烛犹明，一名心腹宫女站在面前。这才醒悟原来是一场恶梦，犹觉喉间哽咽不已，腹部隐隐作疼，一阵紧似一阵，不觉呻吟出声。那宫女见状，知道是公主产期已到，便道："我即刻去唤产娘，好与公主接生。"

公主低声道："切不要声张，那屠岸贾心狠手毒，若是让他知道了，岂能饶过这婴儿？"

那宫女闻言醒悟过来，忙取了所需之物，又去厨房打了一盆开水。此时公主只觉得下腹阵痛，仿佛要将人撕裂似的，豆大的汗珠从额上滚落下来，可她怕被人听见，咬紧牙关，一声呻吟也不敢发出。熬了不

torture for nearly an hour, until a tiny cry was heard —— she had given birth to a strapping baby boy! Fortunately, the night was far advanced, and everyone both inside and out was fast asleep. Nobody heard the baby's first cry. Moreover, strangely enough, after that first greeting to the world, the child did not utter another sound. Swiftly, the princess and her maid, trembling with fear and transported with joy at the same time, severed the umbilical cord, cleaned everything and fed the baby. When they had removed every trace of the childbirth, dawn was already peeping through the papered window. Exhausted by the exertions of the previous night, the princess fell into a deep sleep, with her maid guarding at her side. Halfway through the morning, the heavy tramp of feet was heard outside the window, startling the princess from her slumber. Instantly, she knew that it was an inspection by her captors. It was like:

> The wild wind buffets the vulture on high,
> The cruel frost nips the withered grass roots.

Her maid paled in fright, and fell into a panic. But the princess maintained her composure. Taking the baby from her side, she concealed it in the wide crotch of he undergarment, and covered it with her outer clothing. On top, she spread the thin coverlet, and lay back as before, praying silently to herself. "Oh Heaven, if you do not wish the Zhao clan to perish, please do not let the baby cry. But if it is your will that the Zhaos disappear from the earth, then let it cry. "

No sooner had she settled herself than there came a rap at the door. The maid went to open it. As she did so, a sergeant and a group of soldiers burst in. Straightaway, they searched the room, but did not find the baby. Seeing the princess lying there with a bulging stomach, they concluded that she had not yet given birth, and left to report to Tu'an Gu.

The princess and her maid, sweating with fear, searched out the baby, only to find it sleeping sweetly, not a bit alarmed by the recent disturbance. This calmed the other two down a bit.

到半个时辰，只听一声响亮的儿啼，产下一个壮硕的
男婴来。幸喜是深夜，府中内外人等都在熟睡，无人
听见。说来也奇，那婴儿生出来，只哭得一声，便不再
声响。二人心中又惊又喜，忙着剪脐包裹，洗澡喂
奶。待得收拾完毕，将一切痕迹掩过，再看那天色时，
窗纸上已露进几缕清光。公主折腾了一夜，此时已经
疲累不堪，沉沉睡去，那宫女坐在一边守护。到了半
上午，忽听窗外传来沉重的脚步声，公主惊醒过来，
暗叫不好，定是在府外守护的士兵进来查看。正是：

　　狂风偏纵扑天雕，严霜故打枯草根。

　　那宫女吓得面色煞白，不知所措。公主却面色沉
着，将身边的婴儿放入肥大的裤裆中，用上衣掩了，
再盖上薄被，依旧躺下，心中暗暗祈祷："天若不绝赵
氏，儿子你就别哭；天若要绝赵氏，儿子你就哭吧！"

　　公主刚刚躺好，敲门声已经响起，宫女过去开了
门，一名偏将带着几名兵丁拥入，查看一遍，见公主
躺在榻上，薄被下腹部高高隆起，认定公主尚未生
产，便退了出去，派人向屠岸贾报告。

　　公主和宫女手心里捏着一把冷汗，忙将婴儿抱
出，却见他沉沉熟睡，方才一番折腾，也未将其惊醒，
这才松了一口气。

　　屠岸贾接到报告，道："料那小崽子躲得了初一，

Receiving the report that the princess still had not given birth, Tu'an Gu snarled, "The little whelp can escape my clutches only just so long." He then gave an order that the princess' door be tightly guarded; that if anyone tried to smuggle the child out his whole family to the ninth degree of kinship would be beheaded; that anyone who tried to conceal the child would receive the same punishment. He then gave a cold chuckle, "Why should I let someone else slay the little creature, anyway? The best way to accomplish my purpose is to slaughter it myself!"

When the guards had departed, the maid, seeing that the baby was unharmed, said to the princess, "Mistress, the guards are sure to come back after a while for more inspections. We can't hide the child for long in this place. You must think of some other way!"

The princess knew well that Tu'an Gu was determined to remove all sources of future trouble for himself, and would never allow the orphan of the Zhaos to survive if he could help it. But he had already had notices posted that if anyone dared to hide the baby he would be killed. In addition, he had put a tight guard on the princess' quarters, and anyone bold enough to try to abduct or conceal the child would be arrested for sure. And no matter how hard the princess tried, there was no way to get a message to the outside. She was wrapped in distress, and could think of no way out of her predicament. Truly:

Her heart churning with sorrow, tangled in skeins of sighs.

Drowning in a sea of injustice, bitterness fills the skies.

Soon, it would be noon. The princess told her maid to hide the baby in a closet. She herself took a pillow, and placed it on her stomach in such a way as to convince a casual observer that she was still pregnant. At noon, as usual, the guards came bursting into the room to check the situation. Finding that there was apparently no change, they left to report. The princess and her maid knew that their luck was running out. If the child were to cry out while the soldiers were in the room on one of their regular inspections, all would be lost!

躲不了十五。传我的令：将府门严密把守，若有盗出婴儿者，全家处斩，连及九族。藏匿婴儿及放走偷盗婴儿者，与之同罪！"说毕，又冷笑道："待我捉住那小孽种，亲自用刀杀死，才算称意呢！"

这里宫女见众兵丁去了，婴儿安然无恙，对公主道："士兵过一会儿还要来搜查，小主人藏在府中，不是长久之计。公主快想个办法吧！"

公主心里也清楚屠岸贾意在斩草除根，以绝后患，自然不肯放过这赵氏孤儿。可屠岸贼早已贴出榜文，敢有藏匿或盗出婴儿者诛灭九族。加上这驸马府内外戒备森严，插翅难飞，纵有义士愿将婴儿盗出藏匿，怎奈自己如同囚徒，不得越雷池半步，又怎能将消息传递出去呢？苦思冥想，无计可施。正是：

柔肠千转，愁绪如织。

冤情似海，惆怅漫天。

眼见得快到中午，公主只得先让宫女将婴儿藏入衣柜，自己卷了一个枕头，捆在肚子上，聊以掩人耳目。到了午后，士兵又闯进来查看了一遍，见没有什么异样，才退了出去。公主与宫女好不容易对付过去，心知危险越来越大，倘若那婴儿在士兵查看时哭了出来，立刻就是一场弥天大祸。

But Heaven never leaves no way out. Just as the princess and her maid were plunged into despair, they were informed that a doctor had called to see the princess. The latter was filled with dread and hope at the same time. This doctor, whoever he was, had not been sent for; he had come of his own volition. So he must have had some purpose in coming! As if she were drowning and clutching at a straw, the princess cried, "Quick, ask him to come in!"

The maid lifted the door curtain, and stood in the doorway, ready to repulse any unwanted intruders. The princess lay and watched, wondering who the visitor might be. A thin, bony man in his 40s was shown in. Three tufts of whisky beard hung down to his chest. He had a dark complexion, and his expression was grave. The princess recognized him immediately as a one time member of the household of Zhao Dun; she had seen him often in the Zhao mansion. His name was Cheng Ying.

The princess was overjoyed. She could hardly believe her eyes. She gasped in delight, "Sir, aren't you Mr Cheng who used to frequent the Zhao mansion?"

"Yes, I am," the newcomer replied with a courteous bow.

Let us pause here to explain the background of this man Cheng Ying. His family had dwelt in the suburbs of the capital, and had practiced as physicians for generations. Although his father had been taught by his father, and inherited the family skills, and indeed acquired quite a reputation as a doctor, he felt that medicine was but a petty trade, and longed to make a name for himself in history by serving his country. By the time Cheng Ying was 16 years old he had mastered his father's skills; indeed he had an encyclopedic knowledge of medicine. He had an almost magical healing touch, and was a wizard at the application of drugs. Seeing that his son was so intelligent, capable and meticulous, Cheng Ying's father laid the mantle of his own lofty aspirations on the young man's shoulders. He told him, "Nowadays, the world is divided and in confusion. Men of talent are sorely

也是天无绝人之路，正当公主与那宫女发愁之际，忽报府外有医生前来给公主看病。公主闻言，禁不住又惊又喜，觉得此人不请自到，定有些来历，恰恰犹如在惊涛骇浪中抓住一根稻草，当下道："快快请进！"

宫女当即掀帘迎接，就势站在门外，提防闲人闯入。公主躺在榻上细看来者，只见那人四十开外年纪，身材瘦削，骨格清朗，三绺长须飘拂胸前，面目黧黑，脸上表情沉静，认出正是在下宫经常走动的赵府门客程婴。

公主心中一喜，犹然不敢相信自己的眼睛，急急问道："长者可是常在下宫出入的程先生？"

"小人正是。"程婴施了一礼，躬身答道。

笔者且交代这程婴的来历：程婴世居绛邑城郊，世代行医。其父上承祖先遗教，谙熟医理，医术高明，在方圆几十里内颇有些名气。但心中总觉得行医终是小技，不如辅国安邦可以留名青史，常有几分失落寂寥之感。待程婴长到十六岁，耳濡目染，早将父亲的技艺学了十之八九，妙手回春，药到病除，骎骎然有青出于蓝之势。程父见儿子生性聪慧，精明干练，办事滴水不漏，便将自己此生经邦治国的男儿之志寄托在儿子身上，道："如今列国纷争，天下大乱，正需人

needed. My son, you should spend some years studying. If you can gain an important post you will bring glory on our house, which will be much better than following the example of your father and living your life in obscurity."

Cheng Ying was reticent by nature. Hearing his father's words, he said nothing, but only nodded his head. He chose an auspicious day for starting out, and journeyed to the State of Wei. There he studied for several years, and when he returned to his native Jin his head was crammed full of knowledge. But his character was still introverted and taciturn, and he was slow to reveal his feelings.

Following his father's wishes, Cheng Ying forsook the practice of medicine, and sought his fortune in the capital. For many months, he sought employment in vain, but at last was recommended to the Zhao mansion as a retainer of the prime minister.

The Zhao clan had occupied official posts for generations, and their house was an illustrious one. There were over 100 retainers, well versed in all the arts both civil and military. Among such a distinguished company, Cheng Ying, with his dowdy clothes and homely appearance, went virtually unnoticed. Like a stone tossed into the ocean, he made hardly a ripple in the Lower Palace. Several years passed, and Cheng Ying was still a hanger-on in the mansion of the prime minister. In all this time, he could not fail to notice the upright and loyal nature of Zhao Dun, which made the desire to do something to repay the prime minister for his kindness burn even more fiercely inside him. And this yearning did not leave him even though he was not entrusted with any important task. In the meantime, his shy nature did not allow him to articulate his feelings.

Then one day, Zhao Dun's wife contracted some strange illness. Her pulse was irregular, her eyes were red and her face was puffed up. Moreover, her whole body itched, she could hold down neither food nor drink, and from time to time she would faint. The whole household was in a panic over this. Famous physicians were sent for, but all to no avail. When Cheng

材。我儿出去游学数年,若能做得一官半职,光耀程家门楣,也强似为父这般终生老死林泉,无名竹帛。"

程婴天生内向,听了父亲之言,也不说什么,只点了点头,择日动身,去了卫国。数载之后归来,已是满腹经纶,学富五车,但他性格沉静,却是深藏不露。

程婴归家之后,遵从父命不再行医,转而去绛邑奔走,几个月下来,却无人赏识。最后经人介绍,在赵府做了一名下等门客。

赵氏数代为官,门庭显赫,府上所养门客数以百计,文武济济,应有尽有。程婴衣着普通,相貌寻常,又未显露什么绝技。进了下宫,犹如石投大海,不见一丝水花。一晃数年过去,仍然是一名下等门客。可程婴见赵盾忠义可嘉,心中常存报效之志,虽然未得重用,却也未萌生去意。只是自己天性内向,故而总是请缨无路。

忽一日,赵盾的夫人得了一种古怪病症,脉搏不见异常,但目赤面肿,浑身奇痒,饮食不进,偶尔甚至突然昏厥。阖府上下,好不着急,遍请名医疗治,却不见效。程婴听说此事,遂觑便对赵盾道:"小人前些年从先父那里学了点儿医理,或许能治好老夫人的病。"

赵盾打量一番程婴,虽然宾主相处已有数年,却因程婴平时到不了赵盾跟前,所以看上去面生的

Ying heard about this he plucked up courage to approach Zhao Dun, and explained how he had learned medicine from his father. He thereupon requested permission to try to cure the patient.

Zhao Dun looked Cheng Ying up and down. Although the latter had been in the Zhao household for several years, he had never been formally introduced to Zhao Dun, and so the prime minister looked at him as if he were being confronted by a stranger. However, as his wife's illness had baffled the best medical brains in the State of Jin, with a nod he gave Cheng Ying leave to examine her.

Cheng Ying entered the bedroom of Zhao Dun's wife. After completing the traditional diagnostic routine of viewing, listening, questioning and pulse-taking, it was not long before he had made up his mind what the problem was. He returned to Zhao Dun and asked him, "Midsummer, several years ago, sir, did your wife partake of ginseng by any chance?"

The prime minister turned to the attendants. A maid, after ransacking her memory, said, "Yes, Your Honor, for several years past Madame has suffered from summer heat disorder, with loss of appetite. One of the household physicians recommended that she take ginseng soup. Madame did so a few times."

With perfect composure, Cheng Ying said, "That must be the reason. The lady was originally not ill. But, you see, ginseng is far too nutritious, and she overdosed on it. In addition, taking it at the height of the summer heat brought her system into disorder. Two doses of herbal medicine will soon put her right." So saying, he hastened to make up a prescription.

Zhao Dun was not wholly convinced that Cheng Ying knew what he was talking about. However, he had no choice but to tell his people to concoct the medicine under the latter's supervision. Sure enough, after swallowing the first dose, color started to return to the cheeks of Zhao Dun's wife, and her spirits perked up remarkably. After the second dose, she made a complete recovery.

The prime minister was overjoyed. "Sir, you have a truly miraculous

很。可是夫人情形危急，正所谓病急乱投医，便点点头，道："先生请入内诊治。"

程婴进了夫人卧室，望闻问切，不消一炷香功夫，便心中了然。退出来与赵盾相对而坐，问道："夫人往年可曾在盛夏时服过人参？"

赵盾看看左右的丫环侍从，一个丫环思想片刻，答道："正是，夫人前些年疰夏，恹恹欲病，饮食有减，府里的郎中为夫人开了参汤，喝过几次。"

程婴不慌不忙道："这就是了。夫人本来没有甚么病，却误服参汤，因那人参滋补过分，又于盛夏服用，便种下了病根。待小人开方，下两剂草药就没事了。"说毕，开了个药方。

赵盾听程婴说得中窍，虽然心中还有些疑惑，也只得先命家人煎了试服。没想到，一剂下去，夫人的病便有起色，神情清爽了许多。待两剂服完，遂恢复如初。

赵盾喜出望外，道："先生妙手回春，药到病除，真乃神医啊！"

自此之后，程婴重操旧业，成了下宫的医生，常为赵家老少看病。赵盾自然对他敬礼有加，众人也都刮目相看。真是歪打正着，程婴游学数年，满腹经纶没有派上用场，倒是家传的医术成全了他。

healing touch!" he exclaimed.

After this, Cheng Ying took up the practice of his old trade once more, becoming the physician-in-residence of the Zhao mansion. Naturally, Zhao Dun started to treat Cheng Ying with particular courtesy, and this in turn made the rest of the household see him with new eyes. Thus, it was by a complete fluke that his years of study and his encyclopedic knowledge finally stood him in good stead.

Years passed, and Cheng Ying remained a bachelor. Zhao Dun, ever mindful of the way that the doctor had saved his wife's life, determined to find a spouse for him. At his own expense, he arranged for Cheng Ying to marry a Miss Guo from Guo Shanren in the suburbs of the capital. He also bought a small courtyard house for the newlyweds. Cheng Ying then moved from the Lower Palace and practiced medicine in the capital.

He never forgot his old master's kindness, though, and often paid courtesy calls at the Lower Palace. And whenever anybody in the prime minister's household, no matter what his or her status, fell ill, Cheng Ying would hurry to offer treatment, as previously. He would usually stay at home, waiting for patients, but he also sometimes made house calls. In this way, his skill and knowledge increased greatly, and he gained the trust and goodwill of the people of Jiangyi. In addition, his reputation was enhanced by the fact that whenever a poor person came to consult him, he would often waive his fee and even provide him with medicines free.

More years elapsed, and Cheng Ying grew not only more skillful and famous, but richer too. His only regret was that his wife was frail in body, and although twice pregnant had lost the baby both times. The childless couple grew sadder and more lonely as time went on. Then suddenly, at the beginning of the year Cheng Ying's wife found herself pregnant again. The two of them were overjoyed. Cheng Ying took the greatest care of his wife, dosing her with tonics, and the baby inside her grew. After a few months, her waist started to get thicker and her waistband to get tighter by the day. Her breasts swelled with milk, and her eyes took on a dreamy look. A few

春去秋来，乌飞兔走，转眼之间，程婴已届而立之年，犹自独身。赵盾念他救治夫人的功劳，做主为他娶了绛邑城外郭善人的女儿郭氏，又出钱在城中买了一处小院，从此程婴搬出下宫，与主人分门另住，专在绛邑城中行医。

程婴不忘主人恩德，常去下宫请安问好，赵府中上下不拘谁得了病，依旧请他来看。平时得闲，便在家中坐诊，也常出门到病家把脉。因他医术高明，待人忠厚，遇有穷人来求诊，往往免收诊金，甚至奉送药物，因而在绛邑城中渐渐有了一点儿名声。

光阴似箭，日月如飞，转眼又是几年，程婴医术愈精，名声愈高，日子过得也日渐富裕。惟一遗憾的是妻子郭氏身体单薄，先后怀孕两次，皆因血气不足而中途小产。两口儿称心快意之余，渐渐地添了几分膝下荒凉之感。所喜今年年初，郭氏又一次怀孕。两口儿喜不自禁，小心翼翼，服药调养，终于将胎儿保住。过了数月，眼见那郭氏腰肢日重，裙带日短，乳涨腹高，眉低眼慢，再过几天就是产期。程婴四十得子，欣喜异常，每日里在家中守护妻子，也不出诊，连下宫也有好长时间不去登门。

这一日吃过早饭，家中无事，程婴便上街去买些

days later, she would give birth to a baby. Cheng Ying was beside himself with happiness. He would finally have a son, although he was over 40 years old. Now he stayed at home all day, looking after his wife. He no longer made house calls, and kept away from the Zhao mansion for a long time.

One morning, just after breakfast, Cheng Ying, having nothing to do in the house, went out to do some shopping. At the corner of the street, he bumped into an acquaintance known as Gaffer Zhao, whom he detained, and engaged in polite small talk. Now this Gaffer Zhao was a sturdy and forthright character with somewhat of an old fashioned air about him. It was said that his ancestors and those of the prime minister's clan had had some connection, but the relationship was so distant that he and the other Zhaos had little to do with each other. At one time, Gaffer Zhao's granddaughter, who was the apple of his eye, had fallen gravely ill. Cheng Ying had used all his skill, and had eventually saved the girl's life. Ever since that time, the grateful Gaffer Zhao had often visited Cheng Ying's house, and the two had become firm friends. Having been cooped up inside the house for several days, Cheng Ying was delighted to see Gaffer Zhao, and insisted on taking him into a tavern for a drink and a chat.

Cheng Ying was surprised to find that his normally boisterous friend looked strangely downcast and worried. Refusing Cheng Ying's invitation, Gaffer Zhao pulled him round a corner, and, glancing right and left to make sure that nobody was listening, muttered, "Something terrible's happened at the prime minister's mansion. Perhaps you don't know?"

Cheng Ying was seized with alarm, and gasped, "What's happened?" Gaffer Zhao then related in detail the stories of the flight of Zhao Dun, the massacre at the Lower Palace and Zhao Shuo's suicide by poison. His voice had barely died away when Cheng Ying asked, "But what about the princess? Is the baby she's expecting safe?"

粮米。走到街角，忽然撞见相熟的赵老汉，当即拉着手寒喧起来。这赵老汉为人豪爽仗义，颇有古风，说起他的祖上，还与赵盾的先人有些瓜葛，算是赵氏族中的远支，不过现在已是八杆子打不着的亲戚，双方也早就没有了来往。有一年，赵老汉视如掌珠的小孙女得了重病，亏得程婴细心诊治，这才转危为安，故而赵老汉十分感激，时常来程婴的居处走动，二人遂熟络起来。程婴在家中呆了许多天，见到赵老汉自然是格外喜欢，当下要拉着赵老汉到酒馆小酌快谈。谁知平日里说话高声大气的赵老汉眉宇间隐有忧色，也不答程婴的话，一把将他扯到街角，看看左右无人，才低声说道："相国府上出了大事，只怕先生还不知道吧？"程婴闻言吃了一惊，问道："出了何等大事？"赵老汉遂将赵盾出逃、下宫遭屠及赵朔饮鸩自尽诸事细细说了一遍，话音刚落，程婴便急急问道："公主如何了？胎儿可曾保全？"

原来，公主在年初受孕后，程婴曾为其把脉调养，故而知悉公主有了身孕。赵老汉闻言，气愤地道："听说那屠岸贾尚未敢对公主下手，但派人日夜守护在驸马府前，单等婴儿落地，便要抢走杀死，斩草除根。"说到这里，露出一脸的不屑，道："真是人心莫

Cheng Ying had examined the princess when she had first become pregnant, so of course he knew all about her condition. Gaffer Zhao exclaimed, in a rage, "They say that that dastardly Tu'an Gu dare not raise a hand against the princess. But he has sent men to guard her quarters, and as soon as the baby is born, he is going to whisk it away and put it to death, in order to destroy every last future threat to himself." He added, with great disdain, "He is completely ruthless. And as for his lieutenant Han Jue, at one time he was a regular visitor at the Lower Palace, and was treated with great kindness by the prime minister. But now he aids and abets Tu'an Gu in his wickedness. He is the one who is in charge of the cohort of guards keeping the princess prisoner. Even if you are carrying as much as a blade of grass, they search you from head to toe!"

The blood drained from Cheng Ying's face. He bade Gaffer Zhao a hurried goodbye, and straightaway made for the Lower Palace. When he was only a street away from the mansion, he slowed his footsteps to a leisurely saunter. As he passed the place, he noticed that there were few people in the street, and they hurried on their way with their eyes fixed on the ground. The main gate of the prime minister's mansion was wide open, and the doors themselves were missing. The lofty steps still bore bloody traces of the massacre, although there was no sign of any corpses. Cheng Ying guessed that they had already been borne away and buried on the outskirts of the capital. Two men at arms lounging in the gateway bawled at Cheng Ying to hurry along.

Cheng Ying had seen enough. He went straight home, and told his wife all that he had heard and seen that day. "The Zhao clan have been loyal officials for generations, serving the country wholeheartedly. Tu'an Gu has done this evil deed because he is scheming to seize the throne for himself. The State of Jin will be in turmoil until the day this scoundrel of a minister is eliminated!"

Now although Madame Guo was a woman, she had a sense of loyalty and justice, with which she quietly influenced her husband. Hearing Cheng

测，忠奸难辨。那下将军韩厥以前经常出入下宫，相国待他不薄。如今也助纣为虐，竟成了屠岸贾的鹰犬，亲自带着数十名甲士把守驸马府，带出一根草来也要仔细盘查。"

程婴骤闻大变，脸色阴晴不定，与赵老汉又说了几句，便匆匆分手，径趋下宫。隔着一条街，便放慢脚步，装作闲逛，走过下宫门前。只见街上寥寥几个行人，都是低头疾走。下宫大门洞开，门扇也不知去了哪里，高高的石阶上一片惨憷，都是死难者留下的血迹，尸体却不见踪影，想必是已经拉到郊野掩埋了。两名甲士懒洋洋地站在大门前，见程婴靠近，大声叱喝，要他快快走开。

程婴见事已如此，急忙返身回到家中，将方才的所见所闻一五一十说与郭氏，叹道："赵氏数代忠臣，全力辅佐国家。那屠岸贾意欲篡国，竟然下此毒手。如此乱臣贼子，一日不除，晋国一日不宁！"

郭氏虽为女流，但平时潜移默化，受了程婴的感染，颇有忠义之气。听了程婴的叙述，愤然作色道："古人言，受人滴水之恩，当涌泉相报。你我夫妻二人，若无相国的恩典，哪里能有今日？何况相国一门精忠辅国，如今惨遭杀戮，我们岂能坐视不管，让忠

Ying's grisly story, she burst out in indignation, "The ancients said that if a person receives so much as a drop of water in kindness, he should pay a well worth of water back. Where would we be today, my dear, if it had nor been for the prime minister's kindness? Moreover, how can we just sit back and do nothing when his family, which has been a pillar of the state, has been massacred? Can we allow the grievance of these good and loyal people to go unredressed forever? But Heaven has not turned its face from the Zhaos. Right now, the princess bears within her the seed of the Zhaos. If she can smuggle the baby out, you and I could look after it, and raise, pretending that it is our own, so that in future this scion of the Zhaos can wreak revenge for the clan. It would not be too late for that even if we have to wait ten years. So long as the Zhao line is preserved, sooner or later they will be avenged."

Cheng Ying was surprised that his wife could speak out on such a lofty theme, and could not help bowing to her in admiration. In a quavering voice, he said, "Please accept my humble appreciation, my dear. As a man with warm blood in his veins, how can I not distinguish between loyalty and treachery, and especially since the prime minister has been so benevolent to us? But you yourself are about to give birth. I must give all my attention to you."

His wife replied, "Do not worry about me, my dear. Tomorrow I will go to my mother's house. You must devote all your energies to saving the princess' baby. But that Tu'an Gu is a wicked man. You must be careful!"

Let us turn to General Han Jue. What kind of a man was he? A bold general of the State of Jin, he had once been a subordinate of Zhao Dun. He had a swarthy face and bulging eyes. His demeanor was forceful, and he had a deafening voice. He was known for being trustworthy and forthright, and when Zhao Dun had been promoted to minister, he had been transferred to the troops of Tu'an Gu, whom he served just as loyally as he had served Zhao

良之后沉冤百世？好在老天不绝赵氏，公主腹中已有赵家骨肉，等分娩之后，相公若能救出那孤儿，我夫妻二人抚养其长大成人，便是留下赵氏一条根。君子报仇，十年不晚。只要赵家一脉尚存，何愁将来不能报仇雪恨？"

程婴想不到妻子一个妇人，却颇识大体，说出这一番大仁大义之言。当下向妻子施了一礼，颤声道："贤妻在上，请受程某一拜！程某乃热血男儿，岂能不辨忠奸，何况相国待我恩重如山。只是眼下你身怀六甲，行动不便，眼见得产期临近，叫我怎生割舍得下？"

郭氏道："相公不必为我担心，明日我就回娘家去住。相公尽管出外办事，尽全力搭救婴儿。只是那屠岸贾心狠手毒，相公你务要小心。"

程婴夫妻二人在这里计议已定，且放下不表。这下将军韩厥又是何许人也？原来韩厥曾为赵盾下属，也是晋国的一员猛将。其人生得面如黑炭，虬髯连鬓，眼似铜铃，形状威猛，开口说话，声若洪钟，震耳欲聋。只因他天性忠戆，生就一种直来直去的性子，赵盾升任上卿后，他成了屠岸贾的部下，一样的忠心不二。谁知屠岸贾倒行逆施，残害忠良，渐渐暴露了

Dun. But as Tu'an Gu began his evil maneuvers, bringing harm to good and faithful officials, and making it clear that he had his eye on the throne, Han Jue looked on with cold eyes. His heart was troubled by what he saw, but he kept his feelings to himself.

Cheng Ying had become acquainted with Han Jue in his days in the Zhao mansion. So he knew that the general had been trained under the benign gaze of Zhao Dun, and although he came under the command of Tu'an Gu later, he would never turn against his old master. Despite his bluff manners, Han Jue was not the sort of person to confuse black with white or blur the line between loyalty and treachery. In a crisis, he would not stoop to wickedness.

Cheng Ying was fairly confident of Han Jue's upright character, and he counted on him to allow him to dash into the princess' quarters as soon as the baby was born, and carry the child off to safety. But he reflected that there were two conditions necessary to ensure the success of his plan: One was ensuring the exact date of her giving birth, and the other was the attitude of Han Jue. If the commander refused to cooperate, having thrown in his lot with Tu'an Gu, then the whole enterprise would be ruined. Cheng Ying, being a doctor by training, was able to calculate accurately when the princess was likely to give birth. But as for Han Jue, he decided in the end that he could not take the chance of him turning traitor and denying him access to the princess and the baby at the crucial moment. Cheng Ying made up his mind to attempt his rescue alone. Having made this decision, he felt much easier in his mind. Thereupon, he made his preparations, and awaited the moment to act.

On the day that he reckoned the princess would give birth, he shouldered his medicine bag, and strode off with the stated purpose of going to take the princess' pulse. The guards were only interested in searching people coming out of the mansion, and not those going in, and after a few perfunctory questions allowed Cheng Ying to enter.

夺权篡国的野心。韩厥在一旁冷眼观看,心中渐生不平,只是不曾显露。

程婴昔日在赵府作门客时,曾与韩厥有些交情,知道他曾在赵盾手下为将,承赵盾提携栽培,心怀感激,以后虽然转入屠岸贾辖下,却并非叛离旧主。况且他人虽戆直,但决非颠倒黑白、忠奸不辨之辈,料想在关键时刻不会坏事。

程婴既对韩厥有几分把握,便打算着在公主分娩之日独身闯入驸马府,将婴儿救出,转移到安全的地方。程婴心中盘算:此事若想成功,有两个关键,一是公主分娩的日子,迟早都会误事;二是韩厥的态度,如果届时他翻脸不认人,与屠岸贾相济为奸,则大势去矣。程婴出身医家,掐指一算,便对公主的产期有了八九分把握。至于韩厥到时是否肯不顾身家性命,放自己出门,则终究心中无底。思来想去,心中一横,决心前往驸马府救孤,至于最后能否成功,一凭天意罢了。如此一想,心中反倒平静下来,略作些准备,便只等届时行动了。

这一日,程婴算出公主就要分娩,便背了药箱,大模大样来到驸马府前,声称来为公主把脉。守卫在门口的甲士将注意力都放在搜查从府中出来的人,对入府的人则不太留意,略微盘问了几句,就将程婴

As soon as Cheng Ying came face to face with the princess, the two wasted no time on formalities, despite the difference in their social statues. To the princess, this unexpected visit was like that of a savior star fallen from Heaven. Without more ado, she asked, "Sir, have you come for the Zhao child?"

Cheng Ying nodded gravely. "I have," he said.

Hearing these two words, the princess could not hold back her tears. She said, "Sir, let me first thank you on behalf of the 300 aggrieved souls. I will never forget your kindness and virtue as long as I live. And you will surely be rewarded in the next life."

As she spoke, she bowed from the bed where she lay.

Cheng Ying disavowed her gratitude, and asked her when the child was due, assuming from her bulging abdomen that she had not yet given birth.

The princess hastened to inform the doctor that she had given birth to a baby boy the previous night. She also explained why she had given the child the name of Zhao the Orphan. She then told her maid to bring the baby for Cheng Ying's inspection.

The doctor was overjoyed. "Wonderful!" he cried. "I can take him at once. Although I am a person of no account, I would struggle through fire and flood to uphold loyalty and justice. If my body were mangled and my bones smashed in the process, I would have no regrets." At this point, he paused, seemingly hard put to express something that he wanted to say next.

The princess was astute enough to perceive this, and urged him to continue.

"If I am fortunate enough to save the child," he muttered, "That dastardly Tu'an Gu will for certain ransack this house. When he does not find the baby, he will dispatch his men to interrogate every member of your household, threatening them with the most dire punishments, and

放进去了。

程婴与公主见面之后，二人都是恍然有隔世之感，可在这种情形下，也顾不得寒喧。公主见程婴不招而至，如同天上降下一个救星，急切地问道："先生可是为赵氏孤儿而来？"

程婴沉静地点头道："正是。"

公主听得这两个字，不免感激涕零，道："妾身先替夫家三百余条冤魂谢过先生。先生大恩大德，没齿不忘，来世定当报答。"

说着，就于榻上施礼。

程婴道："公主不必客气，小人已有一计，可将婴儿盗出府外，只不知公主的产期为何推迟了？"原来程婴进屋后先将公主打量一番，见她腹部凸起，显见仍未分娩，是以有此一问。

公主遂将夜间已经生下一名男婴，并取名为赵氏孤儿的事向程婴细说了一遍，又命那宫女将赵氏孤儿抱出与程婴瞧。程婴喜道："如此甚好，小人即刻带他出去。我程婴虽系一介草民，为保忠良之后，赴汤蹈火，粉身碎骨，也在所不惜。"说到此处，顿了一顿，似有难言之隐。公主也是个精明人，看出程婴欲言不言，必有说法，便道："先生有何难处，讲来无妨。"程婴遂道："小人若侥幸将赵氏孤儿救出，屠岸贾必将在府中

not even exempting yourself, princess. If you are unable to withstand their savage torture, you will divulge my name. Now, although the extermination of my whole family would be of little consequence, the real tragedy would be that our attempt to save the child would come to naught. Moreover, even if you yourself are as silent as a clam, how can we be sure that every one of your multitude of servants will remain silent?"

So saying, he cast a glance at the maid servant in the doorway. The princess gave him a wan smile.

"Sir, allay your fears," she said. "Only I and my faithful maid servant there know that the child has been born. You may trust us to handle such a contingency. But there is just one thing that puzzles me: The walls around this mansion are high, and the moat is deep. Guards are stationed outside the gate. How will you, bare-handed, manage to carry the child out of this place?"

Cheng Ying pointed at his medicine bag. "I'll hide the boy in there," he said. "The commander of the guard is General Han Jue, who once served under the prime minister. He is an upright and loyal man. I am confident that nothing will go wrong."

The princess was greatly relieved to hear this. "Heaven has eyes to see, after all!" she cried. "It will not countenance the destruction of an honest and faithful family. There is hope that the wrong done to the Zhaos will be avenged!"

So saying, she cradled the baby in her bosom, as tears fell from her eyes. Cheng Ying, observing this heart-rending scene, did not have the heart to urge the princess to hurry. Eventually, the princess raised her head, and said, "Sir, please wait a little while, until I have suckled the child one last time. Then I will hand it over to you." She then went into a back room, fed the baby, and laid it on one side. Then she untied her waist sash, made a loop in it and attached the other end to the door frame. With tears cascading

大肆搜查，找不到孤儿，定会兴师问罪，对府中之人用刑逼问。公主金枝玉叶，怎禁得住他拷打盘问，万一熬不过酷刑，供出程婴姓名，小人全家问斩倒是小事，只是这'存孤大计'可就付之东流了。纵然公主守口如瓶，这驸马府上宫女侍从一大群，人多口杂，岂能个个都靠得住？"

说罢，又向门外的宫女看了一眼。公主此时已明白了程婴的意思，嘴角露出一丝惨笑道："先生不必为此担心，府中只有妾身与这心腹宫女知道赵氏孤儿出生之事，稍待妾身必有交代。只是还有一事不明，这驸马府高墙深壁，门外又有甲士把守，先生赤手空拳，如何能带着赵氏孤儿逃出龙潭虎穴？"

程婴伸手指了指药箱，说道："小人欲将赵氏孤儿藏在药箱内携出府外，那统率守卫甲士的是下将军韩厥，曾在相国手下为将，况且为人忠厚正直，想来不会有什么意外。"

公主闻言大喜，道："老天有眼，不灭忠义之门，我赵家雪耻有望啊！"

说毕，将婴儿抱在怀中，瞧了又瞧，亲了又亲，两行泪珠纷纷滚落。程婴见她母子情深，心中也感酸楚，不忍催促，站在一旁等待。俄而公主抬起头来，对程婴道："请先生再候片刻，妾最后喂这孩子一次奶，

down her cheeks, she mounted a low stool. In a low voice, she said to herself, "My husband in the nether world, know this, I have entrusted the Zhao orphan to a righteous man. I now come to join you." She kicked the stool away from beneath her, and in no time at all the life had fled from her body.

Meanwhile, Cheng Ying waited for what seemed ages, and when he could hear no sound from the inner room, began to feel uneasy. When he finally hurried inside, it was too late.

The maid servant, viewing the dreadful scene from the doorway, was seized with terror. She fell to her knees, and kowtowed over and over again to the dead princess. Then, turning to the doctor, she produced a pair of scissors from her bosom. With the scissors tightly clutched in one hand, she cried, "Sir, I beg you not to take this amiss. But my mistress was exceedingly kind to me, and now that Zhao the Orphan has been delivered to your care, my life has come to its end." So saying, she plunged the sharp-pointed scissors into her heart, and followed the princess to the netherworld.

With a solemn countenance, Cheng Ying bowed to the bodies of the princess and her faithful maid. Then he turned his attention to the baby. He laid it carefully in his medicine box, and spread medicines lightly over the child to conceal it. Although it was only a few paces to the gate of the mansion, the medicine box felt as heavy as if it contained the very lives of those 300-odd martyrs of the Zhao clan. By this time, it was almost dusk, and most of the gate guards had gone for their evening meal, leaving only two of their number at the gate. General Han Jue sat alone in a small guardhouse outside the gate, seemingly wrapped in thought. Seeing this, Cheng Ying felt a surge of hope, and said to himself, "Truly, Heaven has come to my aid!" However, the sight of the doctor emerging alone from the house, wearing only a thin robe and carrying a medicine box in his hands, roused the suspicions of the two guards. Before Cheng Ying had a chance to say anything,

便交与先生。"说罢，走进内室，将婴儿喂饱了奶水，放在一边。从容解下腰间裙带，结成绳环系在内屋门框上，自己拿了个矮凳站上去，眼中泪如雨下，口中喃喃自语道："夫君泉下有知，赵氏孤儿已托付义士，妾身这就随你来了。"脚下将矮凳一踢，可怜三魂漂渺，六魄无依，一条性命随风去了。

程婴在外间地里候了半晌，听不见响动，心知不妙，进得里间来看时，公主早已投缳自尽了。站在门外的宫女将一切都看在眼中，禁不住心惊魄悸，跪下来向公主拜了几拜，转身从怀中抽出一柄剪刀，紧紧攥在手里，对程婴道："先生尽请放心，公主对我恩重如山，赵氏孤儿已有托付，此时便是奴婢绝命之际。"说罢，手持利剪向胸膛一送，也随公主去了。

程婴一脸肃然，向公主和宫女各拜一拜，转身抱起赵氏孤儿放进药箱，在上面稀稀拉拉盖上些药草，提起来便向府外走去。虽然从屋中到府门只有短短的一段路，程婴却觉得手里沉甸甸的，仿佛提着赵家三百余口人的性命。不觉已来到府门，此时已近黄昏，天色微暮。守门的甲士大多换班吃饭去了，门前只留下二人守卫，下将军韩厥独自一人坐在门外的一座亭子上，若有所思。程婴见状心中一喜，暗道："真是天

they challenged him.

"Hey you! What's in that box?" they yelled. "Open it up, and let's have a look!"

Cheng Ying replied, calmly, "Nothing but medicines, I assure you." But one of the guards barred his way with his halberd, while the other made to snatch the medicine box away from him. Cheng Ying, however, clung to the box for dear life, and a struggle ensued. Just at this moment, General Han Jue called out from the guardhouse, "Bring him here! I'll examine him myself."

Ever since he had been put in charge of guarding the mansion of the emperor's deceased son-in-law, Han Jue had been accustomed to supervising operations and dispatching patrols from the guardhouse, just outside the gate. But at the time that Cheng Ying had entered the mansion he himself had been leading a patrol, and did not know of his visit until later. When it was reported to him that a doctor had come to take the princess' pulse, a pang of disquiet stirred within him. As the doctor emerged from the house, he recognized him as the very Cheng Ying whom he had used to see often at the Zhao mansion. Then, he was convinced that something was fishy; and when he saw Cheng Ying struggling with the guard over the medicine box he was sure of it. At first, he was filled with doubt as to what he should do: on one hand, he wanted to let Cheng Ying go. But if, as was likely, he was trying to smuggle the Zhao child out in his medicine box, Tu'an Gu would be bound to find out. Then, not only would Han Jue forfeit his life, but his whole family, young and old, would be executed along with him. On the other hand, if he examined the medicine box and found the child, he would have to hand it over to Tu'an Gu —— and that would mean the extinction of the Zhao clan. Not only that, but Cheng Ying too would be executed. While he was suffering this agony of indecision, he saw the guard about to wrest the medicine box from the doctor's grasp to examine it. Han Jue hastily ordered the man to desist.

助我也。"不料那两名甲士见程婴独自走出府来，身上衣衫单薄，只有手中所提药箱有些可疑，不待程婴开口，便迎上来喝道："兀那医士手中药箱内装有何物？且打开来看看！"程婴支吾道："药箱中只有药物，并无别的。"那甲士却横戟一拦，另一名甲士伸手便来抢夺药箱。程婴无奈，只能死死护着药箱不放。正在此时，韩厥在亭中开口道："你二人且将那医士押进亭来，待本将军亲自查看。"

　　原来，下将军韩厥自领命守卫驸马府后，便在离大门不远处的一座亭子上坐镇，督察甲士守卫巡逻。适才程婴进府时，韩厥恰好带着一群甲士巡视四周，回来后听守卫的甲士报说有一位医生入府为公主把脉，心中就不免有些疑惑。待到见那医士正是昔日在下宫常常见面的程婴，便知其中必有蹊跷，再见程婴护着药箱不让甲士查看，更是明白了几分。一时间心中好生为难，欲要放走程婴，只怕那药箱里八成藏着赵氏孤儿，将来屠岸贾追究起来，自己难逃一死不说，还要连累全家老小满门抄斩；欲要搜查，如果真搜出赵氏孤儿，不能不交给屠岸贾，到时赵家可就斩草除根，再无子遗了，连带着程婴也要丢了性命，实在有些于心不忍。犹豫不决之际，见到甲士要强行搜查药箱，只得先行喝止，再做打算。

The two guards then escorted Cheng Ying to the guardhouse. The doctor calmly carried his medicine box to Han Jue, and stood before the general to await the outcome of this interview. The latter was in a predicament. He put on a show of bluster, barking, "Who are you, fellow? And what were you doing in the princess' quarters?"

Cheng Ying correctly interpreted Han Jue's harsh tone as a sign that he was pretending not to recognize him, and he knew that he had come to a life-or-death crossroads. Nevertheless, he stared fearlessly into Han Jue's fiercely bulging eyes, and said in a voice that was unwavering, "I am just an ordinary doctor, come to attend the princess."

Han Jue played for time. "What ails the princess? And what medicine have you prescribed for her?" he growled.

"The princess is about to give birth," Cheng Ying explained. "Moreover, she has suffered a tragic turn of fortune. As a result, there is a failure of blood to circulate properly in the pulse, and a slackening in the functions of the meridians and collaterals. I prescribed motherwort soup."

Han Jue glanced at the medicine box in Cheng Ying's hands. "What's in the box?" he asked.

"Medicines ... that's all, General." came the reply.

"You're not smuggling anything out in it, by any chance, are you?"

"Certainly not, General!"

The more bullying the questions, the more serene were the replies. Han Jue was at his wits' end. He couldn't decide for the life of him what to do. Seeing Cheng Ying standing before him, facing danger unafraid, he could not help secretly admiring the man's courage. At the same time, he felt somewhat ashamed of himself. All of a sudden, he made up his mind. With a dismissive wave of his hand, he said curtly, "All right, all right. Off you go!"

Hearing this, Cheng Ying gave a slight bow, and turned to go on his way. But he had proceeded no more than a few steps, when he was startled to

两名甲士听得将军要亲自查看药箱，也就不为已甚，押着程婴进了亭子。程婴不慌不忙，手提药箱来到亭上，站在韩厥面前，且看他如何发落自己。韩厥此时骑虎难下，只得装腔作势，大声喝问道："你是何人？为何来公主府上？"

程婴见韩厥装作不认识自己，反而大声喝问，知道到了生死关头，心情反而平静下来，紧盯着韩厥那双铜铃似的眼睛，沉声答道："小人是草泽医生程婴，前来为公主看病。"

韩厥一时无计，又硬着头皮问道："公主得了什么病？你与公主下得何药？"

程婴答道："公主即将临产，又遭惨变，因而血不归脉，经络涣散。小人下得是益母汤。"

韩厥瞅了瞅程婴手中所提药箱，问道："你这药箱里装着何物？"

程婴答道："回禀将军，尽是些生药。"

韩厥追问道："可曾有什么夹带？"

程婴答道："不曾有任何夹带。"

韩厥心中七上八下，犹如翻江倒海一般，实在难以定夺。反观程婴临危不惧，从容应对，不觉暗暗佩服他的胆量，心中生出几分惭愧，索性将心一横，摆摆手道："罢，罢，罢！你走吧。"

hear Han Jue call out, "Cheng Ying, come back here!"

The doctor's heart began to palpitate, but he had no choice but to halt in his tracks. Slowly turning round, he inquired, "Yes, General. Is there something more I can do for you?"

Hesitation overcame Han Jue once more. Finally, he asked, "Er, what kind of medicines have you got in the box?"

"Oh, nothing but root of balloonflower, licorice and peppermint, that sort of thing."

Han Jue hesitated for a moment. Finally, he sighed, "Well, if that's all, you can go."

With an overwhelming feeling of relief, Cheng Ying hurried on his way. But again he was brought to an abrupt stop by Han Jue shouting, "Cheng Ying, you come back here!"

The doctor knew that Han Jue was suspicious of him but couldn't make up his mind what action to take. So this time he walked back to the guardhouse, set the medicine box on a table and said, "General, please look for yourself, and stop harassing an insignificant fellow like me."

Han Jue stared meaningfully at Cheng Ying, and spoke deliberately, "You say you only have balloonflower, licorice and stuff like that in this medicine box. But if I find ginseng in there you'll suffer for it."

The hidden import of his words was not lost on Cheng Ying, ginseng being a root shaped like a human being. But he stubbornly replied, in a manner guaranteed to confuse his hearer. "The princess is suffering from excessive Fire in the Heart. There is no need to apply the Great Remedial. Therefore, what would be the point of carrying ginseng about with me?"

This exasperated Han Jue, who cried, "Cheng Ying, don't think you're so smart that I can't see right through you. You've got something concealed in this medicine box, and I'm going to have a look and find out what it is!"

程婴闻言微一躬身，转头就走，不料才迈出两步，韩厥却在身后喊道："程婴，你回来！"

程婴心中一颤，只得停下脚步，回头问道："将军还有何见教？"

韩厥见程婴停步，心中又犹豫起来，拖着长腔问道："你这药箱里装着些什么生药？"

程婴答道："无非是些桔梗、甘草、薄荷之类。"

韩厥听了，一时无语，心念一转，说道："既如此，你就去吧！"

程婴只道是虚惊一场，心中大喜，转头又走。谁知未行出数步，又听得韩厥一声断喝："程婴，你给我回来！"

程婴见韩厥几次三番刁难自己，知道韩厥已经生疑，今日之事不能善罢，索性转身将药箱放在几案上，道："将军请亲自验看，也免得三番五次刁难小人。"

韩厥紧盯着程婴，话里有话道："你说这箱里装着桔梗、甘草之类，我若是搜出人参来，你该当何罪？"

程婴听出韩厥话外之意，却只能抵赖到底，故作糊涂答道："公主眼下心火太旺，不宜大补，要人参何用？"

韩厥见程婴到如此地步，还不肯承认，心中不免有几分恼怒，面带愠色道："程婴，你休得自作聪明，以为

Cheng Ying felt a solemn resolution rise in his breast. Stepping forward, he opened the medicine box. "I have something concealed in the box. It is the sole remaining heir of the Zhao bloodline. General, if you are the sort of person who clings to life at all costs, and wants to play the toady to the wicked and ruthless Tu'an Gu, then hand the child over to that monster. I have already put aside all cares about my own life or death. I only fear that you, having been a staunchly loyal and upright man all your life, might make one small lapse now and have your name cursed for generations to come."

Han Jue's mind churned in excruciating turmoil. This tongue lashing from Cheng Ying had cut the ground completely from under his feet. Deliberately, he stretched out his hand, and parted the top layer of medicines in the box, and saw the baby, sleeping peacefully, blissfully unaware that he was facing a moment of life or death. Han Jue bowed his head and pondered deeply. If he handed Zhao the Orphan over to Tu'an Gu, he would be committing a treacherous and heinous act, as bad as assisting the tyrants Zhou and Jie in their savagery. Moreover, he would be regarded for ever as the worst villain in the State of Jin. The thought made his blood run cold.

Observing Han Jue deep in thought and with large beads of sweat pushing through the skin of his swarthy face, Cheng Ying knew that he was feeling the pricks of conscience. Now was the time to add fuel to the fire! He addressed the general thus, "Sir, do you remember the assassin Chu Ni, who preserved righteousness at the cost of his life? He killed himself by dashing out his brains against a tree. And then there was Ti Miming, who wielded his pike so bravely ... and Ling Zhe, who supported the carriage on his shoulder. They both acted in defense of that thing called righteousness. General, when I came here today, I did not expect to leave alive. My only hope was that, by trusting to divine chance, I might rescue Zhao the Orphan, so that a loyal minister might have posterity and his bloodline not be severed. Just before I left the mansion, the princess and her serving maid both committed suicide. They died as martyrs to righteousness, having enjoined me to 'save

我韩厥认不出你。这药箱里定有夹带，本将军今天一定要查看一番！"

程婴闻言，一股悲壮之气从胸口生起，索性自己上前将药箱打开，道："里面是有夹带，夹带的是赵家惟一的血脉。韩将军如果贪生怕死，为虎作伥，此刻便可去向屠岸贼邀功。程婴早将生死置之度外，只可怜你忠直一世，糊涂一时，将来必定遗臭万年！"

韩厥心里本就忐忑不安，被程婴痛骂一番，越发无地自容。下意识地伸手拨开药箱上面的药草，露出白白嫩嫩的婴儿，只见他丝毫不知自己正在面临生死关头，兀然沉沉熟睡，嘴角还流出一条涎水，心中更觉不忍。低头细想，自己今天若是将这赵氏孤儿交与屠岸贾，岂不是不忠不义，助纣为虐，成了晋国的千古罪人！想到此处，只觉背如芒刺，脊梁骨冷嗖嗖的。

程婴见韩厥默然不语，黧黑的脸上沁出了一颗颗豆大的汗珠，知道他此时心中良心发现，天人交战，须得再加上一把火，便接着道："想那钽麑乃一介刺客，前去行刺，尚且能守义舍生，触槐而亡；至于提弥明奋勇挥戈，灵辄单肩扶轮，全都是为着一个'义'字。今日小人前来，本就没有打算活着回去，只想侥天之幸，将赵氏孤儿救出，使忠臣有后，血脉不断。适才出门之时，公主和宫女双双自尽，无非也是以身殉

the orphan and preserve the Zhao clan.' I never thought that you, General, who have always been a man of uprightness and loyalty and in the past rendered valuable services for the prime minister, should today side with a scoundrel and prove weak and irresolute, or that a person with such a manly appearance should turn out to be no better than a woman!"

At this, all Han Jue's selfish thoughts vanished like a puff of smoke, and he was filled with a sense of boldness in the pursuit of justice. In a clear, ringing tone of voice, he said, "Cheng Ying, take your medicine box and depart! I will take care of everything here."

When the doctor showed no sign of leaving, Han Jue, puzzled, asked, "Sir, why do you hesitate?"

With a sardonic smile, Cheng Ying replied, "How do I know that the moment I have gone, you will not report what has happened, soldiers will not pursue me, and I will not fall into one of that villain Tu'an Gu's many traps?"

Han Jue raised his eyes to Heaven, and breathed a long sigh. "Sir, if you never put your trust in any man," he admonished the doctor, "How will you make your way in the world? Enough, enough! By letting you go I have endangered my own life. You may go with an easy mind, but I advise you to leave the capital with all speed. Wean this child, and raise him to manhood, and then I will not have died in vain!"

With a grave countenance, he called to the two guards to him. Not knowing the reason why they had been summoned, they hastened to obey. As the guards stood before him, Han Jue, as swift as lightning, drew his sword and slew them on the spot. Then he drew the razor sharp blade across his own throat, which left a stream of crimson blood in its wake. The sturdy body of the general swayed and tottered, and crashed to the floor.

Cheng Ying kowtowed to the lifeless form of Han Jue, with tears in his eyes. Then he picked up his medicine box, and scurried out of the guardhouse. Fortunately, there was nobody in front of the mansion of the late royal

义，成就小人这一番'救孤存赵'的苦心。没想到将军乃忠义之士，以往多承相国提携重用，今日却认贼作父，优柔寡断，身为堂堂须眉，却连妇人也不如！"

韩厥听了这番言语，不觉将方才的一点儿私念都扔到爪哇国里去了，只感到胸中一腔忠心赤胆，遂斩钉截铁道："程婴，你带着药箱走吧！这里一切都由我一人承当。"

程婴闻言却不迈步，韩厥不解道："先生为何不走？"

程婴冷笑道："我前脚迈出府门，你后脚便去报告。程婴孤身一人，岂能抵挡追兵，逃出屠岸贾布下的天罗地网！"

韩厥闻言，仰天长叹道："大丈夫不能取信于人，有何面目立于世上。罢！罢！我既然放你离去，最终也难逃一死，不如叫你走得放心。先生务须速速出城，日后将这孤儿抚养成人，报仇雪恨，我韩厥也不算枉死了！"

说罢，脸色一肃，向亭外的两名甲士喝道："你二人进来。"那两名甲士不明所以，遵命入内。韩厥闪电一般拔出佩剑，将两名甲士刺死，右手一回，锋利的剑刃从颈上掠过，鲜血喷溅，魁梧的身躯晃了两晃，倒在地上。

son-in-law, and the doctor made his escape as fast as his legs could carry him.

Fearing that Tu'an Gu would mount a full-scale search of the capital for the infant and his rescuer, Cheng Ying did not dare go home; instead, he hurried out of the city gate and headed for the village of Guojiazhuang Village.

Cheng Ying's father-in-law, Guo Shanren, lived in his ancestral village, supporting himself by farming. His wife had died four or five years previously, and there was only the old man and his daughter at home. Guo Shanren had become acquainted with Zhao Dun when the latter had visited the village to encourage the farmers. Later, the prime minister had acted as the go-between for the marriage between Guo's daughter and Cheng Ying. The old man was very fond of his son-in-law, and often visited the couple.

A few days before, his daughter had arrived unexpectedly from the city with news of the massacre of the Zhao clan, and explained that Cheng Ying had remained behind to try to rescue Zhao the Orphan. The old man cursed Tu'an Gu bitterly, and at the same time was filled with anxiety for his son-in-law.

Every day since then, whenever he had time he had gone to the entrance to the village to watch anxiously for the coming of Cheng Ying. That very morning, his daughter had been seized by stomach pains, and was apparently about to give birth, so he had stayed at home to look after her. In the afternoon, she had given birth to a healthy baby boy, to the old man's great delight.

At midnight there had come an unexpected knock on the door. Opening it, Guo Shanren found Cheng Ying standing there with Zhao the Orphan.

He hastily ushered them in. Guo told his son-in-law the glad tidings that

程婴见韩厥自刎死义，含泪拜了两拜，疾忙背起药箱，转身出亭。幸喜驸马府门前空无一人，遂迈开大步去了。

程婴绝处逢生，终于将赵氏孤儿救出。他害怕屠岸贾在城中大肆搜查，不敢回自己家里，风风火火出了城门，直奔郭家庄。

原来，程婴的岳父郭善人，世代居住在郭家庄上，务农为生。家中人丁不旺，老妻已于四五年前谢世，只有一个女儿。早年郭善人与下乡劝农的赵盾相识，后来由赵盾做主将女儿嫁给程婴，对这女婿极是喜爱，时常到女儿家走动。前几日女儿突然从绛邑回来，说起赵氏满门遭难，程婴独自留在城内设法搭救赵氏孤儿的事，不禁将那屠岸贾骂了千遭万遍，又为女婿担心忧虑。这几天里，得空就到村口张望，等候女婿。今天一早，女儿忽然肚痛起来，眼见着就要分娩，故而留在家中照料。到了下午，女儿生下一个大胖男婴，郭善人老怀得畅，笑得合不拢嘴。谁知到了半夜，忽听有人敲门，出来一问，竟然是女婿程婴将赵氏孤儿救出，赶回家中来了。

郭善人将程婴迎进门来，先将女儿生下一个大胖小子的喜讯说了。程婴也将救出赵氏孤儿之事大

his wife had given birth to bonny baby boy that very day. Cheng Ying, in turn, related how he had saved Zhao the Orphan. When he told them of the suicides of the princess, her maid servant and Han Jue, his father-in-law and his wife sobbed uncontrollably. And so, weeping and laughing in turns, they chatted for hours. Cheng Ying took Zhao the Orphan from his medicine box, and laid him beside his new-born son. Gazing at them closely, it struck him that they were as alike as twins, both having fine eyes and eyebrows, straight noses and square cheeks. Guo Shanren was delighted. "What luck!" he cried. "If anybody asks, you can say that your wife gave birth to twins," he pointed out to Cheng Ying.

At that moment, they heard the neighbor's cock crowing. Dawn was breaking already, so the three adults went to bed. As soon as he arose the following day, Cheng Ying planned to go out to buy some nutritious food, such as chicken and duck, meat and vegetables, for his wife to help her recover her health and promote lactation. But Guo Shanren stopped him. "For one thing," he said, "Over the past few days you have been dashing about, and have even plunged into the tiger's lair to rescue Zhao the Orphan. You deserve a bit of a rest. For another, Tu'an Gu will have men out searching high and low for the baby; if he gets wind of your whereabouts disaster will befall us all."

Cheng Ying saw the sense of this, and agreed to lie low for a while. "I'll leave everything to you, father-in-law," he said. "Please hurry back."

Taking some money with him, Guo Shanren went to the nearby market town to make the purchases. There he noticed that the place was not as tranquil and sleepy as it usually was. Knots of people stood here and there, with their heads together, whispering. Fear was written all over their ashen faces. Guo Shanren was curious, but he did not dare ask what the matter was. Before long, he came across a group of people gathered around a notice. Elbowing his way through the crowd, he saw large black characters on a white sheet of paper, which read:

略说了一遍，郭善人与郭氏听得公主、宫女与韩厥先后自尽，才得救出赵氏孤儿，不禁为之歔欷不已。一家人哭哭笑笑，说了半晌。程婴将药箱中的赵氏孤儿抱出，与自己的儿子并排放了，仔细一瞧，都是眉清目秀，鼻直腮方，酷似一双孪生兄弟。郭善人见了大喜道："如此甚好，往后有人问起，就说女儿生的是双胞胎。"

此时已听到邻家鸡叫，看看天色放亮，三人这才躺下歇息。第二天程婴起身，便忙着要出去采买鸡鸭肉蔬，打算着给妻子郭氏补养催乳，以便哺育两个婴儿。郭善人上前道："这个就由老夫去办吧，一则贤婿连日奔波，深入虎穴，救出了赵氏孤儿，尚须略作休养；二则那屠岸贾不见了赵氏孤儿，定会四处搜捕，万一有人认出贤婿，岂不又是一场弥天大祸！"

程婴听岳父说得有理，便不再坚持，只说："岳父大人诸事小心，快去快回。"

这里郭善人取些散碎银两，出门径往附近的市镇，却见那小镇上不似往日平静，人们三五成群，交头接耳，议论纷纷，一个个都是脸色惊惧，面如死灰。郭善人心中奇怪，无奈自己也有心事，不敢开口问人。又走了几步，见一群人聚着围观一张榜文，遂挤进人群，睁大眼睛细瞧。原来是一块白布，上面墨字大书：

Whoever has kidnapped and concealed Zhao the Orphan is hereby ordered to hand over the child to the authorities within five days. If that person fails to do so and is discovered, his whole family to the ninth degree of kinship will be beheaded. Anyone knowing of such a person and not reporting the matter will be treated as an accomplice, while informers will be handsomely rewarded. If the child has not been handed over within five days, every infant below the age of six months will be put to death, without exception. By order.

The previous evening, not long after Cheng Ying had got safely away with Zhao the Orphan, the relief guards arrived at the gate of the mansion of the late royal son-in-law. To their horror, they found the bodies of General Han Jue and the two guards. Two of them rushed off to report to Tu'an Gu, while the others hurried into the mansion. By this time, darkness had fallen, and when they saw that no light gleamed in the house, they were filled with foreboding. Hastily lighting a torch, they entered the princess' quarters, where they found the princess hanging by the neck and her maid lying in a pool of blood. Both bodies were already cold. A careful search revealed nothing else suspicious. Another messenger was dispatched to report this further finding, and the rest of the guards remained at the mansion to await the coming of Tu'an Gu.

When the news reached Tu'an Gu he turned apoplectic with rage. "You useless blockheads!" he stormed. "The princess and her maid didn't kill themselves for nothing; someone must have stolen the Zhao whelp." Then a question crossed his mind. "But Han Jue and the two guards.... How did they come to be killed outside the mansion? Did the kidnapper slaughter them as he fought his way out, I wonder?"

He had no time for further speculation, but hurried off to the

凡盗藏赵氏孤儿者，勒令于五日之内交到官府。若违命不交而被搜出，全家斩首，株连九族。知情不报者同罪，出首者重赏。五日之后不交，则将晋国境内半岁以下男婴尽行诛戮，一人不留！此令。

事情还得从昨晚说起……

程婴盗孤遁走之后，不多时换班的甲士回来，见下将军韩厥与值守的两名甲士都死在驸马府门前，大吃一惊。当下分出二人急赴屠岸贾府上报讯，其余的人一窝蜂拥入驸马府中，径奔公主的卧室。此时天色已黑，却见屋中没有烛光，心知不好，点起灯来闯入屋中，只见公主悬在梁上，地上躺着一名宫女，身下一片殷红的血迹，两人的身子早已冰凉。细细搜查，再无异样。只得先行退出，一面再派人去报信，一面把守屋门，等待屠岸贾亲自来处理。

消息传至屠岸府，屠岸贾勃然大怒，大骂道："一群酒囊饭桶，那公主和宫女无故自尽，定是有人盗走了赵氏孽种！"转而疑惑道："韩厥与两名甲士却为何死在府外，莫非是盗孤者杀死韩厥等人，闯出府外逃走么？"

当下也顾不得细想，疾速带兵驰往驸马府亲自

mansion of the late royal son-in-law with a body of soldiers to inspect the scene for himself. He first examined the bodies of Han Jue and the two guards. He noticed that Han Jue still grasped a sword tightly in his right hand, and his neck had been slashed through to the vertebrae. Blood dripping from the mouths of the two guards indicated that they had been stabbed by someone. Suddenly it dawned on him. "Han Jue must have been in league with the kidnapper! First, he killed the guards, and then, fearing punishment, slit his own throat. The spawn of the Zhaos must have been spirited away." An examination of the princess' body showed that she was no longer pregnant, but there was no sign of a child anywhere. Tu'an Gu ordered the mansion sealed and a thorough search made of the city of Jiangyi. He himself remained at the scene of the debacle, to await news. It was not long before his messengers returned, and reported that nobody had seen a man carrying a baby leave through any of the city gates. The search of the city too had been fruitless. Seized with a fit of uncontrollable fury, Tu'an Gu snatched his sword from its scabbard, and hacked frenziedly at the corpse of Han Jue. He then ordered that all the dead general's family be executed.

Having vented his spleen thus, Tu'an Gu returned home. He sat for a long while deep in thought, his mind greatly troubled. He thought of the man who had risked the extermination of his whole clan to enter the tiger's lair and make off with Zhao the Orphan ... and of Han Jue and the princess and her maid, who had willingly taken their own lives to cover up the plot and save the child. He realized that if Zhao the Orphan were allowed to grow up his very life would be in danger sometime in the future. The more he pondered the matter, the more fearful Tu'an Gu became. He knew that he had to get rid of this threat somehow; but how? The State of Jin had a large population, so at any time there had to be lots of new born babies. Searching every household would be like

验看。先到府外查看韩厥等人的死状，见韩厥右手紧紧地握着一柄宝剑，颈上一道伤痕，深可见骨。那两名甲士每人咽喉上一个血洞，显见是被人刺死。当下心中了然，顿足道："韩厥定是与盗孤者内外勾结，先将甲士杀死，而后畏罪自刎。赵氏孽种必然已被人盗走。"待进了府中，果然见公主腹中空空如也，胎儿不知去向。屠岸贾立命众甲士即刻封锁城门，在绛邑城中大肆搜捕，自己也不回府，就在驸马府外坐候消息。不大功夫，各路人马纷纷回报，言说绛邑城各处城门并未见有人抱着婴儿出城，在城中搜捕亦无结果。屠岸贾一听，心中怒火勃发，难以遏制，拔出剑来将韩厥死尸一通乱砍，又命人将韩厥家属满门抄斩，才算出了一口恶气。

回到府中，屠岸贾心神不宁，独坐沉思，想起那盗孤者甘冒全家灭门之祸，深入虎穴，将赵氏孤儿盗走；而韩厥、公主等三人宁肯自尽，以斩断线索，保护孤儿，可见得如果容这赵氏孽种长大成人，必为后患，将来自己的性命，说不得还要送在这孽种手里。越想越怕，拿定主意要将这后患根除。可是这晋国之内，茫茫人海，初生婴儿不知凡几，若是挨家搜捕，岂不是大海捞针？况且那婴儿脸上又不曾写着"赵氏"二字，就是撞在眼前，又怎能分辨？欲要不管，又担心

looking for a needle in a haystack. Besides, the child wouldn't have "Zhao" tattooed on its face, would it? If he let the matter rest, it would be like releasing a tiger into the wild —— a potential source of untold calamities. Tu'an Gu fretted until he was almost distracted with anxiety, but finally a dreadful solution to his dilemma flashed into his ruthless brain. "It's better to risk killing the innocent than to let the brat escape. That's it! If Zhao the Orphan can't be found I'll have every baby in Jin killed, and then we'll see where that accursed puppy can run to!"

Having made up his mind, Tu'an Gu called for his most trusted henchmen. "I want you to post notices all over Jin," he said. "The notices must say that Zhao the Orphan must be surrendered within five days. After five days, if the child has not been handed in every infant within the boundaries of Jin will be executed." His men forthwith attended to their master's order, and by the following morning the required posters were stuck up all over the country. They caused fear and consternation in all the people of the state, especially in those families which had new-born babies.

Guo Shanren, too, was petrified with horror when he read one of the notices. He stood in front of it for a long time, with his mouth agape and not knowing what to do. Finally, he backed out of the crowd massed in front of the poster, and made his way hastily homeward. When he reported what he had seen to Cheng Ying, the latter was stunned. The whole family, in fact, was stricken with panic.

As he gazed distraught at the two babies lying side by side in their bed, an idea came to the doctor. But he immediately shook his head, and dismissed the preposterous thought. But the more he worried about the problem facing them, turning one scheme after another over and over in his mind, the more he became convinced that this was the only way out. The realization that he could not tell his wife what he was thinking

放虎归山,贻患无穷。想着想着,不免丧心病狂,想出一条毒计来,咬牙切齿地自语道:"宁可杀错,不可放过! 找不到那赵氏孽种,我就将晋国境内的小儿杀个干净,看那孽种向哪儿逃! "

一切想妥,当即将左右亲信唤入,狞笑道:"你等即刻传令下去,在晋国城乡贴布榜文,勒令盗孤者五日内交出赵氏孤儿,过期不交,则将晋国境内半岁以下的小儿统统拘来杀死。"左右不敢怠慢,即刻派人快马传令,到得第二日上午,晋国境内便贴满了榜文。百姓看了榜文,无不心惊肉跳,家里正好生产了婴儿的,更是坐立不安。

郭善人看了榜文,登时惊得张大嘴巴,不知如何是好。呆立了一会儿,拔腿挤出人群,急急忙忙返回家中,将榜文内容告诉程婴。程婴听罢,宛如头上响了个焦雷,也惊得目瞪口呆。一时间,阖家愁眉不展,彷徨无计。

程婴怔怔地看着并排躺在榻上的儿子和赵氏孤儿,心中忽然想起一条计策,马上又摇头自责,打消了这个主意。可是千思万想,只有这个计策能解救眼前的困境。想到这里,又觉得无法向妻子开口,如此再三斟酌,百感交集,悲从中来,不禁放声大哭起

made the pain in his heart even harder to bear. Again he banished the thought from him. But it refused to go away, and in the end Cheng Ying could not help crying out in anguish.

His wife and father-in-law, who had been gazing intently at Cheng Ying, in the hope that he could come up with a plan, were startled out of their wits when he suddenly bawled in sorrow, his face contorted with pain. Little guessing the reason for his son-in-law's bitter wailing, Guo Shanren tried to console him by reminding him that the notice gave them five days' grace within which to think of a plan to save the child and themselves.

But far from bringing him any comfort, his father-in-law's words only served to twist the dagger that seemed to be piercing Cheng Ying's heart. He tried to explain the reason for his agony, but no coherent words came out. His wife guessed that there was a deeper sorrow tearing at him, and urged him to speak out.

Calming down somewhat, and wiping away the tears, Cheng Ying said, "I have thought of a plan, and I beg both of you not to hate me for what I am about to say." Before either of them had time to say anything, he continued. "I know that Tu'an Gu is as vicious as a viper or a scorpion, and that he would stoop to any foul deed. His threat to slaughter all the newborn infants in Jin is no idle one. If we do not hand over Zhao the Orphan we will bring a terrible calamity upon thousands of innocent families. The plan I have thought up will not only save Zhao the Orphan; it will also save the lives of all the babies of Jin. We can do this by surrendering our own child to Tu'an Gu...."

He could not continue, and tears cascaded down his cheeks. After sitting in silence for a few moments, as if she had been struck dumb, Cheng Ying's wife screamed, "You heartless beast!" and abandoned

来。

郭善人和郭氏本来都在眼睁睁地看着程婴，指望他拿出个主意。想不到程婴突然放声大哭，一脸痛楚，不禁大惊失色。郭善人想：女婿定是束手无策，看着甘冒生命危险救出的赵氏孤儿终究难逃此厄，因而急痛攻心，忍不住放声一恸。于是开口劝慰道："贤婿不必着急，榜文上说有五日宽限，且从容思量，必有万全之计。"

程婴耳听岳父劝慰自己，心里更加难过，说道："小婿并非……小婿想……"嗫嚅几次，终究哽咽不能成语。郭氏毕竟对丈夫比较了解，看出程婴另有为难之处，遂道："相公如有主意，不妨说出来商量，憋在心里，没得坏了身子。"

程婴此时慢慢镇静下来，拭泪道："我倒是有个主意，只是说出来岳父大人和贤妻不要怨我。"也不待郭氏父女说话，续道："我想那屠岸贾心如蛇蝎，手段毒辣，如今要杀尽晋国小儿绝非虚声恫吓。若是我们不交出赵氏孤儿，免不了连累千家万户。于今只有一计，一可保全赵氏孤儿，二可救得晋国男婴，那就是拿我们的儿子假冒赵氏孤儿，交了出去，或者可以瞒过屠岸贾……"

说到这儿，语不成声，泪下如雨。郭氏父女闻言，

herself to a paroxysm of weeping. Guo Shanren rubbed his hands in agitation, but said nothing.

Cheng Ying waited for his wife to recover her composure, and then said, "My dear, please don't hate me. We are both nearly forty years old, and only now have we been blessed with a son and heir. The idea of having to part with him tears at my heart just as much as it does yours. But I am afraid that there is no other way to save Zhao the Orphan. Besides, remember how kind the prime minister has been to us both. Think of the massacre of the 300 blameless members of the Zhao clan, and of how the duke's son-in-law committed suicide by drinking poison. Remember how the princess, just before she died, entrusted Zhao the Orphan to me. Then there were the upright Chu Ni, Ti Miming, General Han Jue and the princess' serving maid —— they all gave their lives in the cause of loyalty and righteousness. After all these noble sacrifices of lives and sufferings to save him, if we simply hand over Zhao the Orphan we will be no better than curs or swine. Then how could we face the prime minister again in this life, or his aggrieved ghost in the next? Besides, if we refuse to hand a child over to Tu'an Gu he will barbarously slaughter all the infants in Jin, and both Zhao the Orphan and our own baby together with them! Then our whole venture will come to naught. Please, my dear, think carefully. Is there not reason in what I say?"

Before his wife could reply, her father said to her, "You were the only person I had in the world until the prime minister kindly found a fine son-in-law for me. And now I have a grandson, whom I love dearly. When Cheng Ying talks of sending the child to his death, of course every fiber of my being cries out against it. However, your husband is right. Put yourself in the place of others, and think of how many families in Jin will be left without heirs if that fiend Tu'an Gu carries out his threat. We will not be the only ones to suffer."

犹如一个焦雷打在头上，惊在当地。不一会儿，郭氏缓过神来，恸哭失声，口中说道："相公你好狠的心呀！"一语未毕，又哀哀痛哭起来。郭善人在一旁看着，急得只是搓手，却说不出话来。

程婴待郭氏稍微平静之后，开口道："贤妻不要埋怨夫君，想你我都已年近四十，几次小产，至今未有子嗣。如今好不容易有了这个儿子，却要舍他出去，岂非剜却我夫妻心头之肉？慢说贤妻舍不得，为夫也是肝肠寸断，痛不欲生。可错非如此，又有何策可以救得赵氏孤儿？且不说相国待我二人恩重如山，赵府三百余口无辜枉死，驸马被逼饮鸩自尽，公主临终郑重委托，就是那义士钮麂、提弥明，下将军韩厥并驸马府中宫女，与赵府并无戚谊亲情，却先后丢了性命，只是为了'忠义'二字，故而舍生忘死。如今牺牲数条性命，费尽千辛万苦，将赵氏孤儿救出，倘若将他交出去，岂非狗彘不如，有何面目生见相国，死晤冤魂！如若抗命不交，那屠岸贾必下毒手杀尽晋国小儿，到了那时，赵氏孤儿与吾儿都不能幸免，仍旧大事不成。娘子仔细思量，为夫所说可有不是？"

郭氏未及答言，郭善人先开口道："女儿，按说我只有你一个亲人，由赵老相国作主嫁了一个好女婿，眼见着又得个外孙子，岂有不心疼的？女婿说要将他

Choking back her tears, Cheng Ying's wife replied, "I may be only a woman, but I understand what is right. Yes, it is better that my baby be sacrificed than that the hated Tu'an Gu should murder all the infants in Jin. Nevertheless, I cannot face the consequences of this cruel decision. For if my husband surrenders our child to Tu'an Gu, I am afraid that that wicked monster will kill both of them. How could I bear to lose both my child and my husband in the same day, and end up as a wretched woman alone? How I loathe that evil Tu'an Gu, who has brought harm to loyal and good people, and massacred the innocent! I hate him so much that I could feast on his flesh and drink his blood!" As she spat the words out, her face turned a bright crimson, and her eyes looked as though jets of fire were about to spurt from them.

Cheng Ying bowed deeply to both his father-in-law and his wife, saying, "In order to save Zhao the Orphan, I have dedicated myself to the pursuit of loyalty and justice. To attain this goal, I would submit without rancor to being boiled alive. After I am gone, you must both care for Zhao the Orphan as if he were your own flesh and blood. Raise him to adulthood, so that he can exact payment in full for this awesome blood debt. Then, with my most cherished desire fulfilled, I will lie smiling beneath the ground."

He then picked up his child, and was about to leave the house, when Guo Shanren stretched out a hand to detain him. "Don't be so rash!" he cried. "Tu'an Gu is a cunning devil, and he is determined to get his hands on Zhao the Orphan. If you simply hand over a baby, how do you know that he will believe that the child is the one he is seeking? He may decide to kill not only you and your child, but all the other infants in Jin as well to make sure he has got rid of the right one. Then the two of you will have perished in vain!"

Cheng Ying saw the sense in his father-in-law's words, and stood dumbfounded, not knowing what to do. At this moment, Guo Shanren

抱去送死，乍一听心中万万不肯。可听女婿说的这一番话，着实有理。退一步讲，将心比心，推己及人，想想晋国境内有多少小儿，如果都让屠岸贾杀了，多少人家要断子绝孙，又岂止是我一家的事？"

郭氏听丈夫和父亲说罢，含泪道："我虽是一个妇人，道理却还明白，与其让屠岸贾因此尽杀晋国小儿，不如将我们的孩子牺牲。可我心里实在是舍不得呀！再说相公将孩子送去，那屠岸贾心狠手辣，孩子固然是死定了，相公也只怕难逃厄运。一日之间，死了儿子，又没了丈夫，我一个妇人家怎能心甘情愿！我只恨那屠岸贾残害忠良，滥杀无辜，恨不得吃他的肉，喝他的血！"话才说完，脸已憋得通红，眼中仿佛要喷出火来。

程婴闻言，向郭氏及郭善人深深一拜，道："程婴只为救孤存赵，笃行忠义。纵然因此身入鼎镬，死而无怨。程婴去后，望娘子和岳父视赵氏孤儿如己出，将他抚养成人，报了这血海深仇。那时程婴夙愿得偿，也可含笑地下！"

说罢，抱起儿子就要出门。郭善人却伸手一拦，道："贤婿还须三思而行，切勿鲁莽行事。屠岸贾向来狡诈阴险，对那赵氏孤儿更是势在必得。你如今抱了这个婴儿送去，无凭无据，他怎会相信就是赵氏孤儿？弄

continued, "I think that what is needed now is another hero to act in concert with you. While one pretends to have kidnapped Zhao the Orphan, the other will pretend to denounce him. This charade might deceive Tu'an Gu. But where can we find such a stalwart partner?"

This scheme sounded feasible to Cheng Ying, and he stood deep in thought for a while. Suddenly the image of a man flashed before his mind's eye.

得不好,你父子二人白白送了性命,屠岸贾还是要将晋国小儿全部杀死,贤婿和外孙不是白死了么?"

程婴闻言,觉得岳父所言甚是有理,愣在当地,不知如何才好。郭善人接着道:"依老夫看来,此事必得再找一位义士,与贤婿一唱一和,一个假做盗孤,一个前去出首,演上一出连环戏,方可骗过屠岸贾。只是到哪里去找这搭档的义士呢?"

程婴听罢,觉得岳父之计可称万全,略一沉思,心中蓦地兜上一个人的身影来。

Chapter Five
An Episode of Sterling Devotion

Who was the man whom Cheng Ying thought of to help him accomplish his daunting task? His name was Gongsun Chujiu, and he was living at this time in Taiping Village, near Mount Shouyang.

Gongsun Chujiu had been a senior official at the court of Duke Wen of Jin, a position he continued to hold under Duke Wen's successor, Duke Xiang. But when Duke Ling came to the throne, he found his situation increasingly untenable, as the new ruler surrounded himself with rascally sycophants and wantonly slaughtered innocent people. Seeing the morale at court deteriorating by the day, Gongsun Chujiu, who, despite his advanced age, had a noble and unbending spirit, did not hesitate to rebuke Duke Ling with stern words. Eventually, however, seeing that the duke persisted in the path of folly, and refusing to be tainted by the likes of Tu'an Gu, he resigned his post in high dudgeon and retired to devote himself to farming. His wife, a woman of the Wei clan, was by nature indifferent to fame and gain, but when she saw her husband staunchly and boldly reproving Duke Ling for his wickedness she was afraid that he would bring calamity upon himself. And so, she was greatly relieved when he made the decision to leave the court and go into seclusion in the countryside. With a handful of servants, the pair left the capital to look for a place to where they could settle down in retirement, eventually settling upon Mount Shouyang.

Taiping Village was a charming spot, situated with its back to the mountain and facing water, considered an ideal configuration. Behind the

第五章 肝胆相照

看官不免要问那程婴想起了何人，要与他一起担这泼天价的官司。这人姓公孙，名杵臼，现居首阳山太平庄上。

公孙杵臼早在晋文公时就在朝中为官，任职中大夫。晋文公死后，晋襄公即位，公孙杵臼仍为中大夫。后来灵公即位，宠信奸佞，滥杀无辜，朝纲日益颓弛。公孙杵臼生性刚直，风骨铮铮，虽然此时年纪老大，却是姜桂之性，老而弥辣，看不顺眼，便直言劝谏。无奈灵公执迷不悟，眼见得自己无力回天，又不屑于与屠岸贾之类同流合污，一怒之下，辞官归农。夫人魏氏天性恬淡，不恋富贵，见丈夫生性倔强刚烈，眼里揉不进砂子，多次犯颜直谏，得罪灵公，生怕他招来杀身之祸。今见丈夫弃官归农，心中好不喜欢。老夫妻二人遂带着两三名下人，离了绛邑，择地隐居。挑来挑去，相中了首阳山上的太平庄。

这太平庄倒是好一处景致，其地背山面水，风光幽雅。庄后巍峰横亘，岗峦起伏，巨岩重叠，奇石峭

village marched lofty peaks and precipitous ridges, with fantastic rocks piled one on top of the other. From the heights tumbled cascades and waterfalls, spouting pearly and jade like beads of spray. In spring and summer, the mountain was clothed in lush verdure, with here and there splashes of brilliant color as rare flowers and other plants bloomed. In front of the village, a crystal clear stream of cool water meandered. In the fields, mulberry and elm trees matched the burgeoning crops in grace, and the lotus blossoms were as beautiful as the rosy rays of dawn. The very sight of Taiping Village was gladdening. The most impressive sight of all was the myriad pine trees, which clung to the crags in groups or singly. From close up, they seemed to form a huge green umbrella, and from afar where like an emerald cloak thrown over the land. Whenever a breeze sprang up, verdant billows swept over the pine covered hills, rolling to the horizon. In the still of the night when all else was silent, the murmuring in the pines filled the heart with gentle delight. As soon as he set eyes on this delightful spot, Gongsun Chujiu was overjoyed, and there and then decided to settle down here.

The old couple had never had any children, but they had never missed not having a son or daughter. Gongsun Chujiu was an easygoing fellow. He had never paid attention to amassing property, and although he had served in a high official post for decades, he had not saved up enough money even to buy a house with some land, and so he chose a spot between the mountain and the stream to erect a three-room cottage. Here he settled down, and together with his servants cleared some wasteland, upon which he planted rice and millet. Every day, as the sun rose, he would go out to work on the land, plowing and weeding, planting and reaping, and not return until sunset. In his rare moments of leisure, he would read or play chess. All in all, he was quite content with this way of life. The village was located far from the capital, and no news of the court or of state affairs reached the ears of its simple, unspoiled inhabitants. Gongsun Chujiu made up his mind to spend the rest of his days there. But in spite of making this declaration, there were

立。其间处处飞泉瀑布，喷珠溅玉。每至春夏时节，满山摇苍飞翠，郁郁葱葱，更兼奇花异草，红绿纷披。庄前一条碧流盘曲而下，溪水清洌，田间桑榆共禾苗竞秀，芙蓉与朝霞争辉，令人神清气爽。尤其令人叫绝的是，这首阳山上石岩危崖之间，到处生满了铺地松，一株株，一丛丛，横生斜长，贴地虬曲。近看犹如万千绿伞，密密麻麻；远望又似铺地翠幔，硕大无朋。山风起处，满山松树摇曳起伏，宛如苍海巨涛，滚涌天际。每至夜间，万籁俱静，松涛声不绝于耳，令人心醉神驰。公孙杵臼一眼看见此处景致，便喜欢的不得了，遂在此定居下来。

　　老夫妻俩一生没有生养，无儿无女，倒也无牵无挂。那公孙杵臼为人洒脱，向来不以家产钱财为意，虽然做了几十年官，却不曾聚得钱财，买不起田产宅院，只得在庄后的山间挑了一处枕山际水之地，搭了三间茅屋，住了下来。又带着下人垦出一片荒地，种了些禾黍之类，每日里耕田艻草，下种收割，日出而作，日入而息。偶有闲暇，则读书下棋，怡然自得。此地离京城甚远，当地百姓民风纯朴，朝政国事无人闻问，公孙杵臼乐得清闲，大有终老于此之意。话虽如此说，有时夜深人静，独坐无眠，免不了想起数十载仕宦生涯，遥揣朝中情景，为晋国前途担忧。只是回

times in the dead of night when he would sit up, alone and sleepless, thinking back on the days when he had led the life of an official, wondering how things were going at court, and worrying about the destiny of the State of Jin. When he thought of how he had resigned his post and gone to live in obscurity, he found himself sighing. Truly:

Wakeful at midnight in my humble shack, I hear the soughing in the pines.

By day, leaning on my rickety door, I count the wild geese as they pass.

Several years passed in this way, and Gongsun Chujiu's wife died of illness. His servants, one by one, married and moved away, until he was left with only one boy. The days passed in a leisurely manner. In the early days of Gongsun Chujiu's retirement, his erstwhile colleagues at court had been accustomed to send a messenger from time to time to inquire after him, but eventually such calls became fewer and fewer, until they ceased altogether, except for gifts of clothing and food from Prime Minister Zhao Dun. Like Gongsun Chujiu, Zhao Dun had served three generations of rulers. The two were alike in temperament and spirit, sharing the same deep feeling of loyalty to their country. Serving together, they had become fast friends. When Gongsun Chujiu resigned his position, Zhao Dun had done his utmost to get him to change his mind, but all to no avail. Just as they were about to part, Gongsun Chujiu said, "All my life, I have hated evil. So when I saw wicked villains pulling the strings at court, I did my best to put the situation right. However, I have proved powerless to do so, and my words have fallen on deaf ears. Now the only thing for me to do is to go far away. You, sir, are devoted heart and soul to the welfare of our country, but I must warn you to be on your guard day and night against plots and conspiracies against you." Zhao Dun, who viewed with alarm the attrition in the ranks of all those who were noble and good at the court, was profoundly saddened that his old friend was going away too. Grief-stricken, he could find no words to say, and the two made a tearful but silent farewell.

At that time, Cheng Ying was living in the Zhao mansion, and got to

想自己已经弃官隐居,眼不见,心不烦,也只得付之喟叹而已。正是:

夜眠草屋听松涛,日倚柴扉数雁行。

不知不觉数年过去,夫人魏氏得病死了,几名下人也先后成家,星流云散。公孙杵臼一人带着一名小奚童在太平庄上度日,一主一仆,日子依旧过得悠哉优哉! 朝中旧时同僚起初还有打发人来探望的,日子长了,也都绝迹不来。只有上卿赵盾不时派家人前来问候,有时馈赠些衣物粮谷。原来公孙杵臼与赵盾都是三朝老臣,同朝共事,加上意气相投,一般的忠心为国,故而交情深厚,生死不渝。当年公孙杵臼弃官归农,赵盾百般劝阻,无奈公孙杵臼去意已定,坚执不从。二人临别时,公孙杵臼道:"下官生来嫉恶如仇,实在看不得奸贼在朝中撮弄主君,倒行逆施。只是人微言轻,无力回天,索性远远地躲开去。上卿一心为国,可对日月,也要谨防宵小暗中陷害。"赵盾本来就忧虑朝中忠良凋零,如今见老友公孙也要退隐,悲从中来,一时哽咽不能成语。二人遂洒泪而别。

程婴当日为赵府门客,熟知公孙杵臼之为人,也听赵盾讲起自己与公孙意气相投,是生死之交。眼下走投无路,不由得想起他来,遂对岳父和郭氏说道:"相国大人昔日有一知交,就是以前朝中的老宰辅公

know Gongsun Chujiu well. He heard the prime minister say that he and Gongsun shared the same ideals and were bosom friends. Now, in his great quandary, he thought of Gongsun Chujiu. He thereupon said to his father-in-law and his wife, "The prime minister formerly had a close friend who was a colleague of his at court, named Gongsun Chujiu. He was an upright man who hated evil. Several years ago, he retired to the countryside, to a place called Taiping Village at Mount Shouyang. I met him many times when I was living in the Zhao mansion. I felt that he was the sort of person who would not hesitate to help someone who was in trouble. So I think I should take Zhao the Orphan to Taiping Village and ask Gongsun Chujiu to look after him. Then I will go and surrender myself and my son to Tu'an Gu, letting him think that my baby is actually Zhao the Orphan. In that way, the real Zhao the Orphan will be safe and the infants of Jin will escape slaughter."

Cheng Ying's wife was overcome with distress when she heard this, and choked with sobs. But she knew that her husband's plan was aimed solely at saving the orphan, and so she stifled her grief and kept her tears inside her. Watching this heartrending scene, Guo Shanren was also overcome with sorrow, and very much affected by his son-in-law's high-minded selflessness. He uttered a few words of comfort to his daughter, and then burst into tears. The night was well advanced by this time, and as Cheng Ying intended to set out at daybreak, the three of them did not sleep, but made all the preparations necessary for his journey.

Before cock-crow, taking advantage of the fact that there would be few people about at that time of the morning, Cheng Ying hurried out of the house. As before, Zhao the Orphan was concealed in his medicine box. Guojiazhuang was some 110 *li* from Mount Shouyang by the ordinary flat highway, but Cheng Ying decided to take a longer, mountainous but little traveled route, for fear of meeting prying eyes or government troops. The journey was uneventful. He only met a few woodcutters on the path, and they

孙杵臼,为人刚直,嫉恶如仇,数年前弃官隐居于首阳山太平庄。我在下宫时,与公孙大人曾有数面之交,想他不会见死不救。我欲尽快动身,将这赵家孤儿送到太平庄上,请公孙大人好好收养,然后由他去屠岸贾那里首告,骗那屠岸贾将我父子抓走,赵家孤儿便可保全,晋国境内的小儿也可逃过这无妄之灾了。"

郭氏闻言,不由得柔肠寸断,泣不成声,心知丈夫所作所为,都是为了救孤存赵的大计,只得强忍悲痛,眼泪往肚子里咽。郭善人在一旁瞧着也是痛彻骨髓,深感女婿舍己为人,义薄云天,轻声安慰女儿,不觉间已经老泪纵横。此时已到三更,程婴便要在拂晓动身。三个人索性也不睡觉,将一切关节筹划停当,细细说了一遍。

不等鸡叫,程婴已扎束整齐,依旧用药箱装了赵氏孤儿,趁着清晨行人稀少疾速出门去了。这郭家庄离着首阳山约有百十多里路,一条大路颇为平坦。另有一条山间小路,不但比走大路远着二十里地,而且崎岖难行。程婴害怕大路上人多眼杂,遇上官兵,便拣着小路迤逦而行。一路上果然清静,只遇到了几名上山打柴的樵子,也没有人来盘问。走到中午,已经行了四十里路。程婴找了一处树荫歇下,取出带来的米糊,将赵氏孤儿喂饱,自己则就着山泉吃了些干

displayed no curiosity about him. At noon, he had already covered 40 *li*. He rested beneath a shady tree by a stream. He fed the baby and himself, but did not dare to linger long. Soon he was on his way again.

It was mid-autumn. The path was lined with green-clothed mountains and clear emerald streams. The nearer slopes of the mountains were fiery red, as the maple leaves were in all their glory at this time. On the higher parts of the mountains, the leaves of the smoke trees, clustered in mass ranks, had already been touched by the frost, and were changing color. Little brooks bubbled musically from crevices and flowed down, following the contours of the rocks. Among the trees and by the banks of the streams was a multitude of strange, nameless wildflowers. Impervious to cold, and even frost, they still blossomed gaily in their quiet abodes.

But Cheng Ying gave them no heed, as his mind was preoccupied with his mission. When he did notice the beauty of his surroundings, he felt a pang of disquiet. Retiring to a place like this, surely Gongsun Chujiu must be perfectly content, and his heart must be as pure as water, Cheng Ying thought to himself. Perhaps he was doing wrong to thrust such a dire and important task upon him? Cheng Ying's steps began to falter. But when he remembered Gongsun Chujiu's reputation for being an upright and justice loving man, and moreover a staunch friend of Zhao Dun, he decided that, after all, Gongsun Chujiu was the only person who could undertake this great responsibility.

And so, after much deliberation, he came to the conclusion that there was nothing else for it at this stage but to press ahead and meet Gongsun Chujiu. But as he did so, he noticed that the sun was setting, and dusk was gathering. He did not dare to continue by night, so he sought lodging at a nearby farmhouse. As luck would have it, the woman of the house was a nursing mother, and Zhao the Orphan had his fill of milk that night.

Early the next morning, Cheng Ying bade farewell to his host, and hurried on his way, reaching Taiping Village before noon. Inquiring of the

粮,不敢久憩,站起来又走。

此时正当初秋,一路上青山叠翠,溪水拖蓝,近处的山坡上一片火红,漫山遍野都是黄栌树,树叶经霜变色,迎霞映彩,如火如荼。几股清流从石罅中缓缓溢出,又顺着山势盘旋流泄,淙淙潺潺,水声丁冬。树丛中,溪水畔,长着许多叫不上名来的野花,抗寒耐霜,依然金英灿灿,翠蔓青青,虽不引人注目,却也生机勃勃。

程婴心中有事,无心观景。忽地想起这一带山水佳胜,风景如画,公孙大人选择这样一个处所隐居,定然心静如水,陶然自得。自己突然拿了这件人命关天的大事来搅挠他,岂非太不识相。想到这里,心中又添了几分不安,脚下也不由得慢了起来。转念又一想,公孙大人往日耿直仗义,且与相国是生死交情,舍了他,眼下谁又能挺身而出,担此大任?

程婴心中一上一下,举棋不定。后来又想,事已至此,权且死马当作活马医,好歹要见公孙大人一面。主意已定,眼见红日西坠,暮色渐起,此处人地两生,不敢夜里赶路,就在路边找了一户务农人家住下,恰好主人有个哺乳的儿媳,将赵氏孤儿喂饱了奶水。

次日一早,程婴谢过主人,匆忙上路,紧一程,慢一程,中午以前终于赶到了太平庄。向庄里人问路,

local people, he learned that Gongsun Chujiu did not live in the village itself, but in a hut at the foot of the mountain. He thereupon skirted the village, until he came upon a cluster of thatched dwellings on a south-facing slope. In front was a double fence, adorned with vines and creepers.

Cheng Ying hurried forward, elated that he had at last come to the house of Gongsun Chujiu, after his difficult trek. He was just about to knock at the gate when caution overcame him. "This Gongsun Chujiu was a great friend of Prime Minister Zhao Dun in the old days, sure enough," he thought to himself. "But what if his years of retirement here have made him too fond of peace and contentment to be willing to embroil himself in the perilous cause of justice? What if he refuses to accept Zhao the Orphan? Besides, it is of the utmost importance that this matter be kept as secret as possible. The fewer people who know about it the better. If he shirks the responsibility of looking after it, he may reveal the child's identity to others. I had better keep the baby hidden for the time being."

He then turned away from the gate, found a thick clump of bushes, and hid the medicine box, with Zhao the Orphan inside it, there. Then he straightened his clothing, walked up to the wicker gate, and knocked lightly.

The gate creaked open, and there stood a tall, well poised old man. His eyes were clear and firm. His hair and sideburns were completely white, as was the wisp of beard which hung down to his chest. Cheng Ying recognized him at once as Gongsun Chujiu, whom he had not seen for many years. In spite of the fact that he was in his seventies, the old man seemed alert and in fine spirits. Cheng Ying hastened to step forward and bow, saying, "Sir, you have long been in retirement. I, Cheng Ying, have come specially to call on you."

Now, when the two of them had made each other's acquaintance in the Zhao mansion, they had got along very well together. So Cheng Ying's turning up on his doorstep like this, just as the old man was feeling the loneliness of many years living in seclusion, was as welcome to him as

才知公孙并不住在庄内，而是结庐于庄后的山脚下。程婴于是绕过庄子，见到朝阳的半坡上几间草舍，前面两排篱笆，爬满了萝蔓青藤，右侧植有一片金菊，花容淡雅，意态飘逸，可以约略窥见主人的胸襟情怀。

程婴长途跋涉，一路辛苦，好不容易来到公孙杵臼的居所，本待急步上前叩门，忽地多了个心眼，暗想："虽说公孙大人与相国的交情非同一般，怎奈他隐居多年，心性定然恬静淡泊。若是他贪恋这分宁静，不肯招惹是非，我贸然将赵氏孤儿托付于他，被他一口回绝，倒不好处置了。再者赵氏孤儿是一个天大的秘密，知道的人越少越好，若是他不肯收留，让他看到这婴儿反倒露了消息，往后少了腾挪的余地，还是先将赵氏孤儿暂时藏起为妙。"

想到这里，转身回来，找了一处茂密的草丛，将药箱妥善安置了，这才整衣上前，轻叩柴扉。

只听"呀"的一声，屋门启处，迎出来一位老者，身材颀长，体格潇洒，眉目清朗，鬓发俱白，一绺银须飘拂胸前，正是多年不见的中大夫公孙杵臼。虽说这公孙年逾七旬，却精神矍铄，不减当年。程婴急步上前施礼，道："大人隐居多年，程婴特来看望。"

公孙杵臼当日曾在下宫见过程婴，彼此颇有好

meeting a boon companion in a strange land. Moved, Gongsun Chujiu returned his visitor's greeting, and said, "I am honored by this unexpected visit, Mr Cheng. Forgive me for not coming to greet you on the road. Please come in, and sit down." When they were both seated, Gongsun Chujiu ordered his servant boy to make some tea. Cheng Ying was both pleased and apprehensive about this reception, and was at a loss what to say at first. A thousand things were eager to spill forth from his lips, but he managed to say only, "I trust you are well, sir?"

Gongsun Chujiu smiled and said, "These past few years I have kept myself away from hubbub and uproar. As a result, I have a good appetite and I sleep soundly, and I am never ill." He added, with a laugh, "I am afraid, doctor, that I can't give you any business." Then he said, eagerly, "Tell me, how are the court officials? Has there been any improvement in state affairs, I wonder? You see, moldering in retirement as I have been for such a long time, I hear no more news of the outside world than a deaf person."

Cheng Ying sighed, and said, "I am afraid, sir, that the situation at court has grown worse since you held you post. The duke is a dissipated dunce, evil officials hold the reins of power, and the government gets worse by the day."

Gongsun Chujiu interjected, "But, why don't the ministers censure the duke, and curb the excesses of the degenerate officials?"

"Rascals the like of Tu'an Gu have been known since ancient times," Cheng Ying replied. "Even the reigns of the sage kings Tang and Yu were disturbed by the Four Villains, and conspirators ran rampant."

Gongsun Chjiu's blood, which had been cool and calm for so long, suddenly began to boil and seethe. "But do you mean to tell me that Prime Minister Zhao Dun can do nothing about it?" he spluttered.

This mention of Zhao Dun gave Cheng Ying just the opening he wanted. He launched into a detailed account of how Duke Ling and Tu'an Gu had killed innocent people for sport, turned the palace into a den of lascivious

感，加上多年栖身山门，门前冷落，不意程婴来访，却有些他乡遇故知的感觉，不免有些激动，一面还礼，一面道："原来是程先生枉驾光临，老朽有失远迎，快请进来坐。"待得二人坐定，公孙命小奚童沏上茶来。程婴一则以喜，一则以惧，仓促间不知说什么好，千言万语堵在心头，却说出一句："老宰辅身体可还康健？"

公孙杵臼笑道："老朽身子颇为顽劣，近几年远离尘嚣，反倒吃得下，睡得香，连病也不生，今天你这个医生上门，却是没有生意。"笑话说完，开口问道："朝中各位大人可好？国家政事也不知有无起色。老朽隐居多年，隔绝人世，竟成了一个聋子！"

程婴叹道："如今比不得老大人在朝之日了。昏君无道，奸臣专权，朝政日非啊！"

公孙杵臼道："大臣们何以不劝谏主君，惩治奸臣呢？"

程婴道："像屠岸贾这等贼子自古就有，唐虞圣世也还有四凶作乱，奸贼横行。"

公孙杵臼听了，胸中已经冷却的热血不觉又要沸腾起来，问道："如此说来，相国赵盾也是束手无策吗？"

程婴见他提起赵盾，正中下怀，便滔滔不绝地说起来，将灵公与屠岸贾滥杀无辜、秽乱宫庭、逼走赵

wantonness, driven Zhao Dun into exile and massacred the Zhao clan. As he listened to all this, Gongsun Chujiu's eyes started from his head. In the end, he banged the table and leapt to his feet, saying, "If I were still at court, that blockhead of a duke and those reprobates of officials would not get away with such outrages!"

Cheng Ying was relieved to see that Gongsun Chujiu's old sense of righteous indignation had not withered during his lengthy retirement, and hastened to broach the purpose of his visit. "Fortunately," he said, "The princess was pregnant at the time these disasters struck, and she gave birth to a boy. However, Tu'an Gu, determined to root all possible causes of future danger to himself, put a heavy guard around the princess' quarters."

At this point, Gongsun Chujiu burst out, "Just let me go and bring that baby back to the mountains. I'll raise him until he is old enough to avenge the Zhao clan."

Cheng Ying cried, "Sir, calm yourself, I pray. The child has already been snatched from the jaws of death."

Gongsun Chujiu looked closely at his visitor. From the other man's calm and resolute expression, with shining eyes and keen glance, he began to sense that there was more to Cheng Ying's presence than just a courtesy call. Turning over in his mind what Cheng Ying had just told him, the purpose of the doctor's mission suddenly dawned on him. At once, his fury turned to elation. Clapping Cheng Ying on the shoulder, he said, "You're a splendid fellow, Cheng Ying. So, you wasted no time in performing the heroic deed of rescuing Zhao the Orphan, eh? Well, now I suppose you want to leave him here. Where is the baby now, by the way?"

"To tell you the truth, sir," replied Cheng Ying, "My purpose in coming here was to seek sanctuary for the child. Zhao the Orphan is not far from your gate."

Hearing this, Gongsun Chujiu jumped up and ran outside, closely followed by Cheng Ying. They lifted the medicine box from the bushes, opened

盾、诛杀赵家满门等事细细说了一遍。公孙杵臼听罢，双眼圆睁，拍案而起，道："老夫若在朝上时，断不许昏君贼臣如此猖狂作恶！"

程婴见状，知道公孙虽然隐居数年，仍旧如以前一样古道热肠，早已放下心来，便道："幸好公主怀了身孕，生下一个男婴。可是屠岸贾决意要铲除后患，派兵将驸马府严加把守，扬言要斩草除根呢！"

公孙杵臼闻言，急忙道："待老夫下山将这婴儿抱上山来，养大成人，为赵家报仇雪恨！"

程婴道："大人休急，那赵氏孤儿早已被人冒死救出，转危为安了。"

公孙杵臼听程婴说罢，忽有所悟，细细地将程婴打量一眼，见他沉静如水的表情中透出一股刚毅英武之气，一双眼睛炯炯有神，顾盼如电。再仔细将程婴进门后的言语举止回味一番，便已猜出程婴此番的来意，不觉转怒为喜，拍着程婴的肩膀道："好你个程婴，原来已经捷足先登，抢了这'救孤'的头功。现在来找老朽，只怕是要将他寄养在此处。那赵氏孤儿现在何处？"

程婴道："小人不敢隐瞒，此来正是要投奔老宰辅。那赵氏孤儿就在老宰辅门外。"

公孙杵臼闻言，急颠颠地跑出门去，程婴跟在身

the lid, and looked inside. There was the baby, fast asleep, its chubby face fair and plump. Gazing on Zhao the Orphan, Gongsun Chujiu felt a mixture of emotions surge through him as he contemplated the child's plight —— joy, resentment and pain. He gently lifted it from the box, murmuring, "What a noble countenance you have, little one! Alas, while you were still in your mother's womb your clan was destroyed. No sooner had you been born than you were left without either father or mother. How pitiful is your condition! But when you grow up, and come seeking reckoning for that horrendous blood debt, I am sure that you will mow down your family's enemies like a scythe reaps the barley."

The two men took Zhao the Orphan into the house, and settled him comfortably. Then Gongsun Chujiu said, "It's best if the child stays with me. I will raise him. That dastardly Tu'an Gu will never think of looking for him in this remote, mountainous region."

But Cheng Ying, although he was overjoyed to hear this, looked anguished as he explained, "Sir, I am afraid there is something you do not know. As soon as Tu'an Gu learned that the child had slipped through his fingers, he was so incensed that he ordered posters to be put up, saying that if Zhao the Orphan is not surrendered within five days every newborn infant in the State of Jin will be slaughtered."

Gongsun Chujiu's face turned steely grey with anger. "That wicked monster!" he roared. "I will go straightaway and cast his evil deeds back in his teeth!"

He was so consumed with fury that his silvery whiskers trembled, and he would have rushed off to have it out with Tu'an Gu there and then, if Cheng Ying had not hurriedly stopped him. "Please calm yourself, sir," he urged. "The situation at court is not what it was. Tu'an Gu has gathered all power into his own hands. If you were to confront him alone, that would be tantamount to throwing yourself right into his net. It would be like trying to smash a rock with an egg. You would not only not be helping the cause of preserving Zhao the Orphan, but on the contrary you would ruin the whole enterprise."

后，从草丛中找到药箱，打开二人同看时，只见那婴儿正酣酣熟睡，白白胖胖，宽盘大脸。公孙杵臼见了，心中又喜，又恨，又疼，于是将婴儿轻轻抱起，道："好个堂堂相貌，可惜在娘胎里就灭了祖宗，生下来又死了双亲，着实让人怜爱得紧。长大后报那血海深仇，待要见得你杀人如麻哩！"

二人抱了婴儿转回房中，安置妥当。公孙杵臼当下便道："这孩子就归老夫养活，此处山高路远，料屠岸贾那贼子也未必能找到这里来。"

程婴又转喜为悲，面色凄然道："老宰辅有所不知，那屠岸贾见得有人盗走了赵氏孤儿，恼羞成怒，已于前日贴出榜文，勒令盗孤者五日内交出赵氏孤儿，否则要将晋国所有半岁以下的小儿统统杀死！"

公孙杵臼听了，怒发上指，脸色铁青，道："岂有此理！这贼子怎敢如此猖獗，看老夫下山与他评理。"

说罢，气得颏下银髯不住地抖动，真个当下就要出门。程婴忙劝道："老宰辅息怒，此时朝中大非昔日光景，那屠岸贾重权在握，无人敢与他抗衡。老宰辅单人独马前去找他，无异于自投罗网，以卵击石。不但与事无补，反倒坏了救孤存赵的大计。"

Gongsun Chujiu calmed down and reflected on the position they were in. It was true that he had been about to act rashly, but it was hard to suppress the anger in his heart. "But we can't let Tu'an Gu get away with this," he groaned.

Cheng Ying said, "Right now, the most important thing is to save Zhao the Orphan at all costs. I have discussed it with my wife and father-in-law, and we have formed a plan. But we need your assistance, sir, for it to succeed. It just so happens that a few days ago my wife gave birth to a baby boy —— in fact, only one day after Zhao the Orphan was born. The plan is to pass this boy off as Zhao the Orphan, whom I smuggled out of the mansion of the royal son-in-law. Then you, sir, must hurry to Tu'an Gu, and denounce me as the culprit. You must tell him that I have the baby hidden. Tu'an Gu will have my house searched, and all my family will be executed. Tu'an Gu will then be satisfied, and all the newborn babies in the State of Jin will be saved —— as will Zhao the Orphan. You can then bring up this child, who will avenge the Zhao clan."

Gongsun Chujiu stared at Cheng Ying in amazement and awe. "My dear fellow," he said, "Are you really willing to sacrifice your own flesh and blood for the sake of Zhao the Orphan?"

Holding back his tears, Cheng Ying replied, "I will not deceive you, sir. In middle age I have finally acquired a son and heir. Of course, he is the most precious thing in the world to me. Not to mention, of course, the suffering and pain my dear wife has undergone, through many abortions, to produce a son. Naturally, the very thought of handing my baby over to Tu'an Gu, tears at my heart and entrails. But the Zhao clan has served the State of Jin faithfully for generations. Their meritorious deeds have been magnificent. But now they have fallen into the snares of a villainous official, whose intention is to exterminate all the Zhaos, including the sole surviving male child. How can I just sit back and watch this happen? Besides, in the old days the prime minister was extremely kind to me, and enabled me to become what I am today. It seems to me that if Zhao the Orphan survives,

公孙杵臼冷静下来用心一想，也觉得自己莽撞了，可是心内的愤懑实在难以平息，气哼哼地道："如此就便宜了那贼子不成！"

程婴道："眼下救孤要紧，小人在家中与岳父及拙荆想出一条计策，还要公孙大人赐以援手，才得成功。前日里拙荆正好产下一个男婴，与赵氏孤儿只差一日。小人的意思是将此男婴充作赵氏孤儿，假作是小人从驸马府中盗出。老宰辅可速速下山，到屠岸府将程婴出首，就说程婴藏着赵氏孤儿。屠岸贾必定带人来搜查，小人与自家孩儿一同死了，屠岸贾也就放心了，晋国的小儿由此得救，赵氏遗孤也可保全，从此由老宰辅养大成人，教他报仇雪恨。"

公孙杵臼闻言一惊，不禁对程婴刮目相看，肃然起敬，脱口说道："先生为了救孤存赵，竟舍得抛却自家性命，还搭上亲生的骨肉？"

程婴含泪道："不瞒大人说，程婴中年得子，岂能不爱若珍宝！加上拙荆一向多灾多病，数次小产，子息艰难。如今好不容易有了这个小儿，又要将他送给屠岸贾杀死，自然是痛彻肝肠，心头滴血。只是赵氏几代忠心辅佐晋室，功勋赫赫，竟遭奸臣构陷，落得满门抄斩的下场，但凡有血性的男子，岂能坐视！再

there is hope that justice will be restored to the State of Jin. I will have no regrets about dying, together with my whole family, if I can serve my country on the one hand and repay my debt of gratitude to Prime Minister Zhao Dun on the other."

As he spoke, tears poured down his cheeks. He then sobbed out the stories of the noble deaths of Chu Ni, Ti Miming, Ling Zhe, Han Jue, and the princess and her serving maid. Wiping his eyes, Cheng Ying added, "As soon as I crossed the threshold of the mansion of the royal son-in-law, I consigned the fate of my family to oblivion. My only consideration was that if Heaven has eyes it will not allow loyal and good people to perish utterly. It was thanks to Han Jue, who drew his sword and used it to aid me, that I managed to escape death myself and rescue Zhao the Orphan. Little did I suspect that Tu'an Gu would be so cruel and vicious as to threaten to kill all the newborn infants in the State of Jin if he could not get his hands on Zhao the Orphan. But I don't care if my head is chopped off and my blood runs in streams. Zhao the Orphan must never be handed over to him! But it is because I cannot bear the thought of bringing tragedy to thousands of innocent families in Jin that I have devised this plan, and I hope you will cooperate with me, sir."

Gongsun Chujiu was moved to tears by this declaration. He said, with deep emotion, "This is a most lofty-minded decision. Although I am unworthy to assist you in this noble undertaking, I will raise Zhao the Orphan to adulthood, and instruct him in his destiny, which is to wreak vengeance for his clan." He then hesitated for a moment, shook his head and said, "No, I'm afraid it won't work; it won't work at all. You see, when I was serving as a minister at court I had frequent clashes with that reptile Tu'an Gu. If I suddenly turn up out of the blue with this story, he'll never believe it. I myself don't mind dying, as the price to pay for ruining a great enterprise. But if this plan to save Zhao the Orphan is scuttled, it will mean that you and your child will have died in vain, and that I will have betrayed the

说相国当年待我恩重如山，我程婴才有今日。小人想来，今天救孤即所以存赵，存赵即所以匡晋。小人以一家性命，上报国家，下酬私恩，死而无憾。"

说着说着，早已是泪流满面，又哽哽咽咽地将那"钽麑触槐"、"提弥明死义"、"灵辄扶轮"、"韩厥自刎"及"公主投缳"、"宫女殉难"等情节向公孙杵臼说了一遍，拭泪道："程婴自踏进驸马府之时，就已将身家性命置之度外。总算老天有眼，不绝忠良后代。又幸得韩厥将军拔剑相助，程婴才得死里逃生，救出这赵氏孤儿。不料屠岸贾狠如虎狼，毒如蛇蝎，竟要以晋国的所有新生小儿作代价换取赵氏孤儿。程婴头可断，血可流，但这赵氏孤儿决不能交。却又不忍心连累晋国千家万户，故而出此下策，还望老宰辅成全。"

公孙杵臼听了这一席话，感动得老泪纵横，慨然道："先生舍命破家，定下这救孤存赵的大计，可称义薄云天。老夫忝附骥尾，将这孤儿养大成人，教他报仇雪恨。"话音甫落，忽然又犹豫起来，摇头道："不妥，不妥。老夫当日在朝上时，与屠岸贾那贼子屡有冲撞，如今无缘无故去首告你，他岂肯相信！弄不好坏了大事，老夫死不足惜，只是贻误了救孤大计，不但你父子白白死了，也辜负了韩厥将军等人的厚望。"

great hopes of General Han Jue and the other martyrs!"

This left Cheng Ying nonplused. The two of them stood there for a while in silence, Gongsun Chujiu stroking his beard and deep in thought, and Cheng Ying wringing his hands in distress. Suddenly, Gongsun Chujiu asked his companion, "How old are you now, my friend?"

Puzzled at this abrupt inquiry, Cheng Ying replied, "Forty-five, sir."

"Excellent!" remarked the other. "You see, I am now 75 years old. If I am to raise the orphan until he is old enough to fulfill his destiny, that will take some 20 years. By that time, I will be 95. Who knows? If I die in the next ten years, the boy will still not have reached maturity, and will not be able to accomplish his task. But you, on the other hand, are much younger than I. Even after another 20 years, you will still not be as old as I am now, and you will be able to help him reach his life's appointed goal. Besides, you have never held a court position —— in the old days you were just a client in the household of Zhao Dun. So Tu'an Gu doesn't know you. I, on the other hand, have served three rulers, and together with the prime minister assisted in the business of government for a long time. We were the closest of friends, and foiled Tu'an Gu's schemes many times. It is obvious that he would never believe me no matter what I told him. If you are willing to sacrifice your own son, bring him here to me. Then report to Tu'an Gu that I was the one who spirited away Zhao the Orphan. He will send his men here to kill me and your baby, and that will be the end of the affair. You can then choose to live in some place where you can raise Zhao the Orphan, so that some day he will be ready to embark on his mission of vengeance."

Cheng Ying could not help but admire Gongsun Chujiu's exquisite reasoning. However, he was still inclined to stick to his original plan, until Gongsun Chujiu appealed top him, saying, "Please look at the matter this way: Each of us has his task to perform. Now, which is the most arduous — seeking death or raising the orphan?"

程婴听了公孙杵臼的话，目瞪口呆，一时无言。公孙杵臼将须沉思，久久不语，程婴在一旁看着只是搓手。过了半晌，公孙杵臼突然问程婴道："先生如今多大年纪了？"

程婴不解其意，只得答道："四十五岁了。"

公孙杵臼道："如此正好。老夫现在七十有五，将这孤儿抚养成人，报仇雪恨，总得有二十年光景，到那时老夫已经九十五岁，存亡未卜，倘若早死十年，孤儿尚未成人，又怎能去报仇雪恨！而你如今才四十五岁，再过二十年，也还不到老夫如今这把年纪，可以帮那孤儿完成使命。况且你不曾在朝中供职，当年在赵府也只是个门客，屠岸贾根本不认识你。而老夫是三朝老臣，久与相国同朝辅政，交情颇深，尽人皆知，又曾多次连手挫折那贼子，他岂肯轻信于我？先生若肯舍了自己的婴儿，就将他抱到太平庄来，交给老夫，再去京城向那屠岸贾出首，就说太平庄上公孙杵臼藏着赵氏孤儿，屠岸贾必定带了兵丁来围庄搜人，将老夫与你的小儿一齐处死，从此撂开了这件事。你可择地将赵氏孤儿抬举成人，再行大计，方是长久之策。"

程婴听了公孙杵臼的话，不禁感佩他思理细密，

Cheng Ying pondered for a short while, and then said, "Death is over quickly, but raising the orphan will take 20 years. Of the two, I would say that seeking death is the easier option."

Gongsun Chujiu clapped his hands, and laughed heartily. "Well said," he chortled. "And since I have been moldering away up to my neck in the yellow soil, I'll choose the easier option. You have many years of life ahead of you, and you are still full of vigor, so you should take on the onerous burden. What do you say to that?"

Cheng Ying protested, "But, sir, you have being living in seclusion here in Taiping Village for many years, in peace and contentment, avoiding the mundane world of state affairs. I have not the heart to ask you to submit to death, while a worthless man like myself shoulders such a great responsibility."

But Gongsun Chujiu retorted, "What kind of talk is that, my friend? I have one foot in the coffin already. Death awaits me just around the corner anyway. Besides, if Chu Ni, Ti Miming, Ling Zhe and Han Jue could so generously lay down their lives for the Zhao clan, with whom they had no connection, surely the time has come for me to repay the prime minister for his close friendship with me in the old days."

Seeing that the other's mind was made up, and realizing that he himself had a better chance of convincing Tu'an Gu, and thereby ensuring the success of their mission, Cheng Ying did not persist in opposing the old man, but said sadly, "Sir, your resoluteness in upholding justice at the cost of your life will shine for evermore in the annals of history. But Tu'an Gu is a cruel and ruthless man. He may put you to the most excruciating tortures to try to extract from you the truth about how Zhao the Orphan was snatched away from under his very nose. How could a man of your advanced years withstand harsh interrogation and savage torture? If that fiend Tu'an Gu succeeded in breaking your spirit and extracting the truth, both I and my son would die in vain, and, what would be much more tragic, the effort to save

只是于心不忍，依旧固执己见。公孙杵臼道："请问先生，我二人势必各担一项任务，其中是赴死容易还是抚孤艰巨？"

程婴想了片刻道："赴死只在须臾，抚孤则要忍辱二十年。两者相权，自然是赴死容易些儿。"

公孙杵臼拊掌大笑道："这就是了，老夫已是黄土埋到脖子上的人，就挑个容易的做。先生年富力强，就独任那艰巨的。如何？"

程婴道："老宰辅隐居在太平庄上，悠闲度日，不问世事。程婴不识进退，拿了这件大事来搅挠你，程婴心中已经十分过意不去，又怎能让老宰辅去赴死呢？"

公孙杵臼道："先生说的是哪里话！老夫一只脚已踏进棺材，死在旦夕，早些晚些又有何妨？况且那钼麑、提弥明、灵辄、韩厥等人与赵府并无亲谊，都能慷慨赴死，老夫当年与相国为生死之交，如今正是效力之时。"

程婴见公孙杵臼主意已定，何况如此也更容易取信于屠岸贾，成功的把握也大一些，所以不再坚持，只是忧虑道："老宰辅仗义轻生，定能流传千古，彪炳史册！只是屠岸贾那贼子心狠手辣，抓住大人后，定会痛下毒手，严刑拷打，追问盗孤藏孤的经过。大人已是这把年纪，怎能熬得过那三推六问、绷

Zhao the Orphan would be aborted. "

But Gongsun Chujiu only laughed at this argument. "You may set your mind at rest, " he assured his companion. "I may be old and decrepit, but a sturdy heart still beats in my breast. My pledge is unbreakable. No matter what tortures Tu'an Gu puts me through, he will not get a word out of me. I will resist till the end. "

The trials and fatigues of the past few days as he strove desperately to rescue Zhao the Orphan, and the knowledge that finally he was to lose the baby son he had always longed for, were too much for Cheng Ying, and he abandoned himself to a flood of tears. Gongsun Chujiu too wept. They clung to each other in their grief for a long time, until the older man wiped his streaming eyes, and spoke a few words of comfort to Cheng Ying, "Be assured that your fidelity and service to the Zhao clan, and as a noble benefactor of the State of Jin, will make your name splendid for all time to come. "

Cheng Ying likewise wiped away his tears. "It is because I cannot bear to see wickedness run rampant, riding roughshod over the good and loyal, that I have devoted myself to serving the country's cause and repaying private kindness. Now, the help I have asked you for, sir, means you going to your death of your own free will. I will make sure that in twenty years' time you are repaid for your sacrifice. "

Gongsun Chujiu replied, "To serve the country's cause and repay private kindness —— that is my long cherished wish. And today it has been fulfilled! " So saying, he sent his servant for wine, and he and Cheng Ying drank toasts to the day when Zhao the Orphan would grow to manhood and exact vengeance for the wrongs done to the Zhao clan; when all the treacherous officials would be beheaded; when sacrifices to the Zhao ancestors would be resumed; when Zhao the Orphan would reclaim his inheritance and wield power in the reformed court; and when the State of Jin would once more be a mighty power among the feudal states. Their spirits restored, they

扒吊拷？万一经受不住，如实供认，将程婴牵连在内。到时程婴父子死了没甚么要紧，只可惜这救孤存赵的大计从此中道而废了。"

公孙杵臼哈哈大笑道："先生放心去吧。老夫虽然已是枯皮朽骨，却还有一腔浩然正气，从来一诺千金。任凭屠岸贾那贼子摆出刀山油锅，我只给他一个不开口，岂会有始无终！"

程婴多日来为救孤存赵的大计来往奔波，竭尽心智，艰难险阻，不可胜数，又要舍却自己的儿子，心中自然有无限伤痛。如今终于有了着落，眼见得如无意外，大事必成，不禁感慨万分，胸怀中万般沉郁哀痛，顿时都化作泪水，像江河决堤一般滚涌而出，与公孙杵臼相拥痛哭。哭了半晌，公孙杵臼首先止泪，抚慰程婴道："先生一腔忠义，舍生忘死，乃赵氏恩人，晋国义士。将来必定名垂千古，光照万代。"

程婴拭泪道："小人只是忿恨奸佞逞凶，残害忠良，以此上报国家，下酬私恩。还仗老大人成全，慷慨赴死，才得成事。二十年后，程婴必当有报于老大人。"

公孙杵臼道："好一个上报国家，下酬私恩！也正是老夫夙愿，今日得偿。"说罢，命小奚童摆出酒来，与程婴举觥对饮，憧憬着二十年后赵氏孤儿长大成

encouraged each other to face their trials with confidence.

It was evening when they had finished discussing their plans. Because time was pressing, Cheng Ying proposed traveling back by night to substitute the babies for each other, and bring his own to Taiping Village. Gongsun Chujiu did not try to dissuade him, but on the contrary insisted on traveling with him.

So off these two stalwart men set. A crescent moon hung in the sky. A blustery wind blew from the mountains and made in the pine trees moan. The hearts of the travelers thumped uncontrollably, and the blood roared in their ears. Rounding a mountain, they came to a high plain. Cheng Ying took leave of his companion there, and continued his journey in the moonlight. Watching Cheng Ying's form fade into the distance, Gongsun Chujiu found it hard to suppress a feeling of turmoil in his breast, as scenes from the days when he and Zhao Dun, hand in hand, had battled evil flashed one by one before his eyes.

Duke Ling was not even ten years old when he succeeded to the throne. Shortly thereafter, his mother had been seized by a sudden fit of illness, and died. Now the boy was by nature tyrannical and cruel, and of extraordinary behavior. With his mother gone, and no one else in authority to restrain him, his conduct became more and more erratic; he simply did as he pleased. All day he indulged himself in the pastimes of hunting and cock fighting, together with low companions. He had a callous and brutal streak in him. The court officials observed this, and were fearful that when their ruler grew to manhood, he would turn out to be a profligate tyrant who would care nothing for the welfare of the state. Minister Gongsun Chujiu, being an upright official, did not hesitate to confront the duke with his neglect of duty. At one morning audience, he told the duke, "Filial piety is the basis of a ruler's management of the state. Now that Your Majesty's mother has passed away, Your Majesty should be putting on a display of mourning which would set an example for the common people. So how does it come

人，报仇雪恨，到那时奸臣授首，祭祀祖先，承袭父封，执掌权柄，重整朝纲，晋国威震诸侯的情景，不禁壮怀激烈，相互勉励。

二人商量已定，早到傍晚时分，因限期紧迫，程婴便要连夜下山将赵氏孤儿换了自己的儿子，再送到太平庄来。公孙杵臼也不劝阻，只相随着送他一程。

两位义士并肩走在山路上，一弯明月挂在天边，耳边只听着那山风汹涌，松涛澎湃，忍不住心如海潮，热血沸腾。绕过一处山坡，正是一片高地，程婴请公孙杵臼止步，自己踏着月色去了。公孙杵臼望着程婴远去的背影，心潮翻滚，难以平静。不由得想起多年前自己与赵盾共理朝政、携手抗奸的岁月，一桩桩，一件件，历历在目。

最早灵公初立，还不满十岁，不久之后生母穆嬴就暴病身亡。那灵公天生暴戾寡恩，动静无常，见母亲去世，再无人管束，越发行止乖张，随心所欲。成天走狗斗鸡，狎昵群小，全无悲戚之心，伤痛之状。朝中众大臣见了，不免担忧，惟恐他以后长成，不恤国政，荒淫暴虐。公孙杵臼生性刚直，便当面规谏，于一日早朝时道："主君治国当以孝为本，如今穆后仙逝，主

about that even before the late dowager's bones are cold Your Majesty should be devoting himself to frivolity. Even the common people strictly observe the mourning rites for a deceased parent; how much the more is it incumbent on Your Majesty to do so!"

The duke, who was used to a carefree round of pleasure and abandon, was stung by this rebuke, and would have retorted sharply had he not noticed that Zhao Dun and the other ministers were supporting Gongsun Chujiu in his censure. He did not want to incur the displeasure of the whole body of court officials. Besides, he remembered his mother telling him when he had first come to the throne that Zhao Dun had the power to depose him. So, for the time being he pretended to accept the criticism and to be prepared to mend his ways.

Following this incident, the more the duke thought about it, the more incensed he became. He was the sovereign of a state, after all, monarch of all he surveyed! How dare some petty official take him to task. If things went on like this, what would the world come to? Meanwhile, the cronies and hangers-on who surrounded the duke, seeing that their master was annoyed, seized the opportunity to ingratiate themselves with him by egging him on in his excesses. Duke Ling, already a shameless rake, took his scandalous behavior to extremes under the impact of this encouragement. Naturally, no good counsel could come from a muddle headed ruler surrounded by a coterie of rascals, and before long the pack of them were scheming to get Gongsun Chujiu dismissed from office and facing criminal charges.

A few days later, when Gongsun Chujiu presented a memorial to the throne at a morning audience, Duke Ling deliberately picked out a slight imperfection in the wording, and accused him of disrespect for his ruler and defiance of the ducal authority. He straightaway gave orders to have Gongsun Chujiu stripped of his post and thrown in the dungeons. At this, there was a cackle of approval from the villainous sycophants surrounding the

君当尽孝示哀，以为万民表率。哪里有生母尸骨未寒，儿子便玩乐无度的？枉说主君现在是一国之君，就是平民百姓，家中父母去世，也要依礼服丧，不敢轻忽。"

灵公整日嬉乐，正觉得畅快无比，听了公孙杵臼这几句诤言，十分刺耳，想要发落他几句，却见上卿赵盾等人都纷纷附和公孙，指责自己的不是。知道众怒难犯，又常听母亲说起当年自己即位时的情景，知道赵盾操着废立大权，一时不敢得罪，只好表示改过。

事后越想越气，自己本是一国之主，君临天下，区区一个中大夫也敢教训自己，如此下去，这天下岂不成了他们的了？身边群小见主君不乐，难免趁虚而入，怂恿挑唆。灵公本来就是无恩无义之人，经群小挑逗，越发按捺不住。昏君佞臣凑在一处，哪里能想出什么好主意来，便商量着要找个借口将公孙杵臼罢免官职，罚为罪人。

数日之后，公孙杵臼在早朝时奏事，灵公便故意挑毛病，说他是目无国君，以下犯上，当下就要将公孙杵臼免官，命甲士押去筑城。几个奸臣也七嘴八舌地帮腔，述说公孙杵臼的不是。眼看着公孙杵臼就要沦为阶下囚，赵盾在一旁冷眼旁观，早已明白灵公是

throne. But just as Gongsun Chujiu was about to be led away, Zhao Dun stepped forward from the ranks of the ministers. He had been watching the situation closely, and knew well that Duke Ling was getting revenge for his humiliation of a few days previously. Now he intervened, saying, "Your Majesty, as the lord of your people and the ruler of the state, it behoves you to set an example of filial piety by observing the rites and carrying out the ceremonies fitting to the memory of your recently deceased mother. But you seem to be completely untouched by grief, spending your days gallivanting and sporting to your heart's content. If you continue in this way, how can you gain the trust and sympathy of the common people? I appeal to you, Minister Gongsun is your loyal servant, who gives you honest advice. All for the sake of the State of Jin, he yearns to turn you from the crooked path onto the straight one. But Your Majesty, I am afraid, refuses to heed loyal words, instead lending an ear constantly to the treacherous urgings of base men, and heaping injustices upon true hearted officials. I am very much afraid that you may be following in the doom directed footsteps of the tyrants Jie of Xia and Zhou of Shang. The result will be the ruin of the State of Jin!"

Duke Ling blushed to the roots of his hair. He could find no words to reply to this diatribe of Zhao Dun's, and nor could his gaggle of cronies. The duke had no choice but to rescind his order, and there the matter rested and festered.

Gongsun Chujiu was overcome with gratitude for Zhao Dun's bold intervention, and the two men became the closest of friends from that time on. As the influence of Tu'an Gu over Duke Ling grew, with the former inciting the latter to ever grosser acts of dissipation, Gongsun Chujiu and Zhao Dun worked in close coordination to denounce the duke's excesses. As a result, the two of them earned a wide ranging reputation for virtue. But finally, seeing that his admonitions were all in vain and that Tu'an Gu's evil influence was waxing by the day, unable to bear his indignation any longer, Gongsun Chujiu took the bold step of resigning his post and going to live in

为了前几日的事发作，当下出列道："主君身为万姓之主，一国之君，母后去世，理应遵从礼教，举哀尽孝。如今略无悲戚之意，成日嬉戏游乐，无所不至。如此下去，又怎能体恤百姓，感化万民？这也罢了，中大夫公孙大人一片忠心，直言规谏，希望主君改邪归正，正是为了晋国好。主君不纳忠言，已是不该，又受小人的怂恿，无故加罪于良臣。微臣实在担心主君会重蹈夏桀、商纣的覆辙，导致晋国的衰亡。"

灵公被赵盾揭破心思，面红耳赤，一时说不出话来。几个奸臣见状，也不敢再多说什么。最后还是灵公自己找个台阶下，收回成命，答应改过，此事也就不了了之。

公孙杵臼感激赵盾正直无畏，挺身而出，搭救自己，自此二人结为生死之交。以后屠岸贾渐渐得势，怂恿着灵公胡作非为，公孙杵臼与赵盾桴鼓相应，屡屡规谏，颇得朝野称道。后来自己因见灵公屡谏不改，屠岸贾为恶日甚，终于一怒辞官，激流勇退，回到太平庄过起了隐居生活。如今想来，却有几分惭愧。倘若自己当时也像赵盾那样鞠躬尽瘁，二人戮力同心，或许能挽狂澜于既倒，也不至于让灵公和屠岸贾如此倒行逆施，残害忠良。而今悔之已晚，只能献身于救

obscurity in Taiping Village. But he still had lingering regrets that he had not been as unyielding as Zhao Dun, and continued to join forces with him. Perhaps they could have curbed some of the wild excesses of Duke Ling and Tu'an Gu, and reined in their persecution of good men? But it was too late for regrets, Gongsun Chujiu now reminded himself. The only thing for him was to devote himself heart and soul to the saving of Zhao the Orphan, and in that way remain true to the friendship he had shared with Zhao Dun in the old days.

These old memories stirred a flood of noble sentiments in the breast of Gongsun Chujiu. He looked up at the waning moon. It looked like a sharp curved dagger. The fancy came into his head of plucking it out of the sky and plunging it into the breast of Tu'an Gu. The wailing of the wind in the pines seemed to become the roar of a lion shaking the forests and the gorges, and gradually become a fire of hatred blazing in Gongsun Chujiu's heart. He thought ahead to his thundering denunciation of Tu'an Gu, to his walk to death undaunted. This would be the way he would vent his rage, and leave behind a heroic name for all eternity.

As he stood there lost in thought, the moon dipped and the stars dimmed. Morning dew gathered on his clothing. Only then did he turn, and plod the lonely way back to his cottage.

孤存赵的大计,也算不枉当年与赵盾的交情了。

公孙杵臼追忆往事,心潮澎湃,豪情顿生。抬头看那一弯残月,竟像一把利刃,恨不能手持着刺穿屠岸贾的胸膛。侧耳静听松涛,也一变往日的韵律,仿佛雄狮咆哮,响震林木深谷,渐渐弥漫成一团怒火,在自己的心中燃烧。公孙杵臼由此畅想着来日怒斥奸贼,慷慨赴死的情景,到时出这一口怒气,留下万世英名。

他站在山间想了很久很久,直到月落星黯,晨露沾衣,这才踽踽独行,走回茅舍……

赵氏孤儿

Chapter Six
The Noble Death of Gongsun Chujiu

Cheng Ying walked all night, until he arrived at the village of Guojia-zhuang. He lost no time explaining to his father-in-law and wife the ruse he had worked out with Gongsun Chujiu. He dared not linger too long, and so, after handing over Zhao the Orphan to his wife and putting his own baby son in the medicine box, despite his wife's great reluctance to part with her offspring, he set off immediately on his return journey.

Cheng Ying reached Taiping Village towards evening of the next day. As he caught sight of Gongsun Chujiu's dwelling, there came to his ears the clear twang of a zither. Knowing that the performer must be Gongsun Chujiu, he stopped to listen. At first the notes were like the murmuring of a sequestered brook, or the trickling of a stream across a sandy bed; before long, the strings sent forth a more lively air, reminiscent of the gurgling of waters in spring or the waves rippling across the surface of a pond; then came the crescendo, just like the shattering of silver bottles and the spilling of liquid, the springing forth of cavalry and the clash of swords and lances —— in short, it contained the discordant sounds of battle. Finally, all the strings sounded in harmony, making one think of a bright moon reflected on the e-merald waves of a calm sea. An old saying goes, "The sound of the zither arouses elegant thoughts." According to another, "The zither reproduces the sounds of the heartstrings." The notes of the zither told Cheng Ying that Gongsun Chujiu had made up his mind to face death. The thought filled him with unbearable sorrow. Without more ado, he rushed into the house. The

第六章 公孙死义

　　程婴连夜下山，赶回郭家庄，将与公孙杵臼商量好的结果向郭善人及郭氏说了一遍，不敢在家中停留，将赵氏孤儿交给郭氏，将自己的儿子放入药箱，连夜又赶回太平庄去了。其间郭氏不忍娇儿送死，恋恋不舍；程婴昼夜兼程，往返奔波等情形自不必细述。

　　且说程婴带着小儿，于次日傍晚回到太平庄上，眼见得到了公孙杵臼院门外时，忽听到一阵激越的琴声，知道是公孙杵臼正在抚琴，便停下脚步，侧耳静听。只听那琴声起始犹如幽泉呜咽，溪水下滩；片刻后弦促声急，仿佛春水暗涨，池面生波；再到后来，那声律愈发急促，宛如银瓶乍破，水浆迸裂，铁骑突出，刀枪齐鸣，隐隐杂有杀伐之声；最后数弦和鸣，令人依稀望见海上明月，碧涛潮生。古人云：闻弦歌而知雅意。又说：琴为心声。程婴从琴声中得知公孙杵臼心意已决，视死如归，不禁心中一阵怆然。此时已容不得多想，举步进屋。二人再度见面，自然又有一番勉励。掐指一算，离榜文所定期限，已无多时。程婴

two of them exchanged words of comfort, and then, as time limit set out in the notices was drawing near, Cheng Ying deposited his own son comfortably in Gongsun Chujiu's cottage, ate a hasty breakfast, and set off for the capital of Jin.

Having accepted the baby boy, Gongsun Chujiu began to reflect on the situation, First of all, if he allowed Tu'an Gu to find the baby too easily, it would arouse that cunning fox's suspicions. It would be better to lay a bit of a false trail in order to fool him. At noon the next day, calculating that Tu'an Gu must be drawing near by this time, Gongsun Chujiu climbed a high hill to watch for his approach. Sure enough, before long he espied in the distance a troop of several hundred horsemen. So, Tu'an Gu must have believed Cheng Ying's story, and had dispatched troops to recover Zhao the Orphan! He hurried back to the cottage, hid the child in a cave behind the house, and sat down to await events, to all appearances quite at leisure.

Meanwhile, after ordering the posters to be put up and dispatching spies all over the capital, Tu'an Gu had also been waiting. After a few days, when nobody surrendered Zhao the Orphan or denounced the kidnapper, and when his spies returned with nothing to show for their efforts, Tu'an Gu came to the end of his patience. "Very well," he growled to himself, "if this wretched populace chooses to defy me, I'll put all their brats to death!" He thereupon ordered more posters to be made, and pasted up at the appropriate time. They read:

"Every infant below the age of six months, whether born to an official family or that of a private citizen, within the territory of the State of Jin must be handed over to the office of the commander of the palace guard within three days. Penalty for disobedience: execution of the family to the ninth degree of kinship."

This done, he immediately sent men to search every house for children of the targeted age. Before long, one of his guards announced that a man

略微躺了一躺，见天色已经放亮，匆匆起身，吃了早饭，便下山往绛邑而去。

公孙杵臼送走程婴后，将孩子安顿妥当，忽地想到若让那屠岸贾轻易找到小儿，难免引起他的疑心，不如设些波澜曲折，反倒易于骗得他深信不疑。次日中午一过，公孙杵臼估摸着屠岸贾应该赶到了，便站在高处眺望，不大一会儿功夫，果然远远地望见数百铁骑乌云一般卷到。知道是程婴出头首告，已赚得屠岸贾带兵到此。急忙奔回草房，将婴儿藏入屋后的山洞，自己则从容不迫地在房内等候。

且说屠岸贾自张出榜文，便在府中坐等，同时暗中派人在绛邑城中及四郊打探消息。过了三四天，既不见有人来献出赵氏孤儿，也没有人前来出首，派出去打探消息的人回来，亦是一无所获。屠岸贾见状，心中不免焦躁，咬牙道："刁民胆敢抗命，我索性将国内小儿杀个干净！"于是差人写了数十张告示，只等时间一到，便在全国各地贴出。那榜文上写得是：

晋国境内所有官民人家，凡有半岁以下的小儿，一律于三日内交到司寇府中。违者全家抄斩，九族不留。

布置已毕，屠岸府上下，一片肃然。屠岸贾则忙着安排人手，准备挨门挨户搜捕小儿。忽然门上卒子

named Cheng Ying had come to make a denunciation. "He says that he knows the whereabouts of Zhao the Orphan, sir!"

Tu'an Gu was as delighted as if someone had brought him a treasure. "Show him in at once," he ordered.

The person who was ushered into Tu'an Gu's presence was short of stature, had a swarthy face and bore a serene expression on his face. It was none other than Cheng Ying.

Tu'an Gu put on a show of sternness. "Who are you?" he barked.

His visitor replied, "My name is Cheng Ying. I live in Guojiazhuang Village in the suburbs of Jiangyi. I am a physician by profession."

"You say that you have come to make a denunciation. Where is Zhao the Orphan?"

"The child is concealed in the house of Gongsun Chujiu, in Taiping Village, Your Honor."

Tu'an Gu was by nature suspicious, crafty and sly. His first reaction was to smell something fishy about this report. With a slight frown creasing his brows, he inquired, "How does a country doctor like you come by news of Zhao the Orphan?"

Unperturbed, Cheng Ying replied, "I often go to Mount Shouyang to pick herbs, Your Honor. I have met Gongsun Chujiu several times. Yesterday, while coming back from a herb-hunting trip, I happened to call in at his house for a drink of water. I was surprised to see a baby there, wrapped in a brocaded silk coverlet. Now I know that Gongsun Chujiu is over 70 years old, and his wife is deceased. Moreover, they never had children. So, I asked myself, where did that baby come from? I remembered seeing a poster that Your Honor had had pasted up, so I asked him point-blank, 'Is this the child they call Zhao the Orphan?' He turned pale with fear, and was speechless. And so from that I concluded that he was the one who had kidnapped Zhao the Orphan."

来报："大人，门外有个叫程婴的前来首告，说是他知道赵氏孤儿在那里。"

屠岸贾一听，不禁喜上眉梢，如获至宝，急忙道："快传他进来！"

不一会儿，一个身材矮小、面目黎黑、表情沉稳的汉子被带到厅上，此人正是程婴。屠岸贾声色俱厉地问道："你是何人？"

程婴答道："小人名叫程婴，家住绛邑城外郭家庄上，以行医为生。"

屠岸贾又问："那赵氏孤儿现在何处？"

程婴道："在太平庄上公孙杵臼家里藏匿。"

屠岸贾生性多疑，双眉微微一蹙，问道："你不过是一个草泽医生，如何知道赵氏孤儿的消息？"

程婴从容不迫道："小人常去那首阳山采药，在太平庄上歇脚，与公孙杵臼有数面之交。昨日小人从首阳山采药下来，路过太平庄，到公孙杵臼家中讨些水喝，忽见他房中锦绸包裹着一个婴儿。小人想，公孙杵臼已年过七十，妻子逝世，一生无儿无女，这孩儿是从哪里来的？小人日前曾在镇上见过司寇大人张贴的榜文，要人交出赵氏孤儿，于是便问他：'这小儿莫不是赵氏孤儿？'谁知那公孙杵臼听了，顿时震恐色变。故此小人断定是公孙杵臼将赵氏孤儿藏匿。"

But Tu'an Gu was not so easily convinced. "You lying wretch! How dare you come to me with such a cock and bull story?"

"I assure you, Your Honor, that every word I have said is the truth. If you do not believe me, why not send men to Taiping Village to find out?"

A grimace crossed Tu'an Gu's countenance. "What I want to know," he said, "Is why you are so eager to inform on Gongsun Chujiu, a man against whom you have never had a grievance in the past and do not have a grievance now. Perhaps the two of you are trying to pull the wool over my eyes, eh? Well, if you are telling the truth, all right. But if you are not, I have a sharp sword with which to deal with the likes of you." So saying, he drew his sword from its scabbard with a menacing swoosh, and brandished it under Cheng Ying's nose.

Cheng Ying was prepared for this kind of reception. He knew that Tu'an Gu would bluster and try to frighten him. So he pretended to be intimidated, and whined, "I beg Your Honor not to be angry with me, but to hear me out. It is true, sir, that I have no grievance against Gongsun Chujiu. But I read a notice that Your Honor had had posted, to the effect that if Zhao the Orphan were not found, then all the infants in the State of Jin would be put to death. Now, for three generations there has only been one son in my family. I am now in my 45th year, and have at last managed to produce a son and heir, who is not yet one month old. My wife, who is of a frail disposition, carried him for ten months, and it was a difficult birth. Naturally, she regards him as a precious treasure. If I comply with Your Honor's command, it would mean the extinction of the Cheng line, would it not? So my reason for informing on Gongsun Chujiu is not to save the lives of the other babies of Jin, but to ensure the continuity of my family tree."

As he spoke, Cheng Ying remembered the fate that awaited his child, and tears of grief accompanied his last words.

屠岸贾听罢，忽然脸色一变，喝道："大胆匹夫，你怎敢欺瞒本官？"

程婴道："小人之言，句句是实。大人如若不信，可派人去太平庄上查看。"

屠岸贾冷笑两声，道："我问你，你与公孙杵臼往日无冤，近日无仇，因何要首告他藏着赵氏孤儿？你二人敢是串通了来骗本官？你若是说得在理，万事皆休；说得不在理，我磨快利剑，先斩了你这刁民！"说着，"呛啷"一声，将青锋宝剑拔出鞘来，逼上一步。

程婴早已想到屠岸贾不会轻信，必然对自己装腔作势，虚声恫吓。当下故作惊恐，低声下气道："求元帅暂息雷霆之怒，略罢虎狼之威，听小人诉说原委。小人确与公孙杵臼无冤无仇，只因元帅张出榜文，说是若然找不着赵氏孤儿，便要将全国的小儿统统拘到帅府，尽行诛戮。小人家里三代单传，一向子嗣艰难。今年已经四十有五，千辛万苦，方得了一个儿子，还不满一月。妻子郭氏，素来多病，十月怀胎，实属不易，自然将儿子视若珍宝。可是元帅下令，到时不敢不献出来。若献出来时，我程家不是要绝后了吗？故而我今日来首告公孙杵臼，虽说是为了救晋国的小儿，其实是为了保全程家的后代。"程婴说着，想起自己的儿子行将送命，不由得悲从中来，声泪俱下。

This display of anguish, together with the plausible explanation he had heard from Cheng Ying, more or less convinced the morbidly suspicious Tu'an Gu.

He said, "In the past, Gongsun Chujiu was a colleague at court with Zhao Dun. The two of them were as thick as thieves, and constantly ganged up against me. Having learned of the massacre of the Zhao clan, I suppose he was anxious to raise Zhao the Orphan himself. But he has been in retirement for many years. Without inside help, how could he manage to get the child away?"

As he spoke, he fixed an accusing gaze on Cheng Ying. But the latter was unperturbed. "That I don't know, Your Honor," he replied. "But, as the saying goes, 'The longer the night the more the dreams.' I am afraid that if you delay, Your Honor, the bird may fly the coop."

"All right," said Tu'an Gu. You lead the way. I'll arrest that old fellow Gongsun first, and decide what to do later."

He thereupon gave the necessary orders, and before long a troop of several hundred mounted men, with Tu'an Gu in full armor at their head, was trotting down the road towards Taiping Village, banners flying and swords and pikes gleaming. As they passed, the bystanders averted their eyes in fear.

At their head was Cheng Ying, riding a donkey led by a servant of Tu'an Gu's household. He doggedly led the way, not daring to betray an inkling of the pain and anger in his heart. Reaching Taiping Village after noon, Tu'an Gu ordered his men to put a tight guard on Gongsun Chujiu's house, and then to go in and find Zhao the Orphan and bring Gongsun Chujiu before him.

The soldiers smashed down the gate, and poured into the cottage. Before long, they dragged Gongsun Chujiu out, tightly bound. Their captain went down on one knee before Tu'an Gu, and reported, "Sir, we only found this old man in the cottage. There was no sign of Zhao the Orphan."

屠岸贾虽然狡诈多疑，但听了这番解释，觉得入情入理，又见程婴泪流满面，也就信了三分，道："公孙杵臼当年与那赵盾老儿是一殿朝臣，颇有些交情，又曾屡次搭帮着与我作对，如今见我杀了赵盾一家，自然要代他抚育这赵氏孤儿。只是他多年隐居，若无人作内应，怎能盗出这赵氏孤儿？"

说着，死死地盯着程婴不放。程婴道："这个小人也不知晓，只是那婴儿确实在太平庄上。"

屠岸贾道："也好，就着你来给我带路。"

当下传令集合本部人马，直奔太平庄，捉拿那公孙杵臼。屠岸贾一身戎装，亲自挂帅。只见旌旗蔽空，刀枪林立，一路上风驰电掣，路上的行人见了，莫不侧目而视。

程婴骑着屠岸府家人牵来的一头驴子，走在队伍前面，虽然心中悲愤交集，脸面上却不敢流露半点儿。晌午过后，人马来到太平庄上，屠岸贾一声令下，众甲士里三重，外三重，将公孙杵臼的住处围了个水泄不通。屠岸贾下令道："左右进去搜出孤儿，并将那公孙老儿捉来见我！"

众兵丁打破屋门，冲了进去。不一会儿，便将公孙杵臼五花大绑押出屋来。一名小头目屈膝禀道："报元帅，屋中只有这老儿一人，并不见那赵氏孤儿。"

Tu'an Gu motioned to the soldiers to fall back. He gave a sinister chuckle. "Well," he said to Gongsun Chujiu, "Even at your advanced age you are impatient to meddle in affairs which don't concern you, eh? Do you know what crime you have committed?"

Gongsun Chujiu answered, "I have been living in seclusion, Your Honor, with only the forests and mountains for company. What crime could I have committed? I really don't understand why you have mobilized this great armed force to arrest a harmless old fellow like me."

"Old man," said Tu'an Gu, "You have played a sly trick right under my very nose. Tell me, In the days after the posters were put up by the court, and a search was being made throughout the State of Jin for the orphan, and the country was in an uproar, why did you set yourself up against me and hide Zhao the Orphan?"

Gongsun Chujiu uttered a mirthless laugh. "So it's Zhao the Orphan you are after, is it?" he cried. "I really can't help you there, I'm afraid. Even if I ate the heart of a bear and drank the bile of a leopard, I would still not have the courage to kidnap Zhao the Orphan."

The old man's dignified denial of any wrongdoing enraged his captor. His eyes bulging with fury, he roared, "It seems that you need a good beating before you'll confess." Then, turning to his guards, said, "Come here you men, and give this doddering old fool a sound thrashing!"

His minions rushed to do his bidding. Throwing Gongsun Chujiu to the ground, they started to beat him with clubs.

Just then, a squad of soldiers who had been searching the cottage and its surroundings returned to report that no trace of the baby could be found.

This only increased Tu'an Gu's frustration, and he ordered that Gongsun Chujiu be beaten even harder, until he revealed the whereabouts of Zhao the Orphan.

屠岸贾摆手命甲士退下，"嘿嘿"冷笑道："好你个公孙老儿，竟敢在太岁头上动土，真是活得不耐烦了。你可知罪么？"

公孙杵臼抬头反问道："老夫隐居乡野，与林木作伴，以山水为友，何罪之有？不知司寇大人因何兴师动众来抓捕老夫？"

屠岸贾道："公孙老儿，你竟然胆敢在本官面前耍滑头！我问你，朝廷张榜数日，在国内搜捕那赵氏孤儿，天下莫不震动。你为何公然与本官作对，窝藏那赵氏孤儿？"

公孙杵臼冷笑一声道："原来元帅是为赵氏孤儿而来，那老夫就越发莫名其妙了。我公孙杵臼纵然吃了熊心，饮了豹胆，又怎敢藏匿赵氏孤儿？"

屠岸贾见公孙杵臼不卑不亢，一口否认，心中不觉大怒，眼睛瞪得铜铃一般，喝道："看来你是不打不招。来人哪，给我狠狠打这老儿！"

众甲士闻命，扑上前来，将公孙杵臼按倒在地，舞着棍棒打了起来。正在行刑，又一群甲士在草屋内外搜了一遍，空手来禀道："回元帅，房前房后细细搜过了，并不见婴儿。"

屠岸贾听了这话，越发恼羞成怒，道："给我狠狠地打，问这老儿将赵氏余孽藏到哪里去了？"

As he did so, he gave Cheng Ying a suspicious sideways glance. The latter felt a shiver of fear run through him. He looked furtively at Gongsun Chujiu, and saw that the old man was withstanding the beating stoically. Suddenly, he had an idea. Turning to Tu'an Gu, he said, "Your Honor, this is a region of high mountains and thick forests. Perhaps the old man has hidden the baby somewhere in the vicinity?" This made sense to Tu'an Gu, and he immediately dispatched men to search the countryside round about.

While they were doing so, Gongsun Chujiu said nothing, despite the savage beating he was receiving. But he only uttered, "If you think I have hidden Zhao the Orphan, tell me, who was it saw me do so?"

Whereupon, Tu'an Gu sneered, "It was Cheng Ying here who informed on you."

A look of indignation came over Gongsun Chujiu's face, and he yelled at Cheng Ying, "You infamous villain, Cheng Ying! How many times have I shown you hospitality? Have I ever done anything to harm you? And this is how you repay me for my kindness! With vile slander, you cur!"

Cheng Ying endured this condemnation with lowered head. Not a word did he utter, putting on a show of embarrassment. Gongsun Chujiu kept on pouring out a stream of invective.

In the meantime, Tu'an Gu was getting more and more impatient. He muttered, "If this stubborn old dotard doesn't confess soon, I'll die of apoplexy."

He whirled round on Cheng Ying, who was standing mute nearby, and suspicion stirred within him once more. Frowning, he thought of a new tactic. In a crafty tone of voice, he said to Cheng Ying, "This situation has come about because of your report. Now you beat the old man, and if he doesn't confess you will bear the blame."

说罢，转头用一双贼溜溜的眼睛扫视程婴。程婴心中微微一惊，偷眼再看公孙杵臼，见他忍痛受刑，正气凛然，没有丝毫动摇的迹象。暗暗一想，忽然明白了什么，便向屠岸贾说道："元帅，此地山高林密，莫不是公孙杵臼为了躲避搜查，将婴儿藏到山中去了？"一语提醒了屠岸贾，当下派出甲士搜山。众甲士不敢怠慢，四散开来，拨草分茅，细细搜查起来。

这里屠岸贾继续严刑拷问公孙杵臼，棍棒像雨点儿似的落到公孙杵臼身上，痛入骨髓。公孙杵臼忍痛质问道："你说我藏着赵氏孤儿，是谁见来？"

屠岸贾冷笑道："是程婴出首告发你的。"

公孙杵臼闻言，一脸怒色，大声骂道："好你个程婴，往日来到太平庄上，饮水吃饭，我从不曾亏待过你。而今你竟然恩将仇报，诬人清白，真乃小人也！"

程婴听公孙杵臼大骂自己，只低头不语，做出一副无地自容的样子。公孙杵臼依旧骂不绝口，千"小人"，万"贼子"，将程婴骂得狗血喷头。

屠岸贾见状，愈加恼怒，咬牙切齿道："这老儿死不肯招认，真是气死本官了！"转过头看见程婴在一旁默然不语，似有悲戚之状，不禁疑窦丛生，眉头一皱，计上心来，阴阳怪气地道："程婴，现在就让你来打这公孙老儿，他若不招，本官可要拿你问罪！"

Cheng Ying gazed at Gongsun Chujiu's torn and bleeding flesh. The idea of inflicting even more pain on his friend, by his own hand, horrified him. In a panic he appealed to Tu'an Gu, "Your Honor, I am only a poor country doctor. I am physically weak——why, I don't even have the strength to truss a chicken! Besides, my disposition is to do good. How could I beat somebody? I beg you to rescind your order, and think of some other way."

But Tu'an Gu was unmoved. "Cheng Ying, if you are squeamish about hurting Gongsun Chujiu, I will have to think that it's because you are afraid that he will point an accusatory finger at yourself," was his bland response.

At this, Cheng Ying realized that Tu'an Gu was suspicious of his own role in the affair. There was nothing for it but to steel himself to beat his friend. "Very well, Your Honor," he said.

Picking up a thin stick from the ground, he stepped forward. But Tu'an Gu snorted. "I see that you are careful to choose a club no thicker than a chopstick. So you must be afraid that he'll denounce you if you hurt him!"

Cheng Ying then put the thin twig down, and picked up a thick cudgel. However, the paranoid Tu'an Gu snarled, "Aha! So that's it! You picked up the thin one, hoping that if you did not hurt him he would not betray your complicity in his crime. Now you pick up a thick one, hoping to kill him with it, so that he can't reveal your guilt!"

Cheng Ying was flabbergasted. "Your Honor," he cried, "If the thin one was no good, and the thick one is no good, do you want me to beat him or not?"

"Cheng Ying, stop dithering!" was the reply. "Choose a stick which is neither too thin nor too thick, and get on with it."

Cheng Ying did as he was ordered. Suppressing his distaste for what he was about to do, he began to beat Gongsun Chujiu. The old man, knowing how distressful this must be to Cheng Ying, thought of a ruse to remove

程婴见公孙杵臼早已被打得皮开肉绽，遍体鳞伤，心中正在伤痛，哪里肯亲自动手，雪上加霜，便惊惶失措道："元帅，小人是个草泽医生，生来孱弱，手无缚鸡之力，心有好生之德，怎能行杖打人？恳求元帅收回成命，另想办法。"

屠岸贾道："程婴，你不敢行杖，想来是怕打疼了他将你指攀出来。"

程婴听罢，心知屠岸贾已经起了疑心，不敢再辩，只得硬着头皮道："元帅既如此说，小人行杖打他便是。"

说毕，从地上捡起一根细木棍来，走上前去。屠岸贾却奸笑数声道："你挑来拣去，竟拿起这么一根筷子一般的细棍，莫非是怕打痛了他，攀出你来不成！"

程婴正是不忍下手打痛了公孙杵臼，听屠岸贾如此说，担心屠岸贾看出破绽，忙将细木棍放下，又拿起一根粗木棍来。屠岸贾在一旁看着，又道："你刚才只拣细的，现在你却拿起这根大棍子来，敢怕是想一棍打死了他，来个杀人灭口，死无对证吗？"

程婴左右不是，只得恳求道："小人拿细棍不对，拿粗棍也不对，元帅还是不要让小人行杖便是了。"

屠岸贾道："你就拿那不粗不细的木棍来打。"

程婴只得如言重又挑了一根木棍，狠下心肠，打了

Tu'an Gu's suspicions. Pretending to swoon with pain, when he came to he cried out, "Oh, that was the worst beating I have had to endure so far. Which devil is beating me now?"

Delighted, Tu'an Gu informed him that his tormentor was the man who had informed on him, Cheng Ying.

Gongsun Chujiu raised his head, and glared at Cheng Ying. "There is no quarrel between us, so why are you beating me so savagely?"

Cheng Ying retorted, "You had better confess quickly, Mr Gongsun, to save yourself more suffering."

"Don't talk nonsense," said Gongsun Chujiu. "Why are you trying to pin all the blame on me when you know perfectly well where Zhao the Orphan is?"

Cheng Ying was terrified when he heard these words, and began to tremble from head to toe. He hastily stammered, "The old man has had all his brains beaten out of him, talking like that."

Seeing that not even the prospect of death would make Gongsun Chujiu confess, Tu'an Gu lost all patience. He seized a club himself, and belabored the old man with it. With a pitiful cry, Gongsun Chujiu swooned. Some of the guards fetched a bucket of water, and doused Gongsun Chujiu's head. This revived him somewhat. He mumbled incoherently, "The two of us, . . . together. . . . " Then he lost consciousness again.

Cheng Ying's heart skipped a beat. The alarming thought came to him that Gongsun Chujiu had been beaten so badly that he was talking in a delirium. If that was so, then he might blurt out the truth, and their plan to save Zhao the Orphan would be wrecked.

He blenched at the prospect, and, noticing the doctor's sudden confusion, Tu'an Gu became convinced that some trick was being played on him. "Old man Gongs's stubbornness has finally been broken. He is ready to tell us who his accomplice is, I think."

起来。公孙杵臼将一切都看在眼里,知道程婴是迫不得已,便想为他开脱,故作昏晕,大骂道:"啊呀,挨了这半天打,不似这几棍疼。是哪个狠毒的奸贼在打我?"

屠岸贾得意地叫道:"是首告你的程婴行刑。"

公孙杵臼抬头怒视程婴道:"我与你无冤无仇,为何苦苦相逼,下此毒手?"

程婴道:"公孙大人,我劝你还是快快招供了吧!"

公孙杵臼道:"你不由分说,打得我无处可逃,莫不是你知道那孤儿在何处,却故意往我身上栽赃?"

程婴闻言大惊道:"这老儿被打得说起胡话来了。"

屠岸贾见公孙杵臼抵死不肯招认,心中好不耐烦,自己操起一根木棍,狠命打下,公孙杵臼惨叫一声,晕了过去。一旁的甲士提过一桶冷水,泼在他头上,公孙杵臼打了一个激灵,苏醒过来,迷迷糊糊地道:"我二人一同……"

说了半句,却又咽住了。程婴听公孙杵臼说出这半句话来,心中委实吓了一跳,暗想:"莫不是公孙大人被打得不省人事,昏迷中要说出真相。"

想到这里,不禁心中大恐,脸色剧变。屠岸贾本来就有些疑心,见程婴神色有几分不尴不尬,越发疑云陡生,道:"公孙老儿毕竟不吃打,如今快要供出同谋来了。"

Thereupon, he bent down, and shouted in Gongsun Chujiu's ear, "Old man, just now you said something about 'the two of us together.' Who's the other one? Tell the truth, and I'm prepared to let you live."

The corners of Gongsun Chujiu's mouth twitched. The words came haltingly, "I ... I ... two of us. ..."

The terrified Cheng Ying hastened to interrupt him before he said anything more. "Mr Gongsun," he cried sternly, "Everyone is responsible for his own actions. Don't try to shift the blame onto someone else."

Tu'an Gu gave a hollow chuckle, turned to Cheng Ying, and said, "I think you must be the other person involved, Cheng Ying. Otherwise why are you quaking in your shoes like that?"

With an ingratiating smile wreathing his face, Cheng Ying said, "The old man has been beaten so badly he doesn't know what he is saying, Your Honor."

At this point, Gongsun Chujiu revived again. "What do you have to be afraid of, Cheng Ying?" he asked. "I wasn't implicating you."

Tu'an Gu yelled at him, "If Cheng Ying wasn't one of the two people you mentioned, who was the other one?"

"You have had me beaten so severely, Your Honor, that I hardly know what I am saying," was Gongsun Chujiu's reply. "I don't remember saying anything about two people."

Infuriated, Tu'an Gu drew his sword. Bellowing, "You old reprobate, how dare you trifle with me?" he was just about to chop Gongsun Chujiu's head off when one of his men came running down the mountainside, carrying a baby. "Sir," he cried, "I found this boy child in a cave on the hillside behind the old man's cottage. I think it's that Zhao the Orphan."

On the spot, Tu'an Gu's anger turned to joy. He grabbed the infant, and thrust it before Gongsun Chujiu's face, saying with a wicked smile, "Well, Mr Gongsun Chujiu, do you still deny any role in this affair? Since there is nobody else living around here, I wonder who could have concealed

弯下腰去，凑在公孙杵臼耳边，高声道："公孙老儿，你方才说'二人一同'，你二人一同作什么，那一个人是谁?你如实说了，本府留你一条性命!"

公孙杵臼断断续续道："我……二人……"

程婴惟恐公孙杵臼说漏了嘴，在一旁道："公孙大人，一人做事一人当，你休得冤枉好人。"

屠岸贾怪笑一声，回头对程婴道："程婴，莫非这二人里面有你一个吗?为何惊慌失措?"

程婴满面委屈道："这老儿被打糊涂了，难免要胡说八道。"

这时公孙杵臼清醒过来，道："程婴，你惊慌什么?我又不曾指攀你。"

屠岸贾闻言大怒道："你方才还说是'二人一同'，既非程婴，那一个是谁?"

公孙杵臼道："老夫是叫你打糊涂了，何曾说过'二人一同'的话!"

屠岸贾听了，怒气填胸，拔出佩剑，大喝道："好你个老匹夫，岂敢消遣本府!我叫你即刻丧命剑下!"

说着挥剑就要砍下，忽有一名甲士抱着个男婴冲下山来，道："禀元帅，小的在这老儿屋后的山洞中搜出个小儿来，想来就是那'赵氏孤儿'了。"

屠岸贾当下转怒为喜，一把抓过婴儿，举在公孙

the child if not your goodself, eh?"

The old man uttered a piercing cry. A fire seemed to be raging in his breast. He berated Tu'an Gu in thunderous tones, "You evil miscreant of a court official. You trained that savage hound to attack an honest servant of the court, and drove the prime minister far away. Then you forged a royal decree, and deceived the duke's son-in-law into committing suicide. You slaughtered over 300 members of the Zhao clan, and caused the princess to hang herself. Now, you are going to deprive this orphan —— not even ten days old —— of his life. Surely the world knows few villains as black-hearted as you!"

This indictment cut Tu'an Gu to the quick. In a towering rage, his face contorted like that of a ravening wolf, he hissed, "Gongsun Chujiu, you know not what enmity you have stirred within me. And now, you are going to have the privilege of watching me cut Zhao the Orphan into three pieces. Then, I will deal with you at my leisure."

So saying, he raised his sword on high. As it flashed in the sunlight prior to its deadly downswing, which would end the life of his only son, Cheng Ying felt a pain like a knife twisting in his heart. He could not bear to watch, and closed his eyes. But unexpectedly, Tu'an Gu sheathed his sword. A baleful grin twisted his features as he said, "Cheng Ying, you performed a singular service for me by denouncing Gongsun Chujiu. Now I have a further task to trouble you with. Slay Zhao the Orphan, and I will reward you handsomely upon our return to my mansion."

Cheng Ying was aghast. His whole life had been devoted to healing the sick and saving lives; he had even brought people back to life. How could he take a life, especially the life of his own baby boy? He hastened to make an excuse. "Your Honor," he pleaded, "I am a physician, and the highest aspiration of a physician is the saving of life. I have never taken the life of a living creature in all my decades long career. Besides, I am unworthy to aspire to Your Honor's rewards."

杵臼面前，奸笑数声道："公孙杵臼，你还想抵赖么？这里左右没有人家，这个小儿是谁藏在山洞里的？"

公孙杵臼听着尖厉的啼哭声，胸膛中腾地燃起一团怒火，指着屠岸贾骂道："好你个乱臣贼子，当日你训练神獒，扑咬忠臣，逼得相国离京远逃；又假传王命，害得驸马饮鸩自尽；你杀了赵家老少三百余口，又逼得公主投缳上吊；如今这一个孤儿，生下来不满十日，你也要斩草除根。狠心毒肠，天下少有！"

一番话戳着屠岸贾痛处，止不住恼羞成怒，暴跳如雷，如恶狼一般咆哮数声，露出了狰狞面貌，道："公孙杵臼，我叫你心疼，等我先将这赵氏孤儿砍作三段，再来收拾你！"

说着，屠岸贾将利剑举起，就要砍下。程婴眼见自己的儿子就要丧命，忍不住心如刀绞，闭上双眼。谁知那屠岸贾忽地将利剑收住，奸笑道："程婴，你来出首公孙杵臼，立下首功，本府索性将功劳都给了你，就着你将这赵氏孤儿杀死，回府后也好重重地赏你。"

程婴一生救死扶伤，活人无算，几时杀过人来，更何况这小儿正是自己的亲生骨肉，怎么能下得去手？连忙推脱道："小人一生行医，以医术仁心救人，几十年不曾杀生，不敢贪图元帅的奖赏。"

Tu'an Gu glared at Cheng Ying with malevolent eyes. "Your feeble prevarications suggest to me that you wish this spawn of the Zhaos to live. If it lives, it will grow up, and if it grows up, it will kill me eventually, won't it?"

Cheng Ying had been backed into a corner. He feared that if he delayed obeying Tu'an Gu's order any longer, he would arouse the latter's suspicions again. Hardening his heart, he walked over to the baby, and picked it up with trembling hands. He raised the child above his head, and with all his strength dashed it against a rock. The poor infant, not having been in the world ten days, was reduced to a pulpy mass. Cheng Ying turned with his eyes tightly closed to hold back the flood of tears which threatened to come rushing out. His heart felt as though it were being boiled in oil.

Gongsun Chujiu struggled forward, and cradled the child's body in his arms. At the same time, he cursed Tu'an Gu. "You heinous monster," he cried, "Your wicked deeds make the very skies tremble. The Lord of Heaven will never forgive you. After my death, I will become a ravenous ghost, who will pluck out your black heart and tear out your liver. You will suffer a hideous death!"

But Tu'an Gu stood there with a frightful leer as he said this. Then he said, "Be that as it may, but first I will show you how the brat should have died." So saying, he drew his sword, and chopped the little body into three pieces.

With the blood pumping in his heart, and his eyes swimming with tears, Cheng Ying turned to Tu'an Gu. Furtively wiping his eyes, he said, "I trust in Your Honor's wisdom. Now that Zhao the Orphan has been disposed of, the other infants in the State of Jin are cleared of any taint, and so I take it that I will no longer have to worry about my progeny?"

Gongsun Chujiu took his cue perfectly on time. "You shameless wretch," he shouted at Cheng Ying, "You care not which innocent and good dies as long as you and yours live! Well, don't be too sure of your triumph.

　　屠岸贾用一双贼溜溜的眼睛死瞪着程婴，道：
"你推三阻四，只是不肯下手，敢是想留下这赵氏孽
种一条命，好等他长大来杀本官么？"

　　程婴被逼无奈，生怕再拖延引起屠岸贾的疑
心。只得将心一横，一步步走过去，双手颤抖着抱起
自己的亲生儿子，举过头顶，用尽平生力气，狠命地
摔到岩石上。可怜这程氏小儿，出生不满十日，遭此
横祸，变成了一堆肉泥。程婴转过头去，紧闭双眼，拼
命抑制着就要奔涌而出的泪水，一颗心仿佛在沸腾
的热油里煎熬。

　　公孙杵臼挣扎着扑过来，抚尸痛哭，骂道："屠岸
贾你这贼子，伤天害理，罪恶滔天，老天爷决不会饶
过你。我死后化为厉鬼，也要攫出你的黑心，掏出你
的肝肠，让你不得好死！"

　　屠岸贾闻言狞笑道："我先让你看看这赵氏余孽
怎么个死法，给你一个榜样。"说着挥剑将婴儿尸体
斩为三段。

　　程婴见状，心内滴血，眼中蓄泪，悄悄掉转身子，偷
偷抹了一把泪，道："元帅英明！如今除了这赵氏孤儿，晋
国小儿都可以不受牵连，小人也用不着担心绝后了。"

　　公孙杵臼看了一眼程婴，开口骂道："好一个没

In another 20 years' time Zhao the Orphan will come back to life, and then he will be a grown man. Then he will wreak vengeance upon evil ministers, and then will my heart's desire be fulfilled. "

Cheng Ying knew that Gongsun Chujiu was hinting to him that he must endure humiliation and the heavy burden that had been placed upon him of fostering Zhao the Orphan so that eventually justice would be done. He turned to the old man, and covering an imperceptible nod of the head with a sneer, he said, "Old man, you are facing death. How can you still find time to curse me?"

Gongsun Chujiu understood the hidden meaning in Cheng Ying's words. All his worries were at an end. While the attention of the guards was distracted, he suddenly smashed his head against a large rock. His skull cracked, and blood poured out, and his soul fled from his body. Seeing this, Tu'an Gu laughed out loud with approval.

Turning to Cheng Ying, he said, "This affair has turned out well for you. When we get back to my residence, you will be richly rewarded, I assure you. "

Cheng Ying's mind was a whirlpool of conflicting emotions. He was devastated with grief over the death of his beloved son, and at the same time he was elated at the knowledge that Zhao the Orphan was now safe.

Right at this moment, a tempestuous wind began to blow. It caused the mountain pines to roar like a boiling ocean. Tu'an Gu and the others could not withstand the bone-chilling blast, and made their way back to the capital with all speed.

The corpses of Gongsun Chujiu and Cheng Ying's child —— one old, one young —— lay exposed on the mountain slope, their blood shed in a just cause. The green-clad mountains stood as solemn witnesses, and the clear waters poured forth a lament. Even the sun suddenly started to dim. It was as if they were mourning over the tragedy which had taken place in Taiping Village and which would be commemorated for all time to come. And it was

廉耻的小人，贪生怕死，残害忠良。休高兴得太早了，二十年后，这赵氏孤儿转世成人，又是一条汉子。那时节再找奸臣报仇雪恨，才趁了我的心愿。"

程婴心里知道这是公孙杵臼在提醒自己，别忘了忍辱负重，抚孤报仇。他转过身子对公孙杵臼微微点头，口里却道："你这老儿，死到临头还要咒我！"

公孙杵臼心领神会，再无牵挂，趁人不备，挣扎起来一头撞到一块大石之上，顿时脑浆迸裂，鲜血直流，气绝身亡。屠岸贾哈哈大笑，道："这老匹夫既然撞死了，也就罢了。"

转头又对程婴道："这事多亏了你，回府之后，本官重重赏你。"

程婴听了，心中大悲大喜，百感交集，悲的是自己痛失知己爱子，喜的是终于骗过了屠岸贾，赵氏孤儿从此可以保全。

就在此时，忽地刮起一阵强劲的山风，满山松涛怒吼，犹如海潮汹涌。一时间风声大作，寒气侵肌，屠岸贾等人立脚不住，急忙下山，回京城去了。

公孙杵臼与程氏小儿一老一小的尸体静静地躺在山坡上，鲜血殷殷，倾刻成碧。青山肃立，绿水悲咽，阳光也在刹那间黯淡下来，仿佛都在为太平庄上

not long before news of this atrocity which had "frightened Heaven and Earth, and made even ghosts and spirits weep" spread through the whole of the State of Jin.

这一幕悲壮惨烈、千古传唱的场景哀悼伤痛。而这"惊天地，泣鬼神"的壮烈事迹，也迅速在晋国朝野流传开来。

赵氏孤儿

Chapter Seven
Taking Up Residence in the Tiger's Lair

After his hectic few days, in which he had chased around desperately to snatch Zhao the Orphan from the jaws of death, risked his own life and witnessed the murder of his own son, Cheng Ying's mind was in such turmoil that as soon as he reached home in Guojiazhuang Village, he collapsed on his bed, worn out by fatigue and with a great feeling of relief. That evening, he developed a fever. His whole body boiled, and he babbled in delirium, frothing at the mouth and oblivious to what was going on around him. Guo Shanren and his daughter were in a panic, and towards dawn sent for all the doctors in the neighborhood. The doctors all said that all the seven emotions in Cheng Ying's body had suffered harm. On top of that, he had over exerted himself, and this had brought the ailment to a dangerous stage. All that could be done was to administer a couple of doses of medicine, and wait and see. Guo Shanren hurried off to the nearest town, procured the medicine, prepared it and fed it to his son-in-law. The fever started to subside immediately. Needless to say, this was a trying time for the household, what with Cheng Ying's wife, who had given birth less than a month previously, having to look after Zhao the Orphan and at the same time attend to her sick husband, and Guo Shanren having to dash around summoning doctors and fetching and administering medicine.

After 20 days or so, Cheng Ying had recovered. But although his mind was clear, his limbs were weak and flaccid, and his body seemed

第七章　虎穴栖身

　　程婴连日来奔波劳累，虎穴救孤，首阳定计，目
睹知己牺牲，爱儿惨死，心中大起大伏，悲喜交激。如
今终于救下赵氏孤儿，不由得松了一口气，等到回了
郭家庄，再也撑持不住，一头栽倒，躺在床上。当天晚
上就发起烧来，浑身滚烫，胡话连篇，口吐白沫，人事
不省。郭善人与郭氏见了，当下乱作一团，好不着
急。盼到天明，四处请医生来看，都说是因为七情伤
身，加上劳累过度，病情着实险恶，只能先吃两副药
看看再说。郭善人急急去镇上抓回药来，细细煎好喂
下，幸喜见效，热度渐渐退了。郭氏生产还未满月，也
只得挣扎着起身，一面哺育赵氏孤儿，一面精心服侍
丈夫。郭善人则跑里跑外，延医求药，忙得脚不点地，
自不必细述。

　　过了二十九日，程婴渐渐恢复过来，可心中虽然
清明，只觉四肢瘫软，浑身无力，知道是从鬼门关前
打了一转回来，也只好卧榻安心静养。郭氏每天为丈

drained of strength. He knew that he had been at death's door, and that he needed to rest and calm his mind. His wife prepared special nourishing tonics for him every day. She was constantly in attendance at his bedside, whispering words of comfort.

A month or so passed, and winter set in. Cheng Ying felt fully recovered from his illness, but strength was still lacking in his body. One day, seeing that the winter sunshine was warm and bright, and that there was no wind, he expressed a desire to take a stroll outside. His wife thought that this would do him good after lying in bed for two months, so she wrapped him up in warm clothes and saw him off, with an admonition not to go too far and to come back soon.

Cheng Ying assented, and went for a leisurely walk. At the eastern edge of the village, he saw in the distance a dilapidated temple. The surrounding wall had crumbled in several places. There were also two neglected pavilions, which, as soon as he noticed them, reminded Cheng Ying of something that his father-in-law had told him. It seemed that the people of Guojiazhuang Village had erected a temple with two pavilions in honor of Jie Zitui, who had lived in the time of Duke Wen. They had not been repaired for many years, with the result that they now lay in ruins. This must be the place, he thought, and he quickened his pace. Entering the temple grounds, he startled a flock of jackdaws, which flew away from the tangled grass which was their nesting place. He saw ancient vines and creepers, and a pond of clear water, now frozen over. A feeling of desolation crept over him. He followed an overgrown path. The main door to the temple was missing, and inside the building he could make out the shape of a statue, which he guessed was that of Jie Zitui. The body of the statue was delicately carved, and its posture was relaxed and at ease. Before it was an offering table, heaped with ashes and stubs of candles and incense sticks. As he stood gazing at this scene, a myriad thoughts crowded into his head. He re-

夫做些精细饭食，悉心调养，又守在床前，温言软语地拣些话来宽慰。

约莫又过了月余，时辰早已入冬。程婴觉着自己已基本痊愈，只是身上无力。这一天见冬阳和煦，晴朗无风，便要去外面走走。郭氏见丈夫在床上躺了两个月，也想让他散散心，便为程婴套上衣服，嘱咐他不要走远，快快回来。

程婴口中答应，走出家门，在村中闲步一回。不知不觉来到村东，远远见到有一座荒废的祠宇，四围的墙垣已有多处坍塌，还有一两座荒芜的亭榭，却也有些闲景点缀。猛地想起岳父曾经说过，郭家庄村后有座"介子阁"，原是村人为纪念晋文公时的介子推而修建，如今多年失修，早已荒废了。想来这座祠宇就是了，于是举步入内，见寒鸦惊飞，荒草结寨，枯藤攀缘，一池清水也早已结冰，心中不免生出几分凄凉。沿着一条荒径向前，见那祠宇的大门已经不知哪里去了，正中一尊塑像，正是介子推，骨骼清秀，神态洒脱。塑像前的供桌上积满灰尘，香残烛尽。程婴悄立其中，思绪万千，暗想世人中罕有不慕名利者，恰似凤毛麟角，介子推随重耳出亡，历时一十九年，艰苦备尝。回国后流亡众臣都有封赏，独介子推辞官隐

flected on how rare were the people who scorned fame and fortune. Jie Zitui had followed Duke Wen into exile, suffered every kind of hardship for 19 years, and when he finally returned home, unlike the other exiled ministers, he had refused both reward and rank, and gone to live in obscurity, looking after his mother deep in the mountains. He was truly a man to revere and admire, thought Cheng Ying.

But the long illness had taken its toll on Cheng Ying. He was still not strong enough to walk far, and this sudden burst of emotion made him feel dizzy. His head swam, and his feet felt as heavy as lead. Turning to leave, he found that he could hardly put one foot in front of the other. He groped his way to a clean stone bench in one of the pavilions. But no sooner had he slumped onto it than he fainted.

In the blink of an eye, Gongsun Chujiu floated into the pavilion. In a stern voice, he addressed the doctor, "Cheng Ying, your mission has not yet been accomplished. What do you mean by dawdling in this place?"

Cheng Ying felt an urge to rise and greet his old comrade, but in a flash Gongsun Chujiu vanished. He tottered a couple of steps, when there suddenly appeared before him a faint vision of the naked form of his baby son, covered in blood and wailing. He tried to focus his eyes on the vision, but it was enveloped in dismal clouds and mist, and he could not see it clearly. Then he awoke in a frenzy of terror. He soon realized that he had had a dream, but his mind remained troubled. When he got home, he told his wife about the dream, and said that he had decided that he should go back to Taiping Village, and there give the remains of Gongsun Chujiu and his son a decent burial, with a proper grave mound for each. His wife, however, was horrified at the suggestion. "Are you out of your mind?" she gasped. "That cunning Tu'an Gu is still suspicious of you. While you were ill he sent people to summon you, saying that he had something to talk to you about. But

居,与老母终老于深山,真正可敬可佩……

程婴本是久病之人,身子虚弱,哪里禁得起步行多时,心情激动,不一会儿,便觉得头晕脑涨,两条腿仿佛灌了铅一样沉重,挪不动步。遂转身走出,在一座亭子内拣个干净的石凳坐下来,不一会儿竟然迷糊过去。

方一闭眼,就见公孙杵臼飘飘忽忽来到亭中,厉声道:"大事尚未成功,程婴你怎么竟在此处闲逛?"

程婴方欲起身迎上答话,公孙杵臼却转瞬不见。自己走了两步,隐隐约约见到儿子赤身裸体,满身血污,在前面哭叫。待得定睛细看,一片虚无缥缈,愁云惨雾,什么也看不清楚。猛地惊醒,知道是南柯一梦,恍惚不安。回到家中,与郭氏说起,便打算着要去太平庄掩埋儿子与公孙杵臼的尸骨,为这一老一小筑坟修墓。郭氏道:"相公可是糊涂了?那屠岸贾狡猾诡诈,未必对你没有疑心。前些日子还派人来召相公,说到府中有话要说,因见相公昏睡不醒,这才作罢。相公复去太平庄,万一被屠岸贾知晓,就是一场大祸。且不说这些日来的苦心付之东流,这赵氏孤儿又岂能保得住?公孙大人和我们的儿子岂不是也白白死了?"

since you were still unconscious, they left it at that. If Tu'an Gu finds out that you have been back to Taiping Village, there will be the Devil to pay! Not only will all your sufferings have been in vain, but it will be hard to keep Zhao the Orphan safe. Besides, Gongsun Chujiu and our child will have died for nothing."

Cheng Ying saw the wisdom in her words, so he shelved his plan. Nevertheless, he could not dispel the uneasiness from his mind.

As the pair were talking, there came the noise of the arrival of men and horses. Several soldiers came barging into the house, saying that they had orders to take Cheng Ying to Tu'an Gu.

Cheng Ying and his wife exchange a glance full of silent trepidation.

Having, as he thought, got rid of one big problem with the murder of Zhao the Orphan, Tu'an Gu, upon his return to the capital began plotting to gather both the governmental and military power of the State of Jin into his own hands, and then usurp the throne. But he realized that he had no able men among his subordinates, only base flatterers unfitted for any great enterprise. He thereupon recruited client henchmen from far and wide, to build up his power and raise a revolt when the time should be ripe. To his disappointment, the response was poor. The few men who answered his call he could see at a glance were of low caliber, wretches who wanted free food, that was all. For a long time, he brooded on this problem, when all of a sudden he thought of Cheng Ying. After he had killed "Zhao the Orphan" and returned from Mount Shouyang, he had invited Cheng Ying back to his mansion to receive a reward. Cheng Ying, however, had steadfastly refused to take any reward, saying that the only reason he had informed on Gongsun Chujiu was to save the infants of Jin, including his own child. At that time, Tu'an Gu accepted this with equanimity, and let Cheng Ying go home. Now Cheng Ying sprang to mind again: Wouldn't he make a good ad-

程婴觉得此话有理，只得作罢，心中却是忐忑不安。

夫妻二人正说着，忽听大门外人马嘶闹，正待出门观看，几名甲士已经大摇大摆地闯了进来，道："元帅有请程先生。"

程婴夫妇不禁面面相觑，暗自惊惧。

原来，屠岸贾自从杀了假的赵氏孤儿，回到府中，想着一块心病已去，便思谋着如何将晋国的军政大权慢慢地掌握在自己手中，徐图篡国，却苦于自己左右没有什么人材，虽然也有一些小人前来依附，只会阿谀奉承，办不了大事，于是广招门客，培植势力，准备待到羽翼丰满，便要发难。谁知道屠岸府张榜招贤，过了半月有余，却应者寥寥。就是来的这几个人，眼见得也没有什么才能，只是为了混一碗饭吃而已。屠岸贾只好独自坐在府中生气，一日忽然想起程婴来。当初杀了赵氏孤儿，下了首阳山，屠岸贾便要程婴到府上来领赏。不料程婴一口回绝，说自己只是为了救晋国全境及自家的小儿，才来出首公孙杵臼，并不贪图奖赏。屠岸贾也不在意，听由程婴自己去了。如今突然想起程婴，屠岸府正在招揽人材，无人前来，何不将程婴招来做个门客？一来也就算是赏了他的功劳；二来此番程婴首告，带着自己到太平庄上

dition to his band of clients? For one thing, it would be a way to reward him for his services. For another, ever since Cheng Ying had denounced Gongsun Chujiu and led him to Taiping Village, where he had disposed of both Zhao the Orphan and the old man he had never been able to get rid of a lingering doubt about Cheng Ying; if he could get him into his household, he could keep an eye on him. Moreover, although Tu'an Gu had three wives and six concubines, they had produced no children for the by now nearly 50-year-old Tu'an. He could adopt Cheng Ying's baby son as his own, and when he grew up, the lad could perform great feats for him. That would be killing a whole flock of birds with one stone!

The more he mulled over this plan, the more he liked it. So he wasted no more time, and sent men to summon Cheng Ying from his home in Guojiazhuang Village. Unexpectedly, they came back and reported that Cheng Ying was ill in bed, delirious with fever. Tu'an Gu had no choice but to let the matter rest there, but after about another month, judging that Cheng Ying would be recovered by this time, he sent men with a carriage to fetch him. Just before they set out, Tu'an Gu gave secret instructions to their captain to look closely for signs of anything suspicious about Cheng Ying, and if he noticed any to bring the whole household before him in chains.

Knowing nothing of Tu'an Gu's schemes, Cheng Ying and his wife feared that their part in the Zhao the Orphan affair had been discovered. So they were flabbergasted when they heard the captain of the guards say, "In recognition of your help in the execution of the orphan, the commander-in-chief wishes to raise you to the status of a member of his household. Not only that, but he also wishes to adopt your son. All three of you will move into his mansion, and in due course his adopted son will succeed to his position."

The prospect of being installed in the "tiger's den" appalled the

杀了赵氏孤儿和公孙杵臼，可是自己心中总有一丝隐隐的不安，对程婴不敢放心，如果将他招来府上，正好可以就近监视；三来自己虽然三妻六妾，怎奈命中无子，年近五十，膝下荒凉，正好可以将程婴新生的儿子认作义子，养大后还怕他不为自己出力？正是一举三得。

屠岸贾前后盘算已定，心中得意，当下便命亲信前往郭家庄招程婴前来。不料派去的人回报说，程婴病在床上，不省人事，无法前来。屠岸贾闻言，只得先将此事放下不提。如今过了一月有余，想那程婴早已病好，屠岸贾便派人带车去郭家庄接那程婴。临行前，又对亲信附耳叮嘱一番，要他密切查看程婴神色，如有不妥，便即刻锁拿程婴一家来府。

程婴夫妇二人哪里能想到屠岸贾有这许多花花肠子，只怕是赵氏孤儿的事情败露了。当下听来人道："元帅说你诛孤有功，要抬举你做府上门客，并认你的儿子为义子，让你一家三口儿住进府去，将来还要让你儿子继承他的官位呢！"

程婴夫妇听了，心中惊惧愈甚，想到从此自己一家三口就要栖身虎穴，赵氏孤儿也得认贼作父，每日里小心提防，万一一步走错，马上就是一场弥天大

pair, Zhao the Orphan would have to treat Tu'an Gu as his father, and every minute of the day they would have to be on their guard, for one slip would mean disaster for them all. But Cheng Ying dared not refuse the offer, for fear of arousing Tu'an Gu's suspicions. He well knew that the ruthless Tu'an was capable of having him and his family slain on the spot, and that would be the end of their attempt to preserve the Zhao line. As Cheng Ying hesitated, his quick-witted wife said, before her husband could blurt out something disastrous, "We thank the commander-in-chief for his great kindness."

Tu'an Gu's men were well pleased with the alacrity with which she accepted the offer, and considered their errand satisfactorily accomplished.

Cheng Ying was thereupon forced to pretend to be delighted, and he too accepted, saying, "I never thought that a humble fellow such as I would be the beneficiary of the commander-in-chief's bounty." But while his face was wreathed in an obsequious smile, as if he were conscious of receiving a great favor, his heart had turned to wormwood. After gathering up some things they needed, Cheng Ying and his wife, with the baby, mounted the waiting carriage and were taken to Tu'an Gu's mansion.

They found Tu'an Gu himself waiting for them in the main hall. He rose and came forward to greet them. Tu'an Gu's beaming face seemed to shoot ten thousand arrows carrying loathing and distress into Cheng Ying's heart. He dared not reveal one iota of his real feelings, however, but kowtowed and said, "Many thanks for your boundless kindness, Commander-in-Chief. My wife and I will never forget your goodness."

"Sir," said Tu'an Gu, "You rendered me a great service in helping me get rid of that Zhao whelp. I was most impressed that you refused any reward. As a retainer in my household, I trust that you can be of

祸。欲待不答应，却又怕那屠岸贾暗生疑心，顿时翻脸，将自己一家三口当时处死，救孤存赵的大计转眼毁于一旦。这里程婴正在疑虑，郭氏心思极快，已将此事前后利害想了一遍，怕程婴露出破绽，抢在前面道："多谢元帅盛情！"

来人见郭氏答应得爽快，这才道："像这样的好事，别人打着灯笼也找不着。"

程婴听了，也只得装出一副欢喜的模样，应承道："程某出身寒微，不意承蒙元帅如此抬举。"口里说着，脸上笑容可掬，一副受宠若惊的样子，心里却比黄连还苦。当下车子已候在门外，程婴夫妇稍事收拾，抱着婴儿上车入府。

屠岸贾早已等候在厅堂上，见程婴夫妇前来，亲自起身迎客，堆下一脸笑来。程婴纵然心中悲愤，有如万箭攒心，又怎敢流露出半点儿，当下叩头行礼，口中道："多谢元帅抬举，大恩大德，小人夫妇没齿不忘！"

屠岸贾大笑道："此番除却赵家余孽，先生立了大功，却不愿受赏，令老夫敬佩，不如就在老夫府上做个门客，还有借重之处。况且老夫年近五旬，膝下无儿，想将你的儿子过继了来，这天大的一副家业可

more service to me in the future. Moreover, I am now nearing my fiftieth year, and have no children. So I propose to adopt your son, and bequeath to him my house and rank so that he can carry on my line and inherit my position. I would like to hear your own opinion on the matter."

Flustered, Cheng Ying replied, "Your Honor, I am a man of humble origins, living in straightened circumstances. My wife, myself and our child are lucky indeed to be the objects of your munificence."

Thereupon, Cheng Ying and his wife bowed repeatedly. This pleased Tu'an Gu excessively, and with a smug smile, he said, "Not at all, my dear fellow. You have put my mind at ease. With your help, we shall both come to enjoy wealth and honor." He then took the baby, and asked, "Have you given him a name yet?"

Cheng Ying replied, "Yes, Your Honor. It's Cheng Bo."

Tu'an Gu said, "From now on, in my presence he shall be called Tu'an Cheng, while you may continue to call him Cheng Bo in private. When he gets older, I shall train him in the martial arts, while you teach him his letters. That way, he will grow up accomplished in both civil and military arts, and will surpass all others in his grasp of strategy. When that time comes, he and I will have the State of Jin in the palms of our hands, will we not?"

So saying, he let out a roar of laughter, and his hideous face gleamed and quivered. Despite his feeling of loathing, Cheng Ying could not but chime in with, "Just as you say, Commander-in-Chief. And it will all be because the little one has had the good fortune to meet Your Honor."

From this time on, Cheng Ying and his wife lived in a small courtyard house in the mansion compound. The courtyard was dainty and the house comfortable. Poplars and willows brushed the eaves, and magnolias caressed the steps. Outside the window were two flower beds,

就是他的了。我已一把年纪，也得有个人传宗接代、承袭官爵。只不知先生意下如何？"

程婴慌忙道："小人出身乡野，门庭寒微，不意老元帅如此看重，小人夫妇并小儿三口真是三生有幸啊！"

说毕，夫妻二人又连连拜谢。屠岸贾踌躇满志道："先生何出此言？老夫今日高枕无忧，全靠先生出力，正该共享富贵。"又将赵氏孤儿抱过去看瞧，问道："取了名字没有？"

程婴答道："小儿贱名程勃。"

屠岸贾道："从今往后，这孩子在我这面就唤作屠岸成，在你那面唤作程勃。等他长大后，老夫教他习武，先生教他读书，将来必定文武双全，韬略过人，可为天下第一。到那时这晋国还不是我父子说了算吗？"

说罢，哈哈大笑起来，脸上横肉块块放光，一抖一颤。程婴心中好不厌恶，却也不免附和几句，道："果然如元帅之言，可是小儿命中遭遇贵人了。"

从此以后，程婴夫妇住进屠岸府内的一个小院里。此院小巧精致，房舍齐全，院里杨柳拂檐，幽兰盈阶。窗前又有两方花坛，内植各色花卉，每到春夏之

with exotic blooms of all kinds. As spring turned into summer, the flower beds became a riot of color. To one side was a trellis of roseleaf raspberry which was adorned with dappled snow white blossoms every summer, like a myriad of stars winking in the sky. Tu'an Gu had arranged a study for Cheng Ying, the bookshelves of which were filled with complete editions of the classics. It also contained a large desk with writing brushes, inkslab, etc., in short, everything needed for the education of young Cheng Bo.

As the courtyard was in an obscure part of Tu'an Gu's mansion, Cheng Ying and his wife seldom saw any of the other residents; indeed, they did their utmost to avoid them, in case they should let slip anything that might bring calamity on their heads. And so, they passed their days peacefully enough. But in the stillness of the night, when there was nobody about, they thought of the noble martyrs and their own poor child. Then they were tortured with sorrow, and a nameless feeling of desolation. During the day, when they met Tu'an Gu or other members of the household, they were careful to assume expressions of glowing satisfaction and engage naturally in conversation. Needless to say, this kind of life was a great strain on them.

For several years, Cheng Ying acted as the household physician, going out occasionally in the summer and autumn to gather herbs. His wife attended to the baby and did needlework. Cheng Bo grew up a healthy child, who used to love to run around and play in the courtyard. Tu'an Gu was immensely pleased to see this, and in order to keep him in a good mood the whole household fawned on Cheng Bo.

The tragedy that had taken place a few years before at Taiping Village by now was known to everyone in the State of Jin. The people venerated Gongsun Chujiu for the high-minded way he had gone to his death; at the same time, they despised Cheng Ying as a base scoundrel, and were torn with pity for Zhao the Orphan who, they thought, had

际，姹紫嫣红，绿藤披拂。旁边一架荼蘼，每到夏季，开满白花，斑斑点点，犹如群星闪烁。屠岸贾还特地为程婴设了一间书房，古今典籍，堆满书架，当地一个大几，上置笔墨砚台，专备教那程勃攻读。

因这小院处于屠岸府一隅，平日人迹罕至，程婴夫妇二人又有心事，尽量不与屠岸府中人来往，以免露出破绽，故此日子过得十分清静。只是每到夜静人稀时，不免想起诸位义士及亲生儿子来，只觉痛入骨髓，不啻万箭攒心，凄楚之情无以名状。白天有时与屠岸贾及屠岸府家人见面，还得装出一副欢喜模样，往来酬答，真是苦不堪言。

转眼数年过去，程婴只在屠岸府中为人看病，每到夏秋时节，偶而出外采药。郭氏每日里喂养小儿，做些针线女红。那程勃无病无灾，长得甚是壮硕，在院中跑跳玩耍，十分活泼。屠岸贾见了也是格外欢喜，阖府上下为讨屠岸贾的欢心，更是对他百般呵护。

数年前在太平庄上发生的悲壮惨烈的一幕，此时早已传遍晋国朝野，凡是听闻之人，有敬重公孙杵臼凛然赴死的，有鄙薄程婴为人卑劣的，有可惜"赵氏孤儿"幼年惨死的。文人学士不免发挥想象，添枝

died a tragic death at such an early age. Scholars exercised their imaginations, and produced fanciful tales relating to the incident. Ordinary people too, despite having little learning, made up ballads on the same theme, which were passed from mouth to mouth. Peddlers and other travelers sang the praises of the staunch defender of justice Gongsun Chujiu, who had laid down his life in a righteous cause; and even babes scarcely out of their mothers' arms were taught to excoriate Cheng Ying, who had betrayed his friend to save his own skin and reap a rich reward. When it became known that Cheng Ying was aiding and abetting the evil court officials as a hanger on in Tu'an Gu's household, he was loathed even more intensely. Who could know the pain in his heart?

One day, when Cheng Ying happened to step out into the street, he noticed that all the people he knew avoided him, casting glances of open contempt. It was clear that they wanted nothing to do with him. As he passed them, they would gather in groups and point at him behind his back. Hurrying on with head bent, he happened to see his erstwhile friend Gaffer Zhao coming towards him. But when he hastened to greet Gaffer Zhao, the latter simply spat on the ground and strode away. As he stood nonplussed in the street, he suddenly heard from behind him cries of "It's that villain Cheng Ying!" He turned, to see a crowd of children taunting him. The children then started to throw mud balls and sand at him, and before long he was splattered from head to foot. Cheng Ying had no choice but to flee back to Tu'an Gu's mansion. There he broke down in tears as he related to his wife what had happened. Heartbroken, his wife was worried that this incident might depress her husband so much that he might fall ill again, and she uttered what words of comfort she could. In this way, the weary days dragged by for Cheng Ying and his wife, as they suffered in silence the contempt and insults heaped upon them.

Tu'an Gu, on the other hand, was pleased to see that the pair

加叶，舞文弄墨，润色成篇；便是市井百姓，虽不通文墨，也出口成章，编了顺口溜来传唱。一时之间，贩夫走卒都在颂扬公孙杵臼舍生取义，气节刚强；妇孺孩童亦知指责程婴贪生怕死，卖友求荣。后来人们又见程婴作了屠岸府门客，依附奸臣，越发恨之入骨。却有哪一个知道他一腔的苦衷？

一日，程婴偶尔出门，见到过去相识的街坊都远远用鄙夷的目光看着自己，待他走近，纷纷躲避，明显是不愿与他攀谈。等到自己走了过去，众人却又在背后指指戳戳。只好低着头前行，猛地看见相熟的赵老汉迎面走来，程婴急忙上前寒暄，赵老汉脸上却满是怒色，"啐"的一口唾沫吐在地上，扬长而去。程婴呆立在街上，不知所措，听得后面一阵小儿喊声，翻来复去叫道："小人程婴！奸贼程婴！"程婴一转脸，众小儿抓起泥巴沙石乱扔过来，顿时打得程婴满头满身都是。程婴不禁心苦，叹一口气，疾走躲避。回到家里，在夫人郭氏面前痛哭一场。郭氏也是心痛如割，肝肠寸断，又怕程婴悒郁成病，只好宽言劝慰。夫妻二人忍辱含垢，饮恨吞声，度日如年，也不必细述。

屠岸贾见程婴夫妇在府中安分守己，很少出门，也不与亲友交往，早已疑心尽释，不再提防。

seldom strayed outside, and had cut themselves off from their old acquaintances. His suspicions concerning them finally died down.

One day a message came from Guojiazhuang Village, to the effect that Guo Shanren had fallen seriously ill, and could die at any minute. He wanted his daughter and son-in-law to come home at once.

When Tu'an Gu raised no objection, Cheng Ying and his wife, together with little Cheng Bo, hastily mounted a carriage and hurried to Guojiazhuang Village. There they found Guo Shanren on his deathbed. The old man was unable to speak, but he pointed at the child and gasped. Cheng Ying understood what he meant, and assured him. "Put your mind at ease, Father-in-Law. We will raise him so that someday he will do mighty deeds." Guo Shanren nodded, and his eyes shone brightly for a moment. Then he turned his head, and died. His daughter threw herself on her father's corpse, and wept unconsolably. Cheng Ying too shed copious tears.

It was arranged that the driver would take the carriage back to the Tu'an mansion, leaving Cheng Ying and his wife to attend to the funeral arrangements. The following day, with the help of neighbors, they put Guo Shanren in his coffin and carried it to the grave. The funeral rites completed, they set about tidying the house. As they did so, the grieving Cheng Ying suddenly thought of his son. He had a few quiet words with his wife, and at the crack of dawn the next morning set out for Taiping Village. Now although Cheng Ying had visited the nearby mountains several times searching for herbs, he had avoided Taiping Village for fear that Tu'an Gu might have sent spies after him, or that he might meet somebody who knew him. This time, he felt that he could not pass up the opportunity, and so, choosing obscure paths, he traveled to the village, arriving at Gongsun Chujiu's old cottage the following day. On the mountain slope behind the dismal and dilapidated house were two grave mounds, one large and one small, long since

　　忽有一日早上，郭家庄有人来报，说郭善人得了急病，危在旦夕，想要女儿女婿回去。屠岸贾闻言道："父慈女孝，人之常情。先生可与夫人速速回去探视。"

　　程婴夫妇带着程勃，飞也似地坐车赶回家中，郭善人已在弥留之际，见女儿女婿带着外孙回来，抓着程婴的手却说不出话来，只指着程勃一个劲儿地喘气。程婴知道岳父的心思，当下道："岳父放心，我夫妇二人一定将他抚养成人，干一番大事。"郭善人点点头，双眼中透出一丝光来，头一歪便死了。郭氏扑在父亲身上，哭得闭过气去，程婴在一旁也是泪如雨下。

　　屠岸府跟来的车夫见状，与程婴商量一下，独自驾车回报屠岸贾，程婴一家三口则留下来料理丧事。第二天，由村里的邻居帮忙，程婴夫妇将郭善人殡殓。丧事办完之后，郭氏在家中收拾杂物。程婴则失魂落魄，思念儿子，悄悄与郭氏说了一声，一大早便偷偷出村，赶往太平庄。原来，以前程婴虽然几次上山采药，因怕屠岸贾派人跟踪监视，又怕碰见熟人，未敢前往太平庄上。此次见到是个机会，再也按捺不住心中的念头，不顾一切地要到太平庄上去看

overgrown with grass. Cheng Ying guessed that they were where the villagers had buried the bodies of Gongsun Chujiu and the baby.

He wept silently at the sight, and then, throwing all caution to the winds, wailed and mourned aloud. He dared not remain there long, and was soon on his way back, looking around him all the time. Fortunately, it was a remote spot, and he encountered no other person until he was safely clear.

Back at Guojiazhuang Village, he collected his wife and the baby, and returned to the Tu'an mansion. From then on, every few months, on the excuse of going to the mountains to look for herbs, Cheng Ying would sneak off to Taiping Village, to tend the graves and conduct mourning rites. In this way, he found some outlet for his grief. He was so discreet about this that no one in the Tu'an household was aware of his trips, apart from his wife.

One frosty, blustery autumn night, Cheng Ying lay awake, feeling too cold to sleep. Seeing his wife and Cheng Bo deep in slumber, he slipped out of bed, dressed and went out into the courtyard. There he stood gazing up at the cloudless, moonlit sky, in which the Milky Way glittered. Crickets were chirping in the grass and trees. Cheng Ying felt a sense of desolation creep over him, and a sadness which he could not dispel. An autumn breeze sprang up, making the leaves rustle and fall. The chilly air pierced him to the marrow. He shivered, and went back inside. Still, sleep would not come. He paced his study, and then sat deep in thought. The rustling of the paper in the window, stirred by the autumn wind made the room dreary. Cheng Ying suddenly began to compose a poem:

> The west wind teases the window blinds,
> Stirring the curtains and chilling the sheets.
> Donning a doublet, I gaze on the moon,
> And sorrowing grieve for my lost little child.

看。一路上挑着偏僻的小路行走，第二天上午到了公孙杵臼原来居住的草房，只见三间茅屋早已倾圮，一派破败景象。屋后的山坡上有一大一小两座坟墓，长满青草，想来是太平庄上的农夫将公孙杵臼与孩子的尸体收殓，埋在这里。

程婴见到两座坟墓，早已泣不成声，也不再有什么顾忌，当下大放悲声，祭奠一番。他不敢久留，稍待片刻，便一步三回头地去了。幸喜这里偏僻，倒也不曾被什么人撞见。

程婴回到郭家庄，会合郭氏，带着程勃又回到屠岸府。自此之后，程婴每隔数月，便借口上山采药，悄悄去太平庄洒扫哭祭一番，以略抒胸臆。因做得悄密，屠岸府上下都被蒙在鼓里，只有郭氏一人知道。

这天又到了秋凉风清的时节，程婴躺在榻上，只觉得衾寒枕冷，辗转难眠。见郭氏和程勃都已睡熟，索性轻手轻脚地披衣出门，立于院中，但见万里无云，月色横空，银汉耿耿。院内草丛树畔，一片蛩声叽叽。程婴只觉得心中的悲苦，在胸中弥漫成一片哀情愁绪，排遣不去。一阵秋风吹过，树叶飒飒作响，飘然而下。程婴顿觉寒意砭肌入骨，浑身一冷，打了个寒噤。返身回屋，依然了无睡意，悄悄地转到书房，一个

But he found his heart no lighter for the effort. He recommenced pacing the study floor, and before he knew it, the eastern sky had paled, and the rays of dawn came peeping through the window. Abandoning all thoughts of sleep, Cheng Ying gently wakened his wife and told her that he intended to go once more to Taiping Village to sacrifice to the souls of Gongsun Chujiu and his poor deceased infant son. He thereupon hurriedly packed a few things, and with his medicine box on his back, he left the house. At the gate of the mansion he came across Tu'an Gu marshaling some of his men in preparation for a hunting trip. When he explained that he was going to the mountains to pick herbs, Tu'an Gu airily waved him on his way, and told him to hurry back.

Cheng Ying was very familiar with the way to Taiping Village by this time, and he arrived at the grave mounds in good time. Burning paper money there, his heart was again pierced with grief. But, when he had opened his heart to his departed friend, he felt somewhat better, and left the place with red and swollen eyes.

In the meantime, Tu'an Gu had headed for the eastern suburbs of the capital. As the arrogant procession clattered along the road, with banners flying and armor gleaming, everyone it passed growled in disgust. In the eastern suburbs was a broad flat plain, which made an ideal hunting ground. It was also the perfect season for hunting, being early autumn. The sky was high and the breeze was bracing, the grass was lush and the horses plump. Tu'an Gu, who had devoted all his thoughts and energies during the previous few years to ensnaring loyal and good men, and grabbing more and more power, found himself unusually refreshed and elated on this fine morning. At their master's order, the men-at-arms, each eager to show off his prowess, dashed to form a wide circle. The driver of Tu'an Gu's chariot put his horses through their paces, making them gallop at full speed back and forth and round and round. Then bows twanged, and arrows fell like rain, as the bowmen

人在暗中默坐，又听得窗纸被秋风吹得"特愣愣"地响，好不凄凉，便吟出一首小诗：

西风起兮透纸窗，罗帐飘兮衾枕凉。

披衣出门兮望明月，思念亲人兮心惆怅。

吟罢，仍然有一股悲情横亘胸中，来回在书房内踱步，不觉已是东方既白，曙光入窗。程婴也无心再睡，只悄悄告诉郭氏，想到太平庄上祭奠老友公孙及早夭的孩儿。说罢，匆匆打点一下，背起药箱出门。走到府门，却见屠岸贾正在点校兵士，原来正要出去打猎。程婴上前将自己出门采药的事说了，屠岸贾也不在意，只摆摆手叫他快去快回。

前往太平庄的山路都是程婴走熟了的，依旧来到坟前，烧化些纸钱，不免又痛哭一番，将心中的委屈向老友诉说诉说，心情也因此平静一些，红肿着双眼下山来。

再说那屠岸贾带着数十名甲士，驰出城来向东郊奔去。一路上旌旗猎猎，甲仗鲜明，路人见之，莫不啧啧。这东郊一带，平原旷野，是上佳的游猎之地。此时正是初秋，天高气爽，草长马肥，也正是打猎的好时候。屠岸贾近年来挖空心思，绞尽脑汁，陷害忠良，争权夺利，难得出外行猎，到此不觉心神清爽，全身

showed their skill. Hawks and hounds sprang frenziedly at their prey, while foxes and hares raced away in panic. The well aimed shafts soon left heaps of dead animals where they fell, and filled the air with whirling feathers and tufts of fur. Viewing this scene of bedlam, Tu'an Gu felt his spirits soaring. He himself tried his hand at notching an arrow or two. He whooped with glee, as he made his quarry scatter in all directions. Meanwhile, the circle was tightening, and frenzy seized the animals trapped inside. Tu'an Gu laughed uproariously. But at the height of his joy, disaster struck. From a clump of bushes crept a leopard, its thick fur dazzling in the sunlight. While the nearby men-at-arms stood dumbfounded, the beast, swift as lightning, sprang through a gap in the circle and made straight for Tu'an Gu. As his men yelled frantically, "Kill it! Kill it!" the leopard sprang, and bore Tu'an Gu to the ground, before anyone could stop it. Tu'an Gu's military training stood him in good stead in this emergency, for he instinctively rolled along the ground, and sprang to his feet with his sword drawn. A desperate battle then ensued. Finding itself challenged on all sides, the leopard fought desperately. Time and again Tu'an Gu lunged with his sword, only to stab thin air. Finally seeing an opening, the beast sprang at Tu'an Gu with a blood curdling roar. Tu'an Gu was no longer young, and his body was bloated with gorging himself for many years, and so was not able to dodge the attack. He only managed to jerk his head to one side, and the leopard sank its teeth into his left shoulder, bearing him to the ground. Luckily for him, his men had run up by this time, and they killed the leopard before it had time to finish off their master.

While his attendants were binding his wounds, an order was given to call off the hunt and return to the Tu'an mansion. What had started off as an exhilarating day had ended in disaster. Tu'an Gu managed to stagger to his feet, and totter back to his chariot. He felt humiliated and angry, but there was no way for him to give vent to his spleen on this

舒展。一声令下，众甲士人人争先，个个奋勇，转瞬间已经合围。只见驾车的进退周旋，极尽驰骋之妙；弯弓的矢如雨发，大显神射之能。鹰犬仗势而猖狂，狐兔畏威而乱窜；弓响处血肉狼藉，箭到处羽毛纷飞。其场面好不热闹，屠岸贾精神大振，自己拈弓搭箭，频频发矢。眼见得狐兔四散逃命，屠岸贾得意洋洋，大声呼喝。此时包围圈越缩越小，被围在中间的各种猎物惊慌失措，成了瓮中之鳖。屠岸贾喜得手舞足蹈，哈哈大笑。也是乐极生悲，就在这时，一丛灌木中忽然窜出一只豹子来，细密的毛皮在阳光下耀眼生辉。附近几名甲士一楞，那畜牲电闪一般从人缝里逸出，直扑到屠岸贾面前。屠岸贾胯下的座骑一惊，"希聿聿"一声嘶叫，直立起来，将屠岸贾摔在地上。四周的甲士无不惊呼，一时间不及上前营救。屠岸贾毕竟是武将出身，就地打了一个滚，拔出佩剑，与那豹子翻翻滚滚地厮斗起来。那豹子无法突出包围，只好作困兽斗。屠岸贾几次挥剑刺去，都落了空。那豹子觑了个空隙，凌空扑下，张开血盆大口狠命一咬。屠岸贾因为年纪已大，肥胖臃肿，闪避不灵，只来得及将头一侧，被豹子咬在左肩，顿时扑倒。幸得周围的甲士及时赶到，将豹子刺死，才将屠岸贾救出。

occasion.

When he got back home, the whole household, having heard the news that their master had been mauled by a wild animal, came crowding around him. Tu'an Gu petulently waved them away, saying that he only wanted to talk to Cheng Ying. The summons sent a shiver of fear running down Cheng Ying's spine, but he had no choice but to attend Tu'an Gu on his sickbed. In due course, the latter coughed, cleared his throat, and said in solemn tones, "In the past few years I have been feeling my vigor ebbing away. I am not as nimble as I used to be, and today while out hunting, I was injured. It was only to be expected, I suppose. I have to face the fact that I am getting old, as we all must some day." He sighed deeply as he spoke. Cheng Ying, seeing him so gloomy, uttered a few words of comfort, whereupon, Tu'an Gu uttered a scornful laugh. "Please don't be polite. I remember that at the time I adopted your son and named him Tu'an Cheng, you were given the task of teaching him his letters, while I undertook to train him in the martial arts. The boy is now ten years old, while you and I are growing older by the day. He must be made to master the two branches of learning without delay, or it will be too late." So saying, he glanced at Cheng Ying.

Now the sufferings he had undergone had steeled Cheng Ying's temperament, and the burden of bringing up the orphan while living in the lair of his worst enemy had inured him to insult and degradation. He lived in a state of constant terror of his secret being found out, as if he were walking on thin ice all the time. All these afflictions and pressures had reduced his already frail body to skin and bone. His complexion was pale and sallow, and white hairs had appeared at his temples. He had obviously aged, being the very picture of the harm that worry can inflict upon a person.

Cheng Ying could read in Tu'an Gu's eyes that the latter regarded

众人一面手忙脚乱地为屠岸贾裹伤，一面下令鸣金收兵，打道回府。真是乘兴而来，败兴而归。屠岸贾伤势极重，强自撑持，又感到在众人面前出了丑，满肚子气恼，却也无处发泄，只气哼哼地一言不发。

回到府中，阖府人听说屠岸贾被野兽咬伤，都来探望。屠岸贾却因心绪不快，将余人都打发出去，只吩咐留下程先生说话。程婴闻言，不觉心中惴惴，在一旁坐下，静等屠岸贾开口。屠岸贾咳嗽一声，清了清嗓子，郑重其事道："本官近两三年来渐觉精力不济，身手亦不复敏捷，今日出猎受伤，也是情理中事。毕竟年纪大了，老之将至。"说着，长叹一声。程婴见屠岸贾心中伤感，当下泛泛地安慰几句。屠岸贾苦笑道："先生不必客气。本官记得当年收那屠岸成为义子时，曾言由先生教他读书，本官教他习武。如今屠岸成孩儿已经十岁，而本官与先生却日见老迈，要教他读书习武，再晚就来不及了。"说罢，不觉看了程婴一眼。

原来程婴连续经历了几场人伦惨变，受到强烈的精神折磨，又因肩负抚孤重任，身处虎穴，硬着头皮忍辱含垢，隐痛苟活，成天里提心吊胆，战战兢兢，如履薄冰，惟恐露出丝毫破绽。在这种强烈的精神刺激和无所不在的压力下，他原本不很强壮的身子越发显得

him as old and doddering. He could not suppress a wan smile, thinking to himself, "I long ago started to teach Cheng Bo his letters, but I fear that he has received no training in the martial arts as yet. Now that this villainous Tu'an has raised the subject of giving Cheng Bo an all round education encompassing both the civil and the military arts, he has unwittingly voiced my own heart's desire, for he is simply hastening his own death." Then, out loud, he said, "Your Honor, I will do my best to accomplish this worthy plan. I simply await your orders." This response pleased Tu'an Gu, and he explained that as soon as he recovered from his wound, he would personally instruct Cheng Bo in the martial arts during the day, while Cheng Ying would teach the boy his letters in the evenings.

From then on, Cheng Ying and Tu'an Gu worked diligently hand in hand for the education of Zhao the Orphan. The youngster was diligent at both branches of study, and grew up robust and dignified, attracting the admiration of all around. Every day, as he gazed on this grand young man, Tu'an Gu was filled with delight, thinking that he was raising a hero whom he could depend on to support him in his twilight years. Little did he know that he was digging his own grave.

形销骨瘦，憔悴不堪，鬓边新添了几绺白发，变得苍老多了。忧能伤人，竟然一至于此。

程婴见屠岸贾瞟了自己一眼，知道自己早已老态毕现，被屠岸贾看在眼中。当下不由得淡淡一笑，暗想道："自己早就在暗中教程勃读书习字，只发愁无人教他武艺。今日屠岸贾主动提出要教程勃读书习武，正中自己的下怀，这是屠岸贾自速其死，须怨不得别人。"于是开口道："大人既有此美意，小人正当效力。但凭大人吩咐就是。"屠岸贾闻言喜上眉梢，当下与程婴约定：程勃待屠岸贾伤愈后即开始读书习武，白天由屠岸贾教练武艺，夜间由程婴教他读书习字。

从此以后，屠岸贾与程婴二人同心合力，抚育这"赵氏孤儿"。屠岸贾白日教他练武，程婴夜间教他读书。那赵氏孤儿文武兼习，又出脱得端庄英俊，十分讨人喜爱。屠岸贾每日里见了，只是笑得合不拢口，以为自己终生有靠。他做梦也想不到，他正是在自掘坟墓。

Chapter Eight
The Day of Reckoning

Ten years passed. Cheng Ying was now a white-haired, decrepit old man. Truly:

The days hurry on old age, and time prods youth aside.

But a myriad wordless yearnings in our hearts still abide.

The balmy spring returned to the world, and the flowers began to bloom again. Zhao the Orphan was a grown man by this time. Being possessed of exceptional intelligence, he had profited from the tutorship of both Cheng Ying and Tu'an Gu, and emerged a person of all round talents in both scholarship and the martial skills. He was praised by everyone who knew him, and there were many both at court and outside it. However, their admiration was tempered by the knowledge that he was, lamentably, the adopted son of Tu'an Gu.

Contemplating his adopted son's accomplishments, Tu'an Gu felt his ambition swell inside him, and when he was alone he would often boast to himself, "Sooner or later, my plan will mature, and I will then slay the duke and seize the throne and hand it over to my son Tu'an Cheng. And then my lifelong aim will have been achieved."

Needless to say, while Tu'an Gu was nursing his wicked scheme, Cheng Ying was growing ever more anxious. His intention had been to relate to the youth the whole sad story of who he was and what had happened to his clansmen and their friends. Now that he was a grown man and adept at both learning and martial prowess, it was time for Zhao the Orphan to exact retribution from Tu'an Gu. But as

第八章 报仇雪恨

春去秋来,乌飞兔走,不觉又过了十年。此时的程婴已经是白发苍苍,老态龙钟了。正是:

日月催人老,光影趱少年。

心中无限事,未敢尽明言。

此时正好又到了春暖花开的季节,赵氏孤儿已长大成人。因他生性聪颖异常,又有养父和义父轮番教导训练,故而武艺高强,弓马娴熟,兼且满腹经纶,一胸锦绣,可称是文韬武略,样样过人。朝野中人多有知道者,每加称赞。赞叹之余,不免又因其为奸贼屠岸贾的义子,感到几分明珠暗投的遗憾。

屠岸贾见屠岸成佼佼出众,越发野心勃勃,常在无人处口出狂言道:"待我早晚定计,杀了国主,夺了君位,传给屠岸成孩儿,方遂了平生心愿。"

且不说屠岸贾在那里意得志满,这里程婴却在心烦意乱。原来程婴掐指一算,那赵氏孤儿今年恰恰满了二十岁,已经长大成人,又是文武全才,便欲将前因后果一古脑儿地告诉他,要他报仇雪恨。可是转

he watched the young man practicing his physical exercises during the day and studying in the evening, blissfully unaware of his grim history, he reflected that, as he had never mentioned so much as a word of this to the lad in all the 20 years he had been growing up in the Tu'an household, there was a strong possibility that Cheng Bo would scoff at his tale. He could also see how Tu'an Gu doted on his adopted son, and feared that a strong bond of affection might have developed between them, so that even after he had learned the truth this might prompt him to stay his hand. Another consideration was the fact that Tu'an Gu was a crafty and ruthless man. If Cheng Bo got to know the truth, and then made some rash move, his adoptive father would be alerted to the danger, and would not hesitate to strike first. Then all Cheng Ying's 20 years of painstaking efforts would be wasted. The upshot was that Cheng Ying was at a loss how to tell Zhao the Orphan of his destiny. He was in such a state of agitation that he spent every day either pacing the floor or slumped in his study buried in gloomy thoughts. One night he was sitting in his study, brooding by candlelight and still unable to come to a decision. Suddenly a wave of tiredness swept over him, and he fell asleep with his head resting on the desk in front of him. He seemed to see the candle flare up and then go dim again. As the flame sputtered, Gongsun Chujiu floated into the room, his snow white beard hanging down to his chest. The old man boomed, "The orphan has become a man, and still his task is not fulfilled. Why the delay? You must inform him of his mission of vengeance without more ado, and report the good news to me." He repeated this over and over again, but just as Cheng Ying was struggling to reply, Gongsun Chujiu vanished in the twinkling of an eye.

Cheng Ying awoke with a violent start, unsure whether he had had a dream or not, the experience had been so vivid. He sat there for a long time, his mind blank. Then he put out the candle and went into

念一想，程勃在屠岸府二十年，自己一丝口风也没有漏过，看着孩儿整日里读书习武，天真烂漫，对自己的身世一无所知，只怕突然说出真相，程勃一时难以接受。又见他每日里跟着屠岸贾习武，屠岸贾待他亦是真情实意，一对义父义子亲近非常，并无嫌隙。程婴怕程勃与屠岸贾之间已经产生了感情，在得知真相后下不了手。再者那屠岸贾老奸巨滑，万一程勃得知血海深仇，一时莽撞，打草惊蛇，让那屠岸贾生出疑心，抢先下手，二十年的心血可就要付之东流。因此思来想去，不知如何开口。急得他每日里不是绕室彷徨，便是在书房内枯坐苦想。这天夜里，程婴又在书房中独自挑灯闷坐，想了半天，也拿不定主意。不觉精神倦怠，伏在案上睡了过去。忽见烛光忽明忽暗，闪闪烁烁，公孙杵臼飘然入房，胸前一部雪白的长髯，高声叫道："孤儿已经长大成人，不行大计，更待何时？先生速速教他报仇雪恨，也好将个喜讯儿报我知道。"程婴待要上前攀谈，公孙杵臼却一眨眼不见了。

　　程婴打了一个寒噤，猛地醒来，只觉得方才情景似梦非梦，亦真亦幻。呆了半晌，熄灯回房，将郭氏推醒，把方才梦中情景一五一十地说了，又道："我近日

his bedroom. He woke his wife, and told her of his dream. Then he explained, "Recently, I've been very troubled about this matter. I am already 65 years old, and my days are a torment to me, and I feel as if I am almost eighty. If anything should happen to me and you are left alone, I am afraid that our noble mission would fail. When I see how completely unaware of his background the youth is, and how close he is to that dastardly Tu'an, I don't know how to broach the subject of his earth shaking task. I am vexed almost to death!"

His wife replied, "You are right to be worried, my dear. This matter brooks no delay. It seems to me that what you should do is to paint a picture containing the main strands of the story. Leave it somewhere he is bond to see it, and let it awaken in him a sense of righteous indignation. Then you can tell him the whole truth, and act at the opportune time."

His wife's words were a revelation to Cheng Ying. He nodded several times in agreement, feeling that a great weight had been lifted from his mind. The very next day, he got his wife to search out a sheet of white silk, and set to work painting. For several days in a row, in the dead of night, the two of them painted feverishly. When it was finished, they rolled it up carefully, and left it in a suitable spot.

One day, Cheng Bo rose early to go to the drill ground. Cheng Ying was sitting alone in his study, his cheek resting on his hand, deep in sad contemplation. Outside the window willow trees trailed their golden branches, their buds an emerald green. Peach trees, ablaze with blossoms gave off a heady perfume. A warm breeze wafted through their branches, making the petals shower down like raindrops. But Cheng Ying scratched his hoary head, and sighed. "Time flies, and man's life is bitter and short, like a glimpse of a white colt galloping past a chink in the wall!"

He then unrolled the scroll. The tragic scenes of 20 years flashed

来便为此事烦躁不安，想我今年已经六十五岁，艰难忧患，日月煎熬，看上去倒似个快八十岁的。倘若有一天一口气喘不上来，有个三长两短，扔下你一个妇道人家，岂不误了大事？可眼看着孩儿懵懂混沌，一无所知，又与那屠岸贾十分亲热，不知如何开口将这件天大的事向他说个明白。真正愁死人了。"

　　郭氏道："相公所虑极是，事不宜迟。依贱妾之见，相公不如将前后故事撮其大要，画成图画，瞅便让孩儿看了，令其生出忠勇义愤之心，然后挑明真相，相机行事，岂不妥当些？"

　　程婴听了郭氏之言，如开茅塞，连连点头称是，心中犹如一块大石落地。第二天就让郭氏准备了一匹白绢，开始作画。一连数日，每到夜深人静，夫妻二人便挥毫泼墨，终于将图画完成，细心地卷起来藏在妥当之处。

　　这一日，程勃早早起身到教场习武去了，程婴一人在书房内托腮闷坐。只见窗前柳垂金丝，芽叠翠玉，几株碧桃吐香喷艳，开得如火如荼。一阵暖风吹拂，那红英像雨点儿一般洒落下来。程婴不禁搔了搔自己头上如雪的白发，感慨万千，叹息道："光阴如流，人生苦短，正如白驹过隙！"

before his eyes, scene by scene. Tears cascaded down his cheeks as he thought of all the fine ministers and noble heroes who had gone to their deaths to save Zhao the Orphan, and of the bitter end of his son, not even ten days old. After a while, he rolled the scroll up again and laid it on the desk. Then he took up a zither. The instrument seemed of its own accord to choose notes redolent of pent up grief and rage, like the dropping of tears or cries of accusation. Then the tempo picked up, and became impassioned, fading finally away into a limitless abyss of bitterness.

At this moment, Cheng Bo returned from his martial exercises. He had heard the plaintive music of the zither from afar as he approached the house. He hurried inside, and found Cheng Ying still cradling the zither. Alarmed at the sight of the old man's tear stained face, he hastened to ask him, "Father, why are you so upset? Has somebody acted in a high handed way towards you? Tell me, quickly, and I will make him answer for it!"

The young man's words woke Cheng Ying from his brooding. Startled, he brush away the tears, and with a forced smile, said, "Oh, it's nothing. You go and have your morning meal." But as he turned away he could not help sighing.

Cheng Bo was taken aback at this welcome. He thought to himself, "Usually my father is all smiles whenever he sees me, and is eager to chat. Why is he so cold and distant today? Moreover, he has been weeping, that's obvious. And why did he sigh like that?" Thereupon, he asked again, "Father, have you and my adoptive father had a quarrel?"

Annoyed at this interrogation, Cheng Ying answered sharply, "I have not been quarreling with anybody. If I told you what is in my heart, I'm afraid you would disown your father and mother. Now run along; you must be hungry."

叹毕,取出画卷独自展玩起来。二十年前一幕幕惨烈的场景在眼前闪过,想到为了救孤存赵,多少贤臣义士慷慨就义,就连自己不满十日的儿子也遭惨死,禁不住泪下如雨,泣不成声。许久之后,才将画轴卷起,放在几上,取过一张古琴弹了起来。将一腔悲愤化入琴声,如泣如诉,慷慨悲壮。

正在此时,程勃从教场习武回来,远远听见书房中琴声悲壮,匆匆跑进房内,见到程婴满面泪痕,鼓琴方罢,急忙道:"爹爹为何如此感伤?莫非是谁欺负了你不成?快快告诉孩儿,孩儿去为爹爹出头。"

程婴心潮起伏,正沉浸在对往事的回忆之中,猛听得程勃发问,一时不知说什么好,连忙擦了一把泪,佯笑道:"没有什么,孩儿去吃饭吧。"转过身去,禁不住发出一声叹息。

程勃百思不解,心中暗想道:"往常爹爹见了自己,欢喜不尽,问长问短。今日为何这般冷淡,却又泪痕满面,长吁短叹?"于是又问道:"莫不是爹爹与义父斗嘴,因此不快?"

程婴见程勃追问不休,气恼道:"我并不曾与人斗口。我的心事告诉你,怕你也无法为父母作主。你自去吃饭就是。"

Shaking his head and sighing, Cheng Ying rose and went into the rear chamber. As he did so, his sleeve brushed the scroll from the desk onto the floor. Puzzled at Cheng Ying's bad temper, Cheng Bo picked up the scroll. Out of curiosity, he unrolled it and examined it intently.

There were nine pictures painted one after the other on the white silk. They contained a large number of images of people, depicted in a vivid and lifelike manner. The pictures seemed to be telling a story, and the young man followed the sequence with interest.

In the first picture there was a man dressed in a red robe letting loose a fiercely snarling dog. Its fangs and claws bared, the dog was about to leap at another man, dressed in a purple robe. In the second picture, a stalwart figure had rushed forward to save the man in purple, and was tearing the dog in two. The third picture showed another sturdy man. This one was whipping a horse and lifting a carriage with one hand. The carriage, strangely enough, had only one wheel, and the figure of a man clad in a purple robe could faintly be seen seated in the fore part of it. In the fourth picture too, there was a husky figure, clutching a wicked-looking dagger and pounding his head against a large tree.

Looking at these pictures, Cheng Bo was baffled. He could not even guess what they meant. He puzzled over them for a long while, but couldn't figure out what story they portrayed. He then looked at the fifth picture. It showed a general facing the viewer and in front of him were a bowstring and a short sword. Also in his hand was a wine cup which had just been drained. The young man wondered aloud, "Why on earth would this general wish to kill himself?"

　　程婴说罢，摇头叹息数声，起身径往后堂，临行转身，一只袍袖却将几案上的画卷扫落在地。程勃见父亲无故发怒，径自去了，不禁心中纳闷，随手将地上的画卷捡起来，展开细看。

　　只见一匹白绢上并排画着八九幅图画，其上有不少人物，笔触生动，神情逼真。程勃毕竟年轻，见到图画上仿佛画得是一个个故事，顿时生出兴趣，从头开始一幅幅地看过去。见第一幅画的是一个穿红衣服的人正在放开一条呲牙咧嘴的恶犬，那恶犬张牙舞爪，扑向一个穿紫色衣服的人。第二幅画的是一个大力士冲上前去将恶犬撕作两半，救下了穿紫衣服的人。第三幅图上画的是一位壮士一手举鞭策马，一手扶着一辆车子，那车真是奇怪，只有一只轮子，隐约可以看见先前那穿紫衣服的人坐在车上。第四幅图又是一个壮士，手持利刃，一头撞在一株大树上。

　　看了这几幅图画，程勃心中大感不解，猜不出这是说的什么故事。摸着脑袋想了半天，也得不着一丝眉目，只好再向下看去。只见第五幅图画的是一位将军面前摆着弓弦、短刀两样东西，那将军手中却拿着一杯酒饮下自尽。程勃不禁自言自语道："奇怪，这将军怎么要自杀呢？"

In the sixth picture was a man dressed as a physician, carrying a medicine box on his back. He was receiving a baby from the hands of a woman. In the seventh picture, the same woman had hanged herself in a room, while outside the door was a general cutting his own throat with a sword. The longer he gazed at the pictures the more incomprehensible they seemed to him. Curiosity spurred him on to look at the eighth picture. In it was the red-clad man he had seen in the first picture. He was beating a white-haired, white-bearded old man mercilessly. He was also chopping a baby into three pieces. The last picture showed several hundred corpses of both men and women, old and young, lying in pools of blood in the courtyard of a large mansion. They looked as if they had all been killed at the same time.

Although even when he had examined all the pictures, Cheng Bo still did not understand their meaning, his natural sense of justice and hatred of evil made him boil with righteous anger at the sight of the man in red loosing a savage dog upon a victim, savagely beating an old man and murdering a baby. He even cried aloud, "That heinous monster in red! If he fell into my hands, I'd dispatch him with my sword on the spot!" Then he continued, "Which depraved fiend massacred all those people, I'd like to know? His mind must be infested with evil!"

Cheng Ying, who had been eavesdropping around a corner, knew when he heard this that the young man had viewed the paintings. After a while, he called out through the doorway, "You are perfectly right, my son. Those murders were committed by a black hearted villain indeed!" Cheng Bo hurried in to confront the old man. "Father," he demanded, "Tell me, what story do the pictures relate? And who is that wicked scoundrel?"

His eyes filled with tears, Cheng Ying replied, "The story recounted in that series of pictures is connected with you yourself. I have

　　再看第六幅图，一位医生打扮的人肩背药箱，从一个妇人手中接过一个婴儿。第七幅图上画着方才交出婴儿的妇人却吊死在屋内，门外还有一位将军举剑自刎。程勃越看越是疑心，不知这说的是什么故事。在好奇心的驱使下，又看第八幅图，画的是第一幅图中那个穿红衣的人，将一位白须白发的老者打得皮开肉绽，又举刀将一个婴儿剁作三截。最后一幅图画的是一处大宅院，男女老少数百人倒在血泊之中，眼见的是被人同时杀死。

　　程勃看完图画，虽然不解其意，但他天性善良，嫉恶如仇，见到那穿红衣的人纵犬噬人，殴打老者，又砍死婴儿，不觉义愤填膺，怒道："这穿红衣的人恁地凶恶，如果撞在我的手上，一剑砍杀了也罢！"又道："这是哪个狠心的奸贼，将这一府中的男女老少一古脑儿都杀死了，心肠也着实狠毒了些。"

　　不说程勃正在这里一个人自言自语，程婴料得程勃已将图画看完，放轻脚步回来书房，正走到窗下，听到程勃怒气冲冲地话语，心中暗喜，在门外接口道："孩儿说得不错，这些人都是被一个狠毒的奸贼杀死的。"程勃听到是爹爹说话，忙将程婴迎进门内，道："爹爹快告诉孩儿，这图画说的是什么故事？"

been nursing it in my heart for twenty years, not daring to tell anyone else. "

Cheng Bo stared at him in astonishment. "What can this story have to do with me, Father? I beg you to explain exactly what it all means. "

Pointing to the first picture, Cheng Ying said, "The man in red and the man in purple were once ministers of the same court. But they were as unlike as fire and water —— one was loyal and the other was treacherous. The latter schemed to bring about the downfall of the former. "

Cheng Bo interjected, "How did he manage to do it?"

Cheng Ying then drew his attention to the picture of Chu Ni's suicide. "The villain in red, " he said, "first sent an assassin, a man of honor as it turned out, called Chu Ni. But the would-be assassin was so moved by the devotion to his country of the man in purple that he could not bring himself to commit a deed which he realized would be and affront to Heaven. But to return, his mission unfulfilled, would have meant certain death for him. So he dashed his brains out against a tree. "

At this point, the young man remarked, "You said the name of this upright man was Chu Ni, I think. "

"That's right, " said Cheng Ying. "Remember that name. "

Cheng Bo nodded his assent. Cheng Ying next pointed again to the first picture, saying, "This hound had been sent as tribute from the kingdom of Western Rong. It was terribly fierce. The man in red obtained it from the duke, dressed a straw dummy up in a purple robe, and trained the mastiff to attack and rend it. When it had been fully trained to do so, he took it to the court. There, as soon as it saw the man in purple, it thought that he was the dummy, and it sprang at him. This galvanized a brave man standing by into action. You see

程婴含泪道:"这图画上说的故事,与孩儿却有些关连,爹爹放在心里二十年,不敢向外人说道。"

程勃睁大一双惊疑的眼睛道:"这故事怎地与孩儿关连?请爹爹细细说出原委,免得孩儿疑惑。"

程婴指着第一幅图画道:"这穿红衣的和穿紫衣的,原是一殿朝臣,怎奈两人一忠一奸,水火难容,那奸的便处心积虑要害死那穿紫衣的。"

程勃问道:"那穿红衣的如何害那穿紫衣的?"

程婴遂指着义士触槐的图画道:"那穿红衣的奸贼想着要先下手为强,便派这位名叫钼麂的义士去行刺穿紫衣的。谁知这穿紫衣的忠谨报国,感动了义士,义士遂想着杀害忠良是逆天行事,断断不可。可是空手回去也是个死,便自己一头撞死在这株大槐树上。"

程勃问道:"这位触槐而死的义士原来叫做钼麂。"

程婴道:"正是钼麂,孩儿要牢牢记着。"

程勃点点头,程婴又指着第一幅图画道:"当时西戎国里进贡这只神獒,凶猛异常。那穿红衣的就向国君要过这只狗来,将一个草人扮作穿紫衣的模样,要那神獒扑咬。练的熟了,牵到朝堂上,那神獒见了穿紫衣的,只道是草人,便扑了上去。旁边却惹恼了

him in the second picture. "

Pointing at the figure who had just slain the hound, Cheng Bo said, "Oh, you mean him? What was his name?"

"Yes, " said Cheng Ying. "His name was Ti Miming. When he saw that terrible dog leap at the loyal minister in purple, he was so furious that he tore the beast in two. Sadly, he was pursued and killed by the palace guards. Are you beginning to understand now, my son?"

Again Cheng Bo nodded. "I will remember, " he said, "That this hero's name was Ti Miming. " He then pointed to the third picture, and asked, "Who is this big fellow driving the carriage? And how did it come to have only one wheel?"

Cheng Ying explained, "It's a long story. The man in purple used to go to the suburbs every spring to encourage the farmers. One year, he spied a stalwart yeoman lying on his back beneath a mulberry tree, with his mouth wide open. When he asked the man what he was doing, the reply was that his name was Ling Zhe, and that he hadn't eaten anything for days and was weak from hunger. However, as he was loath to steal somebody else's mulberries, all he could do was lie under the tree with his mouth open and wait for mulberries to fall into it. The honest minister in purple was impressed with the man's integrity, and ordered that he be given food and wine. Later, fleeing from the court after being saved by Ti Miming from the hound, he found that two of the horses had been unhitched from his carriage by the red robed villain's men and one wheel had been destroyed, to make it impossible for him to escape. But in the nick of time Ling Zhe arrived. Supporting the carriage on his shoulder and managing the remaining horses with his right hand, he conveyed the righteous minister to safety outside the capital. "

At this point, Cheng Bo interrupted. "Father, I recognize that

一位壮士,便是第二幅图上画的那个。"

程勃指着撕碎神獒的壮士道:"可是这位壮士么?他唤作什么名字?"

程婴道:"这位壮士,名字唤作提弥明。他见神獒扑咬穿紫衣的忠臣,心中着恼,奋起神勇,将那恶狗撕作两半,可惜后来他也被追兵杀死。孩儿可明白了?"

程勃点点头道:"孩儿记住了,这杀犬的壮士叫做提弥明。"说罢,指着第三幅图画问道:"这赶车的大汉又是何人?这辆车子怎么只有一只轮子?"

程婴道:"这话说来颇长。那穿紫衣的忠臣每年春天里要到郊外劝农,有一年在一株桑树下见到一条大汉,仰面朝天张大嘴躺着,便问那大汉在做什么。大汉道,自己名叫灵辄,已饿了几天,没有力气,又不愿偷摘主人的桑椹,只好张嘴躺在树下,等桑椹掉入嘴中充饥。穿紫衣的忠臣见他是个壮士,便命手下取出酒食来让灵辄吃了个饱。后来那穿红衣的要杀那穿紫衣的,放出神獒来,却被提弥明挡住。穿紫衣的逃出门来,见乘车已被穿红衣的使人卸去二马,拆掉一轮,无法行驶。灵辄适时赶来,右手驭马,单肩扶车,带着那穿紫衣的忠臣逃出城外。"

说到这里,程勃插嘴道:"爹爹,孩儿知道这灵辄

Ling Zhe, in requiting the chance kindness he had received from the minister in purple, was a true man of honor. But what was the name of the wicked knave in red, and who was the upright minister in purple?"

Cheng Ying looked at him, and nodded. "Very good, my boy," he said. "You know well how to distinguish loyalty from treachery. At the moment I am not able to tell you the name of the one in red. But the loyal minister in purple was named Zhao Dun. He used to be the prime minister of Jin —— and there is a connection between you and him."

Cheng Bo said, "I have heard people mention Prime Minister Zhao Dun. But what connection can there be between us?"

"Let me continue," replied Cheng Ying, "And you will come to understand." As he said this, he pointed to the picture of the massacre. "When the man in red realized that Zhao Dun had escaped, he took out his fury on the rest of the Zhao clan, slaughtering the over 300 people in the Zhao mansion."

Cheng Bo cried aloud in outrage and horror at hearing this.

Cheng Ying simply continued, "Only one of the Zhaos remained alive in Jin. His name was Zhao Shuo, and he was married to the duke's sister. The man in red forged an order from the duke that Zhao Shuo commit suicide, offering him the choice of a rope, a sword and poisoned wine. Zhao Shuo drank the poisoned wine. Just before he died, he named the baby in the princess' womb Zhao the Orphan, and his last wish was that the orphan should grow up and avenge the deaths of the 300 odd members of the Zhao clan."

Having reached this stage in his narrative, Cheng Ying felt a pang of grief stab his heart, and he could not hold back his tears.

"But did the orphan manage to avenge the Zhao clan, by killing the villain in red?" asked the young man.

是来报那穿紫衣的知遇之恩，真是一条好汉。那穿红衣的奸臣心肠如此狠毒，他叫作什么？那穿紫衣的忠臣是谁？"

程婴看着程勃，点点头道："好孩儿，知道辨别忠奸。那穿红衣的名字，爹爹现在不能告诉你。那穿紫衣的忠臣姓赵，叫作赵盾，本是晋国的相国，与孩儿还有些关连哩。"

程勃也不追问，只道："孩儿曾听人说起过相国赵盾，他怎地与孩儿有些关连？"

程婴道："孩儿听爹爹说下去，自然就知道了。"说着，指着那尸积如山的图画道："那穿红衣的见相国赵盾走了，便将他一家三百余口统统杀死。"

程勃听了，失声叫道："这奸贼怎地心黑，如何就下毒手将人家三百余口杀个干净！"

程婴也不接口，只道："那赵盾一家三百余口尽皆死了，只留下一个儿子，唤作赵朔，娶了国君的姊姊，是个驸马。那穿红衣的假传君命，将绳索、短刀和毒酒赐于赵朔，要他挑一样自尽。赵朔被逼无奈，将毒酒饮下，临死前为公主腹中的胎儿取名赵氏孤儿，要那孤儿长大后为赵家三百余口报仇。"

说到此处，程婴心中悲痛，不觉泪流满面。

Instead of answering, Cheng Ying pointed to the sixth picture. "Having got rid of Zhao Shuo," he continued, "The man in red dispatched General Han Jue to mount a tight guard on the royal son-in-law's mansion, so that as soon as the princess gave birth to Zhao Shuo's child it should be taken from her and put to death. Now, there had been a retainer at the Zhao mansion, a doctor from the countryside called Cheng Ying. . . ."

"Father, that's you!" cried Cheng Bo.

Cheng Ying realized that he had made a slip of the tongue, and hurriedly tried to cover up his mistake. "Oh, er, well, there are lots of people with the same name in this world," he stuttered. "This was another Cheng Ying."

But Cheng Bo was not convinced. "A man called Cheng Ying, who also happened to be a doctor," he mused. "Of course there are many people with the same name, but this seems to be too much of a coincidence. Almost certainly, that man was my father!" However, he did not say this aloud, but urged Cheng Ying to continue with his story.

"This doctor went to the mansion of the royal son-in-law. There, the princess handed the newborn child to him. She then hung herself. The doctor was intercepted and searched by General Han Jue as he tried to smuggle the child out of the mansion. Fortunately, the general was a man of loyalty and integrity, burning with indignation at the way the evil red-clad court official had attempted to destroy the loyal prime minister, allowed the physician to escape. He thereupon cut his own throat, and died on the spot."

Cheng Bo let out an exclamation of awe. "So many loyal and good people died for this Zhao the Orphan!"

Cheng Ying took up the tale once more. "But the villain in red did not take the loss of the orphan lying down. He issued a decree

程勃急急问道："那孤儿可曾将那穿红衣的奸贼杀死，为赵家报仇？"

程婴却不答话，手指着第六幅图道："那穿红衣的奸贼将赵朔逼死，又派下将军韩厥带兵将驸马府牢牢守住，只待公主生下孩儿，便要抢去杀死。那赵府原有一个门客，是个草泽医生，唤作程婴。"

程勃听得提到爹爹的名字，插嘴道："这医生便是爹爹了。"

程婴一时疏忽，将自己的名字说出，忙掩饰道："天下同名同姓的人多着呢，这是另一个程婴。"

程勃听了，心中暗想："偏偏这人唤作程婴，却也是一个医生，天下同名同姓的人虽多，哪里有这般巧法？十有八九便是爹爹。"口中却不敢说出来，只催促程婴接着讲下去。

程婴道："这个医生来到驸马府中，公主将赵氏孤儿交付于他，自己却悬梁自尽了。医生遂抱着赵氏孤儿出府，却被下将军韩厥搜出。那韩厥也是个忠义之人，不忿那穿红衣的奸贼残害忠臣之后，将医生放过，自己却拔出剑来在脖子上一割，当下死去。"

程勃听到这里，叫声"哎呀"，道："为了这赵氏孤儿忠良之后，死了这许多人。"

demanding that the person who had spirited the baby away hand it over to him; otherwise he would seize every infant under the age of six months within the territory of the State of Jin and chop it into three pieces. In that way, he would be sure that Zhao the Orphan would not escape. Now it just so happened that the wife of the doctor who had abducted Zhao the Orphan had just given birth to a son herself. What the doctor did was to pretend that his own son was the orphan, in the meantime handing the orphan over to Gongsun Chujiu —— the old man with white hair and a white beard in that picture there. The o-riginal plan was for Gongsun Chujiu to denounce the doctor, and fool the red robed villain into executing the doctor and his newborn baby. Gongsun would then raise the orphan to manhood so that he could wreak revenge for the Zhao clan. "

"Who, in fact, was Gongsun Chujiu?" asked the young man.

Cheng Ying said, "Gongsun Chujiu was originally a fairly high ranking official who served at court along with Prime Minister Zhao Dun. They were bosom friends. He said to the doctor, 'I am advanced in years, and could die at any time. I am afraid I will not be able to raise the orphan until he reaches adulthood. It would be better if you handed your own child over to me, and denounced me as the kidnap-per. When that red garbed monster has executed both me and your son, you can raise Zhao the Orphan, so that he will eventually avenge his wronged clan.' And so, the physician gave his own child to Gongsun Chujiu, and then went to the villain in red and denounced Gongsun Chujiu as the person who had stolen Zhao the Orphan. The villain in red, together with a great troop of men and horses, seized Gongsun Chujiu and the child. He submitted the old man to fearsome torture to try to get him to reveal who his accomplice was, but the stalwart oldster uttered not a word to incriminate the physician, even though he knew he was threatened with death. Gongsun Chujiu finally

　　程婴道："那穿红衣的奸贼见赵氏孤儿被人救出，不甘罢休，下令盗孤的将孤儿交出，否则便要将晋国境内所有半岁以下的小儿全都抓来，斩作三截，料那赵氏孤儿也难逃过。那抱走赵氏孤儿的医生无法，恰好自己也在此时生了一个小儿，只得将自己的小儿与赵氏孤儿掉了一个包，抱给公孙杵臼，便是图画上那白胡子白头发的老者。要那公孙杵臼去出首，将医生告发，骗得那穿红衣的奸贼将医生与小儿一起处死，公孙杵臼便可将赵氏孤儿养大成人，再来报仇。"

　　程勃问道："那公孙杵臼又是何人？"

　　程婴道："公孙杵臼原来是晋国的中大夫，与相国赵盾一殿为臣，结下了生死交情。他对那医生道：'我已老迈不堪，怕有个三长两短，不能将这孤儿抚养成人。不如你将自家的小儿舍出来，交给老夫，你却前去出首。待那穿红衣的奸贼将老夫与医生的小儿杀死，你则将那赵氏孤儿拉扯大，给他父母报仇。'二人商量妥当，那医生将小儿交给公孙杵臼，自己到那穿红衣的奸贼处首告。那穿红衣的奸贼带着人马，将公孙杵臼与小儿抓住，严刑拷打，要他供出盗孤的

killed himself by dashing his brains out on a rock. The wicked fiend then forced the doctor to beat his own son to death." The remembrance of his infant son's tragic end was too painful for Cheng Ying to continue his tale for a while, and he abandoned himself to a flood of tears. Cheng Bo took this opportunity to ask, "How could the doctor bear to kill his own son?"

Wiping away his tears, Cheng Ying replied, "To save the life of Zhao the Orphan, he would have been willing to sacrifice his own life, let alone that of his child."

Cheng Bo stiffened, and his eyes blazed with rage. "That red-robed villain is so depraved as to stoop to any wickedness!" he cried. "I beg you, Father, to tell me his name, so that I can help Zhao the Orphan to avenge the wrongs done to him and to his clan. I will chop that red-wrapped renegade into ten thousand pieces!" So saying, he drew his sword and fixed his gaze on Cheng Ying.

Instead of replying directly, Cheng Ying, holding back his tears recited the following:

Why tarries the strapping hero, master of civil and martial skills?

His grandsire has fled in a carriage, his household's cruelly killed.

His mother, imprisoned, hung herself, his father, blameless, was slain.

A strange hero indeed is he who neglects to avenge his family's pain.

He then uttered a long sigh, and said, "I have long been afraid that you would not understand when the day came for me to explain all this, my son. But that Zhao the Orphan is now twenty years old. He, in fact, is as far away as the horizon and at the same time right under my nose."

Cheng Bo heard these words in a state of growing and over-

同谋。公孙杵臼抵死不说，自己撞石而死。那穿红衣的奸贼将小儿搜出，逼着医生亲手将自己的孩儿摔死了也。"说到此处，程婴想起惨死的儿子，不觉痛彻肝肠，老泪纵横，哽咽着无法再说下去。程勃借机问道："那医生为何舍得将他的小儿去送死？"

程婴拭了一把泪，道："为了救这赵氏孤儿，他连自己的性命都舍得，何况是他的小儿！"

程勃倏地站起身来，一双眼中怒火喷涌，道："这穿红衣的奸贼着实可恶，竟然如此心狠手毒！爹爹且告诉孩儿那奸贼的姓名，看孩儿助那赵氏孤儿报仇，将那奸贼砍成万段。"说着，拔剑在手，一双眼睛紧盯着程婴。

程婴却不答话，只含泪朗吟道：

相貌堂堂七尺躯，学成文武待何如？

乘车祖父归何处，满门良贱尽遭诛。

冷宫亲母悬梁缢，法场慈父引刀俎。

冤恨至今犹未报，枉为人间大丈夫。

吟罢长叹道："原来说了这一日，孩儿还不明白！那赵氏孤儿如今已经二十岁，远在天边，近在眼前。"

程勃猛地听了这话，惊疑不定，心中却料定那赵氏孤儿必定与自己有极大关联，因道：

whelming agitation, as the connection between Zhao the Orphan and himself began to dawn on him. He cried out, "Father, tell me the truth! Don't leave me groping in the dark any longer!"

Cheng Ying drew a deep breath, and intoned, "The man in red is Tu'an Gu. The man in purple is your grandfather. The royal son-in-law was your father, and the princess was your mother. I myself am that Dr. Cheng Ying who sacrificed his own son to save Zhao the Orphan."

"Is that true?" cried Cheng Bo, aghast.

Cheng Ying was too choked by sobs and tears to reply in words. He simply nodded vigorously. Cheng Ying's wife, who had crept in unnoticed and had heard these last words, then announced her presence. She uttered a strangled gasp, in which the words "My ... my ... Oh my poor ... child!" could just be discerned.

Cheng Bo could refuse to recognize the truth no longer. With a cry of "So I am Zhao the Orphan! This anguish is too much to bear." He fell down in a swoon.

Cheng Ying and his wife rushed to help him, and after a flurry of distraction on their part, the young man gradually revived. The first thing he did upon regaining consciousness was to rave that he was going to have it out with Tu'an Gu. But Cheng Ying managed to calm him down by saying, "Please don't be rash. If you are to avenge the deaths of your clansmen the three of us must lay long term plans. If that black hearted villain Tu'an Gu gets wind of what is afoot, he will not hesitate to strike first. In that case, my twenty years of agony will all have been for naught, and the sacrifices of your real father and mother, as well as those of the other martyrs in your cause, will all have been wasted."

Hearing this, Cheng Bo realized that he must bide his time. He looked carefully at Cheng Ying and his wife, and noticed how worn out with age they were, with wrinkled skin and white hair. They

"爹爹快将真相告知孩儿，不要叫孩儿云里雾里，摸不着头脑。"

程婴长叹一声，道："那穿红衣的就是屠岸贾，穿紫衣的就是你公公，驸马正是你父亲，公主正是你母亲。爹爹就是那舍子救孤的医生程婴。"

程勃闻言大惊，道："此话当真？"

程婴此时涕泪交流，说不出话来，只是拼命点头。其时郭氏也早已进房，听到这里，"哇"的一声哭了出来，道："我…我…我那可怜的…孩儿啊！"

程勃到此已不由得不信，大声喊道："原来我就是那赵氏孤儿，好不气杀人也！"话音方落，只觉胸中气血上涌，急怒攻心，晕倒在地。

程婴和郭氏连忙救治，乱了半晌，程勃才悠悠醒来，大喊大叫，要去找屠岸贾拼命。程婴庄容道："孩儿不可莽撞，赵家三百余口的性命全靠你来报仇，且待我一家三口从长计议。屠岸贾那贼子狡猾奸诈，心黑手毒，若让他觉察了什么风吹草动，先下手为强，爹爹二十年的心血便要付之东流，孩儿的亲生父母和诸位义士也就白白死去了。"

程勃听罢，只得暂时隐忍。转脸见程婴和郭氏两人老态龙钟，鸡皮鹤发，犹如风中残烛，想起他们舍

looked, he thought, as frail as stumps of candles flickering in the wind. When he recollected how they had given up their own child to save him and had devoted themselves to bringing him up, he was overcome with emotion, and there and then he fell to his knees and kowtowed to them, begging them to accept this gesture of his reverence.

Cheng Ying and his wife could control themselves no longer, as the memory of their twenty years of bitterness and hardship welled up inside them. The three of them clung to each other, weeping. Fortunately for them, the courtyard was in an out of the way place, and no outsider witnessed this scene.

That night, while all the rest of the household was asleep, Cheng Ying, his wife and Cheng Bo held a whispered discussion. The upshot of their deliberations was that the following day they would approach the duke and reveal to him who Cheng Bo really was, and ask him for soldiers to help the young man to arrest the rascally Tu'an Gu and wreak vengeance for the massacre of his clansmen. When this had been decided, Cheng Bo declared, his hair standing stiff on his scalp and his eyes glaring, "When we have denounced that blackguard to the duke and had him arrested, his seal of office removed and his official robes stripped from his back, I shall tear out his tongue and pluck out his eyes, and then chop him into ten thousand pieces. I'll make him suffer all the agonies he inflicted on others. But even when I have had my blood vengeance, it will still not be enough to appease the sense of injustice I feel in my heart."

Early the next morning, Tu'an Gu, as usual, went with a troop of soldiers to summon Cheng Bo to the drill ground. But Cheng Ying intercepted them, telling them that the young man had caught a chill the previous night, and was ill in bed with a headache and a fever. "He begs to be excused from practice today," he informed them. Tu'an Gu, suspecting nothing, assented and departed.

子相救、抚育教读的好处来，心中一阵热流翻涌，当时扑身下跪，道："爹娘在上，请受孩儿一拜。"

程婴和郭氏再也按捺不住，二十年的酸甜苦辣涌上心头，三人相拥而泣，痛哭失声。好在这座小院地处偏僻，倒也无人知晓。

入夜后，三人在一屋睡下，唧唧哝哝说了一夜的话，定下明日便去面见国君，将程勃的身世和盘端出，求国君做主，派兵助程勃除贼报仇。计议妥当之后，程勃头发上指，双眼圆睁，发狠道："待我奏过主君，把那老贼擒下，摘了他的官印，剥下他的官服，五花大绑，拔舌抉眼，千刀万剐，而后铡头剁脚，让他受尽人间苦楚，再取他的狗命。报了我的血海深仇，却也解不了我心头之恨！"

次日一早，屠岸贾全不知情，像往常一样派人来叫程勃前去教场练武。程婴对来人道："孩儿昨夜里受了风寒，头痛发热，起不得身，今日且歇一天。"屠岸贾闻报，不知是计，道："既如此，孩儿好好歇着吧。"说罢，自己带兵去了。

程婴与程勃等屠岸贾走远，急忙出门，径往上宫去见国君。

As soon as they had gone, Cheng Ying and Cheng Bo hurried to the palace to request an audience with the duke.

Duke Ling had died many years before, worn out by a life of debauchery. He had left no heir, and the senior ministers had made Cheng the duke. Cheng had been of a weak constitution, and had also passed away after a short reign. The present ruler was Duke Dao, who, although not a man of great talent or vision, was devoted to the welfare of the state and its people. For some time he had been appalled by the tyranny and arrogance of Tu'an Gu, and harbored an anxious desire to have him removed from power. But, in consideration of Tu'an Gu's hold on the military forces, his mastery of the bow and the warhorse and his large band of diehard followers, Duke Dao had no choice but to bide his time and wait for the right moment to strike.

On this morning, right after the customary audience, as the duke was scanning official documents, alone in the royal quarters, his attendants announced that "Zhao the Orphan" wished to see him.

The duke was puzzled, and asked who "Zhao the Orphan" was. When he was informed that he was Tu'an Gu's adopted son, a feeling of disquiet came over Duke Dao, but he ordered that the young man be admitted to his presence.

After Cheng Bo had finished kowtowing, the duke noticed that he was a fine figure of a man, with a dignified bearing. Yet he had an air of great sadness about him, and his eyes were red and puffy. Duke Dao said, "I heard that your original name was Cheng Bo, and that as Tu'an Gu's adopted son you go by the name of Tu'an Cheng. Why today do you call yourself Zhao the Orphan?"

The young man wailed, and collapsed on the ground, weeping copious tears. "Your Majesty," he cried, "There has been an injustice done which cries out to Heaven for redress! My grandfather was a senior minister of Jin, named Zhao Dun. He and Tu'an Gu were as unlike as fire and water. Whereas he personified loyalty, Tu'an Gu

却说当日灵公荒淫无度，数年后暴病身亡。因他没有子嗣，众大臣遂拥立成公。成公身体孱弱，不上几年就病死了，现下晋国是悼公执政。这悼公虽无雄才大略，倒能克己奉公，勤政爱民。近年来见屠岸贾恃势专权，骄横跋扈，早就有心剿除他。却顾忌他握有兵权，娴熟弓马，广有死党，因而投鼠忌器，只得等待时机，再作打算。

这一日早朝已罢，悼公正在内宫独自披览奏章，听得左右传报，道："赵氏孤儿求见。"

悼公听报，心中诧异，问道："这赵氏孤儿又是何人？"

左右禀道："就是司寇屠岸贾的义子屠岸成。"

悼公听说，暗忖其中定有蹊跷，道："传他进来。"

程勃闻召进宫，叩拜已毕，抬起头来。悼公只见他虎背熊腰，仪表堂堂，却是神情悲愤，双眼红肿。悼公开口问道："寡人听说你本名程勃，被司寇认作螟蛉之子，又唤屠岸成，今日为何自称'赵氏孤儿'？"

程勃长号一声，哭倒在地，启禀道："真是天大的冤屈！主君，小人的祖父赵盾原是晋国上卿，领班大臣，与屠岸贾冰炭不容，忠奸分明。屠岸贾遂定下毒计，驯练神獒来扑咬他。逼得小人祖父脱身逃走，不

personified treachery. Tu'an Gu hatched an evil plot to have a savage mastiff attack Zhao Dun. My grandfather was forced to flee, and no one knows where he is now. Pouring slanderous lies into the ears of Duke Ling, that ruler allowed Tu'an Gu to slaughter all the 300-odd people in the mansion of the Zhao clan. He also drove my father, Zhao Shuo, to suicide. Moreover, in order to remove all future danger, he imprisoned my mother, who was pregnant with me at the time, and caused her to hang herself. The Zhao line was only saved from extermination by the fortunate intervention of a loyal hero who sacrificed his own son to save me. This good person raised me to manhood. Now I have come to beg Your Majesty to champion the cause of the Zhao clan and have that scoundrel Tu'an arrested. Only with his death will the souls of the murdered Zhao clansmen be avenged."

Duke Dao had heard of the Zhao affair, but he had been unaware that the orphan still lived. Now he was overjoyed to hear Cheng Bo's testimony, realizing that this was just the charge he needed to bring about Tu'an Gu's fall. He asked in a low voice, "Do you have evidence for what you have stated?"

Cheng Bo replied, "The man who raised me, Cheng Ying, knows all about this affair. He is outside the palace at this moment, awaiting your summons, Your Majesty."

Duke Dao ordered that Cheng Ying be brought in. After making the ritual obeisances and greetings, Cheng Ying stood up and unrolled the painting scroll, and explained in detail Tu'an Gu's crimes against the Zhao clan. When he had finished, the duke, with a brow like thunder, roared, "Ten thousand deaths would not atone for that villain's crimes in leading his ruler into the ways of wickedness and reducing the state to disorder!" Then he assigned General Wei Jiang and 500 men to assist Cheng Bo in the execution of Tu'an Gu.

Outside the palace, Cheng Bo and General Wei Jiang discussed

知身归何处。灵公听信谗言，任屠岸贾猛下毒手，将赵家满门良贱三百余口尽行诛戮，又矫命逼死小人的爹爹赵朔，还要斩草除根，将怀有身孕的母亲关进冷宫，害得小人的母亲自缢身亡。幸有忠臣义士献身舍子相救，方才保住赵氏一点儿血脉，养得小人长大成人。今日来恳求主君与赵家做主，擒拿屠岸贾，定罪处死，替赵家三百口人报仇雪恨。"

悼公以前对赵家的事也曾略有耳闻，只不知那孤儿还活在人间。如今听了程勃的诉说，大喜过望，想着正好借此发落屠岸贾那奸贼。于是俯身问道："你所说的可有见证？"

程勃答道："小人的养父程婴尽知此事原委，现在宫外听宣。"

悼公立传程婴进宫，程婴叩头行礼后，站起身来，展开那轴画卷，将那屠岸贾如何惨害赵家的故事细细向悼公说了一遍。悼公听后，不由得大发雷霆道："这贼子如此狠毒，竟敢导君作恶，害国乱政，万死难辞其辜！"当下颁诏，派将军魏绛率五百兵士，助程勃诛杀屠岸贾。

魏绛领命，与程勃出宫，商量如何擒拿屠岸贾。程勃道："那屠岸贾每日里从教场回来，必路过东城集市，将军可在那里伏下兵卒，将屠岸贾所带甲士尽

how best to go about their mission. Cheng Bo said, "When Tu'an Gu returns from the training ground every day, he has to pass the Eastern Market. You can leave soldiers in ambush there, to separate him from his guards as they pass by. I will then dash out and seize him when he least expects it. That is the safest way to ensure that he does not have the chance to raise a rebellion."

The general agreed to this with a nod, and stationed his men in ambush in the vicinity of the Eastern Market. Meanwhile, Cheng Bo, armed with a sword and with a determined scowl on his face, stood waiting at a nearby crossroads.

It was nearly noon when Tu'an Gu returned from the drill ground. With his usual arrogant pose, he rode at the head of a group of a couple of hundred guards. As the gaudy procession drew near, and Cheng Bo spied his foe, his eyes blazed with crimson fire. As swift as an arrow, the young man stepped in front of Tu'an Gu's steed, his blade glittering like autumn frost. Tu'an Gu was dismayed at finding his path blocked thus by Cheng Bo, with drawn sword and a countenance made fearsome by anger. "Tu'an Cheng, my boy!" he cried, "What are you doing here?"

"What do you mean, Tu'an Cheng?" growled the young man. "I am Zhao the Orphan! Twenty years ago, you massacred all the rest of my clan. Now I have come to take your worthless life, and make you repay the blood debt!"

These words struck Tu'an Gu like thunderbolts. For the moment he was at a complete loss what to do. Then he suddenly heard a commotion behind him. Turning round, he saw General Wei Jiang and his men close in and cut him off from his retinue of men-at-arms. He was surrounded, but he tried to brazen the situation out. "My boy," he cried, "Don't be foolish. Who has lured you into harming your adoptive father?"

行隔开。然后由小人出头，出其不意，将屠岸贾擒下。如此可防屠岸贾举兵变乱，以保万全。"

魏绛闻言点头称是，遂率五百名精兵，埋伏在东城集市附近。程勃一人手持钢刀，横眉立目，站在路口等候。

却说那屠岸贾将近晌午时从教场返回，因他一向目中无人，骄纵傲慢，故而独自骑着一匹骏马走在前头，一二百名甲士紧随其后，耀武扬威，仪仗鲜明。程勃远远望见，正是仇人相逢，分外眼红。待得屠岸贾跨马驰近，程勃一个箭步上前，手持秋霜似的利刃，拦在当路。屠岸贾忽见程勃双眼血红，一脸怒色，横刀拦住去路，不觉心中奇怪，问道："孩儿为何在此？"

程勃双眼圆睁，怒道："谁是你孩儿？我乃赵氏孤儿！二十年前，你将俺一门良贱斩尽杀绝，我今日来取你的狗命，报仇雪恨来了！"

屠岸贾听了这话，宛如头上响了个霹雳，一时失魂落魄，不知所措。忽听身后一片喧闹，回头一看，原来是魏绛带着兵士蜂涌而出，将自己所带的甲士隔在身后，包围起来。心知大事不好，只得硬着头皮道："孩儿莫要胡来，你是听谁陷害义父？"

"Cheng Ying has revealed the whole truth to me. Don't try to wriggle out of it, you dastardly villain!"

Hearing this, Tu'an Gu's face turned ashen. He realized that he had made a terrible mistake in raising a tiger cub, which was now fully grown and had turned on him. With Cheng Bo and his sword blocking his way forward, and General Wei Jiang's men blocking his retreat, Tu'an Gu knew that he would have to fight to the death with the young man. However, there was a slim chance that he might come out of this alive, he thought. So he flung a challenging sneer in Cheng Bo's face. "So, you wretched whelp, you skulked in my house for twenty years, did you? How blind I was to raise a little viper like you! But today is not too late to kill you!" So saying, he made to draw his sword and close with Cheng Bo.

But the young man was too quick for him. Cheng Bo leaped lightly forward, and dragged Tu'an Gu from his horse onto the ground. What with being startled out of his wits, as well as being old and portly, Tu'an Gu was no match for Cheng Bo. Moreover, the tumble had stunned him. It was too late now to repent of his wicked life, during which he had killed people like flies. All he could do was to sit there helplessly, awaiting execution.

Seeing their chieftain captured, Tu'an Gu's men threw down their weapons, and fled in panic. But before long they had all been rounded up by General Wei Jiang's soldiers.

General Wei and Cheng Bo brought Tu'an Gu, bound hand and foot, before Duke Dao. The latter pronounced sentence, "This monster's heinous crimes are too well known to warrant special investigation. Take him immediately to the market place for execution!" General Wei and Cheng Bo thereupon escorted Tu'an Gu to the market place, where they made preparations for the execution in a clear space. When news of the death sentence passed on Tu'an Gu spread through the capital there was not one person who did not clap with glee

程勃道："程婴爹爹亲口对我剖说明白，老贼休想抵赖！"

屠岸贾闻言，脸色大变，犹如死灰，心中只恨自己一时糊涂，养虎遗患。眼见程勃横刀立目，拦在面前，身后又被魏绛断了退路。知道二人来者不善，今日只得拼了老命，或者还有生机，心中一横，骂道："原来你这个孽种藏在我府中二十年，可恨我瞎了眼睛，将你这小贼养大。今日取你的性命也不算迟！"说着，便欲拔剑搏杀程勃。

程勃岂能让仇人逞凶，当下跃起，轻舒猿臂，一个回合便将屠岸贾擒下马来，摔在地上。屠岸贾一来慌了手脚，二来到底年老身重，根本不是程勃的对手，早被摔得发昏。可叹他横行一世，杀人如麻，此时却只得束手就擒，坐以待毙。

跟在屠岸贾身后的甲士见首领被擒，顿时大乱，抛下兵器四散逃走，被魏绛率兵全部擒下绑了起来。

魏绛与程勃将屠岸贾绑成粽子似的，押着回到宫中向悼公缴命。悼公道："此贼恶贯满盈，无须审理，绑到东市上斩了就是。"魏绛与程勃于是又押着屠岸贾来到东市，清出一片空场来，准备行刑。京城

and run around to tell others. The whole populace flocked to the execution site.

With General Wei's soldiers standing guard all round, Tu'an Gu was brought forward. The general addressed him thus, "Tu'an Gu, today you have been arrested for slaughtering loyal and good people. As you face death, do you have anything to say?"

Tu'an Gu was degenerate by nature, an out and out blackguard. Even though he knew there was no escape from death this time, he was unrepentant. "Win, and you become a king," he snarled. "Lose, and you're regarded as a bandit. My only regret is that I did not exterminate that Zhao brat, but let him live to bring ruin upon me. Well, seeing as it's come to this, kill me and be done with it!"

Hearing this, Cheng Bo was suddenly filled with fury. "So, you fiend, you want to die quickly, do you? Well, you will not have your wish!"

General Wei Jiang then gave a command, "Nail the criminal to the wooden donkey. Then slowly apply the three thousand cuts. When his flesh is all stripped away, cut off his head!"

At this point, Cheng Ying and his wife appeared, just in time to see the sentence being carried out. First Tu'an Gu's ears were sliced off; then his eyes were gouged out; his tongue was torn out, and bit by bit the flesh was stripped from his body. Tu'an Gu screamed in torment, unable alike to live or to die. The bystanders clapped and cheered, feeling that only now was their sorrow appeased. Finally, after two hours, when Tu'an Gu had suffered all possible pain, his head was cut off and his chest ripped open. Truly:

It's been 20 years, since those wicked deeds were done.
But a tyrant's been beheaded, and justice has finally won.

Joy spread throughout the State of Jin as people learned of the

百姓听说国君下令诛杀奸臣屠岸贾，无不拍手称快，奔走相告，纷纷前来观看。

魏绛派兵士四面把定，命人将屠岸贾押上来，问道："屠岸贾，你这残害忠良的奸贼，今日被擒，死在临头，还有何话？"

屠岸贾生性阴狠，桀傲不屈，自知今日难逃一死，遂发狠道："成则为王，败则为寇。恨只恨让那赵氏孽种逃脱，留下后患。于今事已至此，惟愿速死！"

程勃在一旁听了，怒气冲冲道："老贼想要速死，我偏不让你如愿！"

魏绛闻言下令道："给我将这贼子钉到木驴上，慢慢地剐他三千刀，皮肉都尽，再断首开膛，取他性命。"

此时程婴夫妇二人也赶来观看，只见行刑军士遵命将屠岸贾割耳挖眼，揭皮钩舌，一刀一刀细细剐削。屠岸贾痛苦万状，凄号惨叫，求生不得，求死不能。程婴等人在旁看了，不由得拍手称快，大声叫好，觉得这才出了一口怨气。直有一个时辰，屠岸贾受尽了苦楚，才被枭首开膛，气绝身亡。正是：

忠臣受屠戮，沉冤二十年。

今朝戮奸贼，方知冤报冤。

execution of Tu'an Gu. As General Wei Jiang and Cheng Bo made their way back to the palace, they were met by a group of ministers, with Shi Ji at their head. At the court, Duke Dao announced, "Tu'an Gu deserved ten thousand deaths for murdering loyal and faithful people, and throwing the government into chaos. I declare all his property confiscated, and sentence his whole household to execution —— not even a chicken or a dog must be spared. In addition, Zhao the Orphan may use his real surname once again, and I give him the name Zhao Wu. He shall succeed to his grandfather's rank at court, and have command of the army. Moreover, he shall have the Lower Palace as his dwelling. As for Cheng Ying, who sacrificed his own child to save Zhao the Orphan, I grant him ten acres of land, and he shall be supported in his old age by Zhao Wu. As Han Jue lay down his life for righteousness, I grant his descendants the rank of general. For Gongsun Chujiu, who showed an inspiring devotion to justice as he faced death, I will have a tomb mound raised and a stele placed before it recording his merit. And on the heroes Ling Zhe and Ti Miming I will bestow honors and praise."

Everybody present kowtowed in gratitude, and cried, "Long live the duke!" The people of Jin were delighted when they heard about the duke's munificence. They all agreed that Tu'an Gu had got his just desserts for his murderous career, and that Cheng Ying was a model of selflessness and lofty virtue for all time.

Zhao Wu, having succeeded to his rightful title, repaired the Lower Palace and went to live there together with Cheng Ying and his wife. Despite his youth, Zhao Wu was experienced in the ways of the world and prudent. In both the literary and martial arts he was outstanding among his generation. Every day he combined the training of the soldiers with the handling of state affairs. Returning home, he would chat and joke with the old couple, and attend to their needs as if he were their own son.

消息传出，朝野一片欢腾。魏绛与程勃等人一齐回朝复命，恰逢士季等大臣前来为赵氏孤儿求封。悼公于是下令道：

"屠岸贾残害忠良，挠乱朝纲，罪该万死，将财产一律没收充公，并将其阖门老小一概诛除，鸡犬不留。赵氏孤儿复其本姓，赐名赵武，并承袭祖父官爵，位列上卿，执掌兵权，仍将下宫为官邸。程婴舍子救孤，赏给田地十倾，并着赵武养老送终。韩厥以身殉义，着人寻访其后代，仍为将军。公孙杵臼慷慨赴死，大义凛然，为其立碑造坟，以旌功德。灵辄、提弥明等义士一概予以表彰褒扬。"

众人当下叩拜谢恩，山呼万岁。消息传出，朝野上下欢声雷动。晋国百姓闻知此事，无不欢欣鼓舞，都道屠岸贾残害忠良，终得报应；程婴高义伟节，万代敬仰。

且说赵武承袭官爵，将下宫修葺一番，与程婴夫妇一同住了进去。他年纪虽轻，却老成持重，文韬武略，高出侪辈，每日里整训三军，戮力国事。回到家中，便在程婴夫妇前说笑，承欢膝下，极尽孝道，和亲生儿子一般无二。

Strangely enough, after he was awarded a farming estate and moved into the Lower Palace, Cheng Ying became morose and taciturn. Whenever he had spare time, he would sit by the window deep in thought, occasionally letting fall a tear. Seeing him so withdrawn and distracted, and even from time to time muttering to himself, his wife and Zhao Wu tried to cheer him up, saying, "We three have been through so many trials and tribulations together that now we should revel in our good fortune. Why are you so depressed?" But Cheng Ying simply fobbed them off with the excuse that he was getting old and his wits were befuddled. He preferred solitude, he said. The other two were content to leave it at that, and inquired no further.

Dear readers, what do you think was on Cheng Ying's mind? Well, the fact was that even after Zhao Wu had executed Tu'an Gu, and got his revenge, and after Cheng Ying had been awarded a grant of land, and had started to live in the Lower Palace, clothed in silks and satins and waited on hand and foot, the latter could not help constantly casting his mind back 20 years. Whenever he did so, he felt both proud and remorseful. He was proud of the fact that for 20 years he had endured shame and humiliation in order to raise Zhao the Orphan to manhood so that he could get revenge for the injustice which had been visited on his clan. But he felt remorse that so many upstanding and loyal officials had lost their lives in the course of those years, while he alone survived, living in the lap of luxury. It pained him to think of his only son, not yet ten days old, whom he had beaten to death with his own hands. It pained him to think of his old friend Gongsun Chujiu, whose bones were lying alone in a remote grave and whose soul had gone alone to the Yellow Springs of the underworld. At such times, he would murmur, "I should have died 20 years ago. The only reason for me living on for all those years was to make sure that Zhao the Orphan grew up and fulfilled his duty of vengeance. But now that the evil minister has been beheaded and the

奇怪的是程婴自从受封得赏,住进下宫之后,便有些神情郁郁,寡言少语。每日里得闲,便一个人坐在窗下沉思冥想,时时忽然堕泪。赵武和郭氏见他神情痴迷,意态凄然,不时喃喃自语,都劝说道:"我一家三口历尽艰难,方有今日,应当高兴才是。为何反倒闷闷不乐?"问了几次,程婴总是推说年纪大了,精神不济,喜欢清静。赵武和郭氏探不出究竟,也只好让他去了。

各位看官,你道这程婴是在想些什么?原来程婴自从赵武杀屠岸贾报仇,自己受封得赏,一同住进这下宫,每日里锦衣玉食,婢仆如云,便将二十年来的往事反来复去地思想不停。想到深处,不觉喜愧交加,悲痛凑集,喜的是自己二十年忍辱含垢,终将赵氏孤儿养大成人,报了大仇;愧的是当年多少忠臣义士含恨献身,而今自己独享荣华富贵;悲的是亲生儿子生下不满十日,竟被自己亲手摔死;痛的是老友公孙杵臼慷慨赴死,于今独卧野坟,黄泉寂寞。于是喃喃自语道:"程婴当死于二十年前,所以隐忍偷生至今,全是为了将那赵氏孤儿抚养成人,报仇雪恨。如今权奸授首,赵氏复兴。我再苟活于世上,将来有何面目去见公孙老友与那许多忠臣义士?"想来想去,

fortunes of the Zhao clan restored, how could I face Gongsun Chujiu and all the other loyal worthies if I continued to live in this world?" After much contemplation, he came to a decision.

One day, Cheng Ying told his wife and Zhao Wu that he intended to journey to Taiping Village to offer a sacrifice at the grave of Gongsun Chujiu and let him know that Zhao the Orphan had accomplished his task of wreaking vengeance. When Zhao Wu expressed the intention of accompanying him, Cheng Ying said, "No, my boy. You must stay here and continue your daily training. It is sufficient if I go alone." His wife's pleas were likewise brushed aside, and the following day he set out, with his medicine box on his back.

When he reached Taiping Village, he noticed that two stone tablets had been set up in front of the large and small grave mounds, respectively. On the offering tables, there was fresh fruit and burning incense. Sitting in front of the tombs, Cheng Ying felt a wave of sadness flow over him, and he burst into tears. Pulling himself together, he stood up, took a small knife from his medicine box. Facing the mounds, he slit his throat and fell down dead. When the local people discovered the body, they sent the news to the capital with the utmost speed. Zhao Wu was at first dumbfounded, and when he had recovered from the first shock, he was racked by a paroxysm of weeping. Cheng Ying's wife, too, was so affected that she fainted several times.

Early the next morning, Zhao Wu reported the tragedy to Duke Dao, and asked for leave to go to Taiping Village to give the man who had raised him a decent burial. The duke, in admiration of Cheng Ying's adherence to righteousness even at the cost of his life, gave permission for him to be interred in the same tomb as Gongsun Chujiu on Mount Cang.

Zhao Wu hurried off to Taiping Village, where he gathered the bones of Gongsun Chujiu and re-buried them on Mount Cang, together

终于拿定了主意。

这一日,程婴忽地向郭氏和赵武提起,说是自己要到首阳山太平庄上公孙杵臼的坟前祭奠一番,也好将赵氏孤儿已经报仇雪恨的喜讯告与公孙老友知道。赵武听了,便要随程婴一道去。程婴却说:"孩儿每日要上教场练兵,爹爹一个人去就够了。"郭氏也来劝说,程婴却执意不从,次日早上背了药箱独自上路了。

到了太平庄上,见到一大一小两座坟墓,新立了两块石碑,供桌上香花鲜果,烟雾缭绕。程婴坐在坟前,不觉悲从中来,大哭一场。哭罢立起身来,从药箱中取出一把短刀,就于坟前自刎而死。太平庄上的农夫见了,飞报京城。赵武惊得目瞪口呆,过了半晌方回过神来,哭得死去活来,哀哀欲绝。郭氏自然也是痛哭不已,接连昏晕数次。

次日早朝,赵武将此事奏闻悼公,要去首阳山收敛义父。悼公亦深感程婴重义轻生,正气凛然,便下令将公孙杵臼与程婴合葬于藏山。

赵武奉命,亲自到了首阳山,将公孙杵臼的骨殖收拾了,与程婴一齐埋在藏山,四周广植松柏,坟前立碑刻文。后人遂称之为"二义墓"。

with the body of Cheng Ying. Around the tomb mound, he planted fir trees and cypresses, and in front erected an inscribed tablet. Later generations called it the "Tomb of the Two Worthies."

After he had observed the customary three years of mourning by the tomb of the man who had been a father to him, Zhao Wu devoted himself to looking after Cheng Ying's widow for the remainder of her days, as if she were his own mother. When she died, he set up a shrine for her, at which he offered sacrifices for her every spring and autumn, year in and year out. To this day, in the region east of the Yellow River, when members of the Zhao clan perform rites for their ancestors on the main festival occasions, they always include sacrifices to the Two Worthies Cheng Ying and Gongsun Chujiu.

Zhao Wu's descendants continued to hold high offices, including those of general and prime minister. Eventually, the State of Jin was divided by its powerful clans into three parts. The Zhao clan set up the State of Zhao, which lasted for over 100 years in the area of present-day Shanxi and Hebei provinces, as one of the seven powerful states of the Warring States Period (475-221 B. C.).

后来赵武为程婴守孝三年，奉侍郭氏如同亲生母亲，为其养老送终。并建立祭邑，春秋祀之，世世不绝。至今河东一带，赵氏逢年过节、初一十五祭祀祖先，总要一并祭祀程婴、公孙杵臼二位义士。

赵武之后，赵氏子孙世世为官，出将入相。后来三家分晋，赵氏建立赵国，拥有今山西河北部分地区，立国长达一百余年，为战国七雄之一。

图书在版编目(CIP)数据

赵氏孤儿:汉英对照/(元) 纪君祥著;王建平,任玉堂改编.—北京:新世界出
版社,2000.10

ISBN 7 - 80005 - 565 - 5

Ⅰ.赵… Ⅱ.①纪… ②王… ③任… Ⅲ.英语 - 对照读物,小说 - 汉、英
Ⅳ.H319.4:Ⅰ

中国版本图书馆 CIP 数据核字(2000)第 54047 号

赵氏孤儿

原　　著: 纪君祥(元)

改　　编: 王建平　任玉堂

审　　订: 刘幼生

翻　　译: 保尔·怀特

绘　　图: 李士伋

责任编辑: 张民捷

装帧设计: 贺玉婷

责任印制: 黄厚清

出版发行: 新世界出版社

社　　址: 北京阜成门外百万庄路 24 号　邮政编码:　100037

电　　话: 0086 - 10 - 68994118(出版发行部)

传　　真: 0086 - 10 - 68326679

电子邮件: nwpcn@ public. bta. net. cn

经　　销: 新华书店、外文书店

印　　刷: 北京外文印刷厂印刷

开　　本: 850×1168(毫米)　1/32　字　数:　188 千　印　张:　11.625

版　　次: 2001 年 1 月(英、汉)第 1 版第 1 次印刷

书　　号: ISBN 7 - 80005 - 565 - 5/Ⅰ·050

定　　价: 26.00 元